THE
BATTLES
THAT
CHANGED
HISTORY

Danube R.

ADRIATIC
SEA

•Rome

ILLYRIA

THRACE
Constantinople

•Neapolis

•Beneventum   Tarentum
Asculum

Heraclea

MACEDON

EPIRUS

TARENTINE
GULF

THEBES

Athens

Carthage

SICILY

•Syracuse

CORINTH

AEGEAN
SEA

Sparta

MEDITERRANEAN SEA

CRETE

Alexandria

LIBYA

•Oasis of Siwa

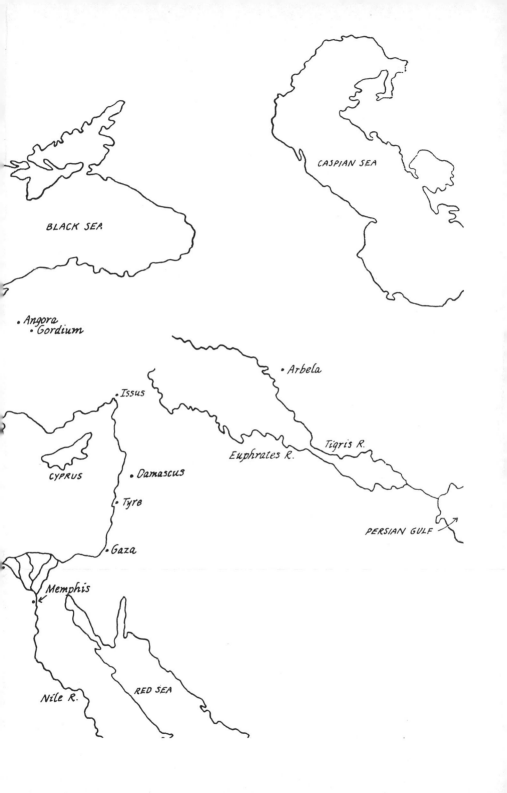

BLACK SEA

CASPIAN SEA

• Angora
• Gordium

• Arbela

• Issus

Tigris R.

Euphrates R.

CYPRUS

• Damascus

• Tyre

PERSIAN GULF

• Gaza

Memphis

Nile R.

RED SEA

THE
BATTLES
THAT
CHANGED
HISTORY

Fletcher Pratt

DOVER PUBLICATIONS, INC.
Mineola, New York

Bibliographical Note

This Dover edition, first published in 2000 is an unabridged republication of the work originally published in 1956 by Hanover House, Garden City, New York. Maps and typography by Edward Gorey.

Library of Congress Cataloging-in-Publication Data

Pratt, Fletcher, 1897–1956.
    The battles that changed history / Fletcher Pratt ; [maps and typography by Edward Gorey].
        p. cm.
    Originally published: 1st ed. Garden City, N.Y. : Hanover House, c1956.
    Includes bibliographical references and index.
    ISBN 0-486-41129-X (pbk.)
    1. Battles. 2. History, Military. I. Title.

D25.5 .P73 2000
904'.7—dc21
                                                                99-054547

Manufactured in the United States of America
Dover Publications, Inc., 31 East 2nd Street, Mineola, N.Y. 11501

CONTENTS

LIST OF MAPS

A Few Words in Introduction

Viewing a wide and accidented landscape, it is sometimes necessary to half close the eyes to determine what are the most important features involved. If one is to make any sense of history as a whole, the process is somewhat similar. Putting in all details and qualifications adds up to accuracy and is indispensable for analysis, but often leads to analysis of minor features only and prevents the perception of the really outstanding features, around whose sides cluster so liberal an accumulation of minutiae.

The present volume is a half-closed-eye view of one aspect of Western history. From such a viewpoint one of the most striking features of Western European culture has been its ability to achieve decisive results by military means. It may even be the critical factor, the reason why that culture has encircled the world. Not that the Far East and Africa have been lacking in great battles or great victories, but their results have had less permanent effect on the stream of world history. The conquests of China are a classic case; they resulted in nothing but the absorption of the victors, and the resultant cultural pattern was transmitted only to the narrowest range of peripheral areas. The seepage through the Afghan passes into India would have taken place without any accompaniment of military events, and more importantly, did little either to change the basic patterns of Indian life or to extend them to other areas. The genuinely decisive wars began when the peoples of Western European culture (and those who acquired it by osmosis, like the Arabs) discovered that it was possible to change the course of history on the battlefield.

There will be ample room for disagreement as to the choice of the battles named here as decisive, and it is therefore worth while explaining the basis on which the choices were made. The first criterion was that the war in which the battle took place must itself have decided something, must really mark one of those turning points after which things would have been a good deal different if the decision had gone in the other direction. It would be possible, for instance, to introduce a battle or two from World War I, and on the technical side to discuss the vast changes that conflict made in the ideology and technique of combat; but the war itself decided nothing, and it had to be fought all over again in twenty years. Moreover, certain decisions taken in battle have turned out to be reversible. Tsushima is an instance; anyone writing this book in 1930 might well have set it down as decisive, and someone did; but the subsequent course of history has not allowed this to be the case.

The second requirement in compilation was that the battle in question represent a positive decision. History is full of negatives, of things prevented from happening. Creasy's *Fifteen Decisive Battles*, the first book in the series of which this is a member, includes Châlons and Tours, fought only a small distance apart, both of which were preventive decisions. But the special genius of Western European culture when it takes up arms is that for really changing the course of history in battle, not merely arresting a movement, but completely altering its direction. The battles described all did this, regardless of whatever subjective regrets one may have in the individual case.

It was also necessary to impose a limitation to keep this from being a general military history of the Western world, approximately as long as the Encyclopaedia Britannica. This limitation was achieved by omitting all those cases where the battle or campaign, although decisive, could hardly have had any other result, given the forces engaged. There will doubtless be some disagreement as to the choices on this ground also, but the point may be illustrated by the case of the Battle of Tenochtitlán, in which Cortés overthrew the empire of the Aztecs. In view of the small number of Spaniards engaged, there was certainly an element of doubt about the outcome of the immediate operation, and Tenochtitlán was preceded by a battle which was definitely a Spanish defeat. But the European technical and logistic background was so superior, with the seagoing ship, the horse, the sword, the musket, armor, and knowledge of how to use all five, that even if Cortés' force had been destroyed it would have been no more than an accident in the tide of conquest.

The sweep of the Vikings over England had a similar inevitability, not through superior technological equipment, but more efficient social organization. Hastings decided nothing but the names of the Norman families that were to rule England, and the change in basic system was really very slight. In the reverse case the decaying Byzantine Empire could have been preserved against the Turks only by a decisive victory which never took place, and the Battle of Manzikert, generally taken as the deathblow of that empire, merely confirmed an existing trend.

The battles listed here may thus be described as decisive in a counterdeterminist sense. Not all of them reversed existing tendencies, although this is a very common case among the battles chosen. It is quite clear that the absorptive power of the ancient Persian Empire on Greek civilization could have been neutralized only in battle; as it was, after Alexander's victory at Arbela the absorption was turned in the other direction.

The question then became one of the extent of the absorptive power of the Greek system. It is often held that the severest test of the Roman system came in the great struggle with Carthage, but I think that close examination will not allow this to be the case. Carthage was a tremendous opponent and she was served by one of the greatest geniuses of military history, but the fundamental structure beneath the Carthaginian effort was flawed. Defeats for Carthage in those wars were always disasters; defeats for Rome only called forth more effort from the incomparably strong and resilient polity that supported the effort. That polity was menaced only once, at Beneventum; when it came in contact with the Greek system that was the heritage of Alexander, and which itself contained elements of permanence that the Carthaginian system never had.

After this the development of the Roman Empire was inevitable; all the battles, however otherwise decisive, were made up of predetermined elements. There is no real point at which one can say that the basic structure of Western civilization was altered by a single event, off the battlefield or on it, for many generations. Even the failure of the Roman effort to conquer Germany was in the cards; the Romans never developed a real technique of forest warfare, and it would have taken a decisive battle, which did not occur, to change matters. The Nike sedition, the first true crisis, the point at which there might have been a fundamental change, occurred late in the game (532 A.D.), and in Constantinople, which had already become the seat of whatever Rome there was left.

After this more than one deluge came down and beneath them the long ground swell of the barbarian invasions or, more properly, infiltrations. It was an age rich in changes and personalities, but not one in which there were basic changes in the cultural pattern. One can point to developments, but to no such abrupt shift of direction and emphasis as that following Arbela. When the Battle of Kadisiyah did effect a change, it was at a tangent to the flow and not a reversal; and it is necessary to understand Kadisiyah to comprehend why the newly risen power of Islam became a threat to the developing European system. That threat was brought to a halt in Western Europe through Spain for reasons explained in the text; it was the reversal of the threat in this area and the manner of the reversal that counted.

Far more serious for the West was the Islamic drive up the Danube valley, where the Turks had developed not only a better military system than any Islamic predecessors, but a military-political system capable of indefinite expansion. Vienna was a reversal of tendency; when the tide rolled back down the Danube, there passed with it the last chance that an exterior system would be imposed on the European, and the decisions henceforth were within variations of that Western European culture.

The farther we are from the peaks, the higher they must be to become visible. After Vienna the line is easier to follow, the parts become more integrated. It is possible that the story of the relief of Orléans should have been placed in that later complex instead of where it is set down for chronological reasons. But this would have involved pulling out of position one of the key facts in connection with Vienna, that the Turk was a greater danger to Charles V than the Protestant Reformation.

No apology is offered for construing the term "battle" in a rather loose sense. Not all military decisions have hinged on the result of a single clash of arms. The Vicksburg campaign is the best illustration; it was thoroughly decisive, but none of the five battles can be said to have done more than emphasize the character of the campaign itself. The abiding interest is in the command decisions and the rush of Grant's hurrying columns, so disposed that at every contact Union forces were in the field in numbers that made victory a foregone conclusion.

If it seems that a considerable proportion of the battles cited deal with the American scene, it can be replied that the emergence of the United States as a world power is one of the great facts of history as it stands today. The emergence of the Soviet Union is another; but the decisions in favor of that entity were seldom made on the battlefield (which, after all, does not determine everything), and the record in many cases has been so deliberately befouled for propaganda purposes that no honest account can be given.

THE BATTLES THAT
CHANGED HISTORY

1. Arbela and the Man
Who Would Be God

I

The Greeks had to go imperial to make it stand up.

This was something that Demosthenes, like many liberals insulated within the circle of his own rightness, failed to understand. He was a genius and he spoke in the name of an admirable ideal; the ideal of democracy, that the state is the collective will of all its individual components, achieving the united decision through free discussion. What he failed to see was that even in Athens this remained an unattained ideal, a precarious balance subject to destructive forces both from above and below, from within and without.

The achievement of Athens in the arts, philosophy, every intellectual pursuit, was magnificent and the democratic ideal was always present, but she was no more of a real democracy than Renaissance Florence, where there was also intellectual achievement. Democracy was in the hands of a small body of citizen voters, an island in the vast sea of slaves, metics, and unnaturalizable residents of exterior origin. There was a fatal inconsistency in Demosthenes' doctrine; his banner might more accurately have read, "Democracy—for Athenians only." Athens differed from Sparta, frankly an oligarchy, only in cultivating things of the spirit and in placing fewer restrictions on the personal habits of the individual. To be sure, this subtended enormous cultural differences, but they were not political differences, and the important decisions were made in the political field.

By its self-imposed limitations the Athenian democracy was incapable of real co-operation with any other state. It could form alliances, but only on a strictly temporary basis and in the face of imminent danger. It could take a place in no organization larger than itself, for this would involve the recognition of exteriors as equals, and the whole theory of Athenian democracy was that no one else had reached or could reach its own level. When Athens formed a league, it was the League of Delos, and its members were subjects. They were admitted to the sacred company of Greeks, the only civilized people in the world, but as second-class Greeks, like the lumpish Boeotians or the soft Corinthians.

This was not merely provincialism; there was in it a certain pride of attainment, and the general view, both at the time and since, has been that the attainment was very real. The narrowed view of democracy, however, did deprive Athens of one of the specific advantages of democracy—its defense mechanism. A monarchy or a dictatorship is in a very happy position at the beginning of a war; it has unified command, the co-ordination of all efforts to a single purpose, and unlimited control of resources. But the experience of the ages has been that in the long run these do not overmaster the resilience of democracy, its ability to adopt on a temporary basis whatever variations from the norm of practice may be needed for military efficiency, and the ease with which ability makes its way to the top through the looser structure of a democratic organization. In the closed circuit of Athenian democracy ability did not find it easy to reach the top or to stay there, and nobody thought of looking for it in a slave or a metic. Resilience was wanting; Sparta, organized for total war, had more of it.

The defense mechanism is always necessary. That of the Greek city states as a group grew out of the very thing that made their democracy imperfect—the common recognition of all as Greeks, possessing the *homonoia*, and having a common duty to help each other against the great, menacing world of the barbarians. The mechanism worked reasonably well for a time, thanks to several factors. One of these was psychological: the devotion of every Greek to his own city, his own group; his relation of mutual reliance within that circle to the *homonoia*, and its relation to him. Two factors were technical: the development of good iron armor, good iron spears and swords; and the fact that these were made to a common pattern, permitting the employment of groups of identically armed men as units. One was tactical: the fact that out of their mutual reliance the Greeks had learned to march in step.

The last came to the fore at Marathon in 490 B.C., and at Plataea in 479 it was decisive. In both battles the Asiatics, strong and courageous men, made their fight in the manner tribesmen usually do, in little knots of ten or a dozen, rushing one part of the line or another. At the point of contact they were always outnumbered by the Greek infantry, all in line, they were outreached by the long pikes, they could not get through Greek armor when they did close and, with light targets that would keep out an arrow but not much more and no body armor, had little defense of their own. At Marathon the Persians were driven in rout; at Plataea they were crushed, and even that cavalry which was the pride of Persia could make nothing of the hedge of spears.

Yet Thermopylae, Salamis, Marathon, Plataea were not decisive battles. In each case they decided nothing but that Greek civilization would not be submerged this time, and they determined nothing but the fact that the Greeks had developed a highly superior tactical technique. The Greek victories were backed by nothing so permanent as the fact that the conquest of Indians by whites in America was supported by a technology which could produce muskets and swords. Persians as well as Greeks could manufacture iron armor and eight-foot pikes and train men to use them; the Persians were quite as capable as Greeks of learning how to march in step, and some of them did when they found what a good trick it was.

Even devotion was no monopoly; and in the century that followed Plataea the Greek kind began sensibly to decline through the long series of conflicts that collectively bear the name of Peloponnesian and Corinthian wars. The citizen-soldier turned out to save his home, but as it began to require almost daily salvation over a period of years, he became more of a soldier and less of a citizen, and in the intervals of peace that spaced with those of combat, he tended to find he had no home and became a mercenary.

It is unnecessary to go into the complicated history of that century. But the main line is clear: Greece was gradually succumbing to Persia, not by force of arms—which had been defeated—but from the political impact of a system which could digest small units into larger ones. Under Xenophon, 10,000 Greeks marched through Asia Minor without anyone's being able to stop them, but they were mercenaries in Persian pay. When Sparta established her hegemony in the Greek world, it was overthrown among the islands at the Battle of Cnidus in 394 by a Greek fleet; but the fleet was paid from Persia and at least technically under the command of a Persian satrap. In the "King's Peace" of 386 the Greek cities of continental Asia Minor were turned over unconditionally to Persia, and perpetual Persian interference in Greek affairs was recognized as a right. Sparta, Thebes, and even Athens successively took Persian money for the furtherance of projects which in the long run could benefit only Persia.

That is, for all the formidable character of their armies and the skill with which they were used, the Greeks had found no answer to the Persian system of government, its way of life on high levels. They were becoming adsorbed to it, and the process would become absorption as soon as Greek internal conflicts had produced sufficient weaknesses. The collective defense mechanism of the Greek culture was failing and had, indeed, already failed.

II

In 367 a younger son of the King of Macedon, named Philip, was sent to Thebes as a hostage to guarantee the good behavior of his father's turbulent little kingdom toward the Greek cities along the coast. Thebes spoke for them because she was enjoying a brief period of leadership. Four years before at Leuctra the Thebans had inflicted an utterly astonishing defeat on one of those hitherto invincible Spartan armies, killing the king who led it and ending Sparta's lordship in continental Greece, as it had earlier been lost among the islands.

The whole air of Thebes at this date was electric, and there must have been a good deal of discussion of how the Theban farmers had pulled off their incredible feat. It was due to their general (and leading statesman) Epaminondas, people said. Confronted by that Spartan army, the very announcement of whose approach produced utter despondency in his home city, he did not draw out the hoplite infantry in parallel order, as the custom was. Instead he ployed the best of his men into a massive column, fifty men deep, on the left wing, and flung it well forward before the rest of the armies could close. This huge battering-ram of men sheared through and crushed the Spartan right, and all the Spartans not left on the ground were soon going somewhere else.

It was as simple as that to most of them. Probably the fifteen-year-old boy from Macedon was one of the few who saw that it was not quite as simple as that, that before the huge block of Thebans made contact there had been some sharp cavalry fighting in the wings and the Theban horse, which was always very good, had driven off the Spartan cavalry, which was always very weak, then turned in on the flank of the enemy line just as the Theban battering-ram struck it. It was the sort of observation the fifteen-year-old boy would make; he belonged to a race whose princes made war their only profession, partly through force of circumstances and partly because they liked it.

The Greeks generally regarded Macedonians as not quite in the *homonoia;* barbarians who had acquired a veneer of Greek culture and spoke a Greek dialect. In fact, they were mainly Dorian Greeks who had stopped off in the plain of the Haliacmon during the great southern movement of the tribes and intermarried a little with the original inhabitants. The intermarriage was nowhere near as extensive as that of the southern-going Dorians with the Achaeans who preceded them, and the Macedonians never did participate in the movement from the eighth century to the fifth, in which the city states developed various forms of aristocracy, oligarchy, and democracy. Politically Macedon was intensely conservative; it kept the old king-and-council system and the people thought of themselves as Macedonians, not citizens of the towns of Pella or Larissa. This was one of the things that made them un-Greek.

Philip's Theban visit lasted three years. He returned to Macedon, was given a small and remote province to govern, and proceded to grow up a vivid, rip-roaring blade, with a strong taste for women (he rather rapidly accumulated six wives) and a still stronger one for wine. There is something very like the Vikings about all the Macedonians, and most especially about Philip; the hoopla attracted attention, and nobody noticed that underneath it he was making some rather remarkable alterations in the army of his province, or that no matter how much of a hang-over he had in the morning he was out drilling with the troops.

In 359, when Philip was twenty-three, his elder brother, King Perdiccas, was killed in a fight with some Lyncestian highlanders, leaving an infant son and a formidable harridan of a queen mother, who had been regent before and wanted to be again. This sort of thing was not new in Macedonian history, and all the surrounding hill tribes—Illyrians from the west, Lyncestians and Paeonians from the north, Thracians from the east—moved in to collect the usual plunder from the cities of the plain while the royal family was weak. A Macedonian king —again like a Viking—was supposed to be a military leader; the council of higher nobles asked Philip to take the crown, a step doubtless encouraged by his own previous arrangements.

He bought off the Paeonians and Thracians by money payments, drove out the Lyncestians with the normal local levies, and secured the support of Athens (temporarily dominant in Greece) by ceding any right he had to their revolted colony of Amphipolis; the rest would have to wait. That winter Philip opened up a gold mine at Mount Pangaeus to fill up his treasury, a key event, then sent to south Greece and Greek Italy for technical experts, and began organizing and drilling his army.

The completion of that last process took years, and owed something to what he had learned from the Thebans and a good deal to what he heard from people who were not Thebans; but the essential elements in it were Philip's own, and the most essential of these were that it was the first standing army in the world, based on universal service, and that it was the first army in the world that did not take local levies just as they came, but deliberately trained for and combined all arms.

The core of this new model was the phalanx of heavy infantry; they were armed with a longsword and a spear, the sarissa, considerably longer than the usual Greek model, between twelve and twenty feet, according to which source you choose. They were trained to stand at three-foot intervals, but could close up to receive cavalry. For mobility the Greek hoplite's breastplate was discarded in favor of a leather jerkin, but he kept the shield and helmet. They were divided into regiments of 1,536 men, and Philip gave this phalanx weight by arranging them sixteen men deep instead of the eight or twelve of the normal hoplite formation.

One of the weaknesses of the pre-Philip block of infantry was its flanks; to cover those of his phalanx Philip attached a corps of his own invention, the hypaspists, later very famous as the "Silver Shields." They were spear-and-sword men, but the spears were shorter and the shields lighter than in the phalanx; a corps of maneuver, which could extend or mass. For skirmishing and light work there were archers and javelin men, still more mobile; the latter chiefly Agrianian tribesmen from the hills, the former mostly hired out of Crete, which had a great reputation as a nursery of bowmen.

But the heart of the army and its striking force was the heavy cavalry, the *hetiaroi*, or "King's Companions." They had helmet, shield, breastplate, and spear, but as stirrups were not yet invented the spear was used for thrusting and not as a lance. Service in the Companions was honorific, and most honorific of all was to be a member of the squadron of 250, which always rode on the extreme right, the post of greatest danger, and was known as the Agema, or "King's Own." Finally Philip had heard that among the Greek cities of Italy they had machines that would batter down the brick and timber walls that surrounded most cities; he imported engineers from that area and had them set up a mobile siege train, the first in history.

All these formations were kept with the colors until they had very thoroughly learned their drill, making route marches of thirty-five miles a day with full kit. By the spring of 358 the king had 10,000 trained infantry and 600 of the Companion cavalry and turned on the hill tribes which had been such a nuisance. The Paeonians collapsed after one not very hard fight; the Illyrians were strong enough to stand a battle in the formal Greek style, and Philip showed them something new in military tactics. He held his left refused while the hypaspists and phalanx closed on center and right, and when a satisfactory stage of front line confusion had been produced, charged on his left with the Companion cavalry and nearly wiped out the enemy.

After this the hill peoples were quiet and furnished a good many of the recruits which made up the growing body of the national army, a process which simultaneously assisted the unification of Macedon, since the men were not brigaded in the usual way according to districts and races, but formed a unified force. There were some incidents with various city states (Philip took Amphipolis by storm, for instance, to the indignation of Athens), but nothing really important for another six years, during which the king matured his army and his project, which was nothing less than an attack on the huge empire of Persia. This attack he did not intend to make merely as King of Macedon, but as commanding general for a league of all the Greek states. In fine, he had discerned what Demosthenes missed, that the Greek cultural system must ultimately be rooted out by the Persian if the former remained so divided and the latter so extensive and wealthy. It is somewhat more than probable that Philip intended no more than setting up a solid state in the area populated by Greeks; that he was not looking for conquest, but coexistence.

What Demosthenes did not miss was the implications of the early steps in this process, the drive toward the unification of Greece. To his mind this involved the suppression of democracy (including the privilege of each democratic city to go to war with any other). When, by a carefully arranged request, Philip intervened in one of these local wars and came out of it as official head of the confederation of Thessaly, the orator delivered his First Philippic. He kept on delivering them as long as he lasted.

At this point it is necessary to note that although Philip was a diplomatic liar on a large scale, a lecher, and a drunken viking, his civil administration was quite as sharp as his military. He gave good government. The gold mines he had opened allowed him to pay for everything on the nail; there was justice in his courts and people were prosperous under his administration. What the hell was the use of democracy when you lived better under Philip? There was thus a strong pro-Philip party in most cities and Demosthenes had an uphill job. It is unnecessary to trace all the steps in the complicated double dance that followed, but in 338 the allied armies of Athens, Thebes, and some of the lesser cities met that of Macedon at Chaeronea. Thebes was wiped out and Athens terribly crippled.

To the surprise of the defeated, the conqueror, instead of going in for the expected exactions and proscriptions, called a conference of the powers of Greece at Corinth, even including Athens and Thebes. He presided at that conference and, recognizing that Greeks thought with their tongues, let them talk as long as they pleased. The issue was a general agreement prohibiting wars within Greece and naming Philip as captain-general of a League of Corinth to enforce. Since such a league must have a purpose beyond the mere police function, there was implied in its statute the idea that the fundamental reason for the League was a war of revenge on Persia for the aggressions begun by military means 150 years before and continued by other devices since. This idea was of no small help to the pro-Macedonian parties; no concept could have been more popular than a union of the *homonoia* against the great power which did not recognize it.

III

In 357 Philip married, as his seventh wife, an Epirote princess named Olympias, whom he had met at Samothrace during the celebration of the mysteries there. She was an Orphic priestess and a bacchanal, who claimed descent from Achilles, indulged in strange rites and a friendship for snakes. In a sense she became his only wife, a woman who could keep step with him. The night the marriage was consummated she dreamed that thunderbolts fell on her womb, and in due time was delivered of a son named Alexander.

Alexander's earliest tutor was a man of extraordinary strictness, who made him march half the night to gain an appetite for breakfast and eat a light breakfast to have an appetite for dinner. When he passed beyond the grammar school age, Alexander was turned over to Aristotle. The training was both philosophical and military; he early developed such strength, such address, such extraordinary good looks, such quickness of intelligence that in view of his mother's close connection with mysterious deities tales began to circulate that he might be of no human origin. As he grew up at the court he drank to keep the others company, but not very much. He exhibited an extraordinary continence and walked out of the room with a sneer when his father caused a courtesan to be placed in his bed; he did not care for games. At the age of eighteen he commanded the Companion cavalry when it delivered the decisive charge at Chaeronea. When he was twenty, and an advanced corps under the old marshal, Parmenio, had already secured a beachhead at the Dardanelles for the attack on Persia, Philip was assassinated and Alexander became King of Macedon.

The leading Greek cities of the opposition, Athens and Thebes, expressed a delight over the death of the monster which quickly cooled when Alexander came through the passes at the head of his army. He was elected Captain-General of the League in his father's room, and turned back to northern Macedon, where, to secure his base before attempting the great adventure against Persia, he conducted two whirlwind campaigns to the Danube and in Illyria. These campaigns are ill-documented, but they were key events. It was not only that Alexander broke the tribes so thoroughly that they gave no more trouble for a generation, but the manner in which he did it. He marched the men harder than Philip ever had; he was in the middle of every battle, and always with the arm with which he intended to strike the decisive blow—once with the phalanx, once with the Companions, once with the hypaspists, and once even with the light-armed javelin men. That is, he had a new concept of tactics. His maneuvers were astonishing and somewhat outrageous to the old officers who had served with Philip for twenty years; but they had to admit that everything came off as planned, and there developed a bond of confidence between the youthful commander and his army.

While Alexander was on this expedition, Darius III Codomannus, who had become King of Persia and was by no means ignorant of what the Macedonians intended, tried the old infallible trick of subsidizing the Greeks to fight each other. Sparta, not a member of the Corinthian League, took his money; so did Demosthenes for Athens, though the city officially refused; probably Thebes collected also. A story was spread that Alexander had been killed in the north and witnesses were produced to prove it. Thebes rose and attacked the Macedonian garrison in its citadel; Athens was discussing doing something serious when Alexander and his army dropped out of the clouds, stormed Thebes, killed 6,000 of its people in street fighting, and ordered the place leveled to the ground. Athens he treated with the greatest consideration, not only from the emotional reason that he regarded her as the center of Greek culture, but also for the practical one that she had a powerful fleet. He usually had two reasons for doing things. The Greek base was now secured. In the winter of 335, Alexander went to the Straits, recalled Parmenio from the beachhead, and began his own preparations for the invasion. It is quite certain that from the beginning he had discarded his father's concept of a war of limited objectives for the preservation of Greece and was aiming at nothing less than the conquest of the Persian Empire and the whole system supporting it. He expected to be away from Greece for a long time; in charge of Macedonian-Greek affairs he left the other marshal, Antipater, with military authority and 9,000 Macedonian troops. Olympias, the queen mother, theoretically had charge of civil affairs, although the authority of the two somewhat overlapped. They hated each other, and could be counted on to achieve some sort of dynamic balance.

The invading force consisted of 30,000 infantry and 5,000 horse. In addition to the Macedonian regular army it included a strong contingent of League troops, normal Greek hoplites, and a body of cavalry from Thessaly, second in value only to the Companions. In all previous wars the central idea had been to find the enemy field army, beat it, and then take his cities; Alexander brought to his task something quite as novel as Philip's combination of arms—a master strategic plan. For a twenty-one-year-old who conducted his movements with a celerity indicating impatience it was a distinctly surprising plan: to clear out the whole west coast of Asia and, by depriving the fleets serving Persia of their bases, to prevent any counteroffensive against his lines of communication or home areas. Alexander was perfectly aware of the looseness of the bonds produced by the Persian principle of local autonomy, the fact that the provinces would change allegiance easily in the presence of force, and the fact that it would take time for Darius to assemble an army to deal with him.

He set out, then, down the coast of Asia Minor; and at the river Granicus, a stream with steep banks, met the first opposition in the form of 20,000 Asiatic horse and 20,000 Greek mercenary infantry commanded by Memnon of Rhodes, gen-

eral for Persia in those parts. Memnon made the mistake of trying to hold the bank with his cavalry while the Greek spearmen were in the rear. Alexander broke the horse by a charge
of the Companions, the phalanx gained the crossing and cut
the mercenaries to pieces. Not enough of the Persians were left
to keep most of Phrygia from falling under the king's control.
Now he moved south through Asia Minor, taking cities, with
a turn back to Gordium and Angora in the central plateau,
then moved south through the mountains to the coast of
Lycia.

Darius had meanwhile gathered an army of several times the
Macedonian numbers and, well advised at least in strategy, suddenly brought it through the passes onto Alexander's rear in
the plain of Issus, the date being October 333. The Persians
were so cramped between hill and sea that their numbers did
them no good; Darius' army was reduced to fragments in a
battle of hard Macedonian charges, and what was left of it dissolved, while Alexander moved on down the coast. Of the
cities only Tyre held out; it took an eight-month siege to reduce the place, but when he had it Alexander also had command of all the Phoenician fleets and the waters of the eastern
Mediterranean.

Gaza also stood a siege, but Egypt made hardly any resistance, and Alexander rolled through it to visit the famous oracle
of Zeus-Ammon at the oasis of Siwa. This was a key event; the
priest on duty greeted him as the son of Zeus without previous
recognition and they went in together to visit the altar of the
god, where Alexander received revelations he never afterward
discussed. But from this time onward the story of his quasi-
divine origin became more and more firmly established. There
was nothing unreasonable about this to the age; everyone, including probably Alexander himself, believed in his descent
from Achilles on his mother's side and from Heracles on his
father's. Also he was coming into frequent contact with Orientals, among whom divine kingship was a rooted and normal
institution; a king was not a king at all unless he had some
special connection with the gods, even in Israel. And in Greece

31

royal divinity had very special uses; the antimonarchial tradition among the city states was very strong and had been one of
the main reasons why it was possible to arouse opposition to
Philip. But it became quite a different matter if, instead of dealing with a king, you were being ordered about by a demi-god.

At Memphis, Alexander made a governmental reorganization
that was to become a pattern with him, placing the civil administration in the hands of local talent, to rule according to
traditional usages, and the military administration and garrison
commands in the hands of Macedonian officers. It was now the
spring of 331; reinforcements from Greece, mainly mercenaries, met the army at Memphis and Alexander turned back
northward, meeting his fleet at Tyre and sending a strong
squadron back to Greece to keep an eye on the Spartans. He
struck inland through Damascus, crossed the Euphrates at
Thapsacus, and made for the upper waters of the Tigris, which
was spanned north of the ruins of Nineveh, whereupon the
Macedonians moved down the left bank of the river. Alexander's intelligence organization, like all his subsidiary services,
was good; he had learned that Darius was approaching with all
the men he could gather, intending to fight in the open plain
east of the Tigris; and the invader meant to oblige.

I V

Darius Codomannus does not seem to have been much of a man
of war himself, but he had a certain talent as an employer of
experts, and under their advice he had made the best possible
use of the vast potential of the empire. The whole two years
of Alexander's campaign along the eastern Mediterranean had
been spent in assembling a vast host—Bedouins from the Red
Sea, Armenians, Parthians, Hyrcanians, even Pathans from dis-
tant India, in addition to the home forces. The size of that army
is given by several ancient authors as a million men, which is
certainly an overestimate meaning a "very large number," but
it cannot have been smaller than the least figure given, which is

45,000 cavalry and 200,000 infantry, against the 40,000 infantry and 7,000 horse Alexander now had.

The Persian advanced base was established at Arbela, from which Darius moved thirty-five miles west to where an already extensive plain was rendered still more suitable for his operations by the leveling of hummocks and the removal of all obstacles. He had two hundred scythe-chariots, weapons with which the Macedonians were totally unfamiliar and which could be very formidable. These he placed in his first line, with the idea of disorganizing the phalanx. Midway along that line and directly in front of Darius' own post were stationed fifteen war elephants from the Indus. It was as certain as anything could be that Alexander would strike for the Persian king, as he had at Issus, and that he would be leading the Companion cavalry; the elephants were supposed to break up this formation.

An accurate picture of the rest of Darius' formation has come down from the fact that his order of battle was later captured. On the left, under the eastern satrap Bessus, one of the employed experts, there were thrown well forward the Bactrian and Scythian armored horse archers; next to them a big block of the Persian royal horse guard. Out on the extreme right, under another expert, named Mazaeus, were the Armenian and Cappadocian heavy cavalry. In the center of the second line was a solid formation of Persian foot spearmen, the "Kinsmen," trained like Greeks and with golden apples on the hilts of their spears; on either flank they were supported by formations of Greek mercenaries, the only troops who could be expected to meet the phalanx on foot, but who would (it was hoped) encounter it after it had been shaken by the scythe-chariots in front and charges of cavalry into its wings. Left of this solid infantry center were more cavalry formations, Bactrians and Persians; right of it, still more cavalry, Persians, Indians, Hyrcanians, Parthians, mostly of the steppe variety. Behind, marshaled according to their tribes, whose names do not matter, were the various infantry levies, mostly ill-armed, mostly ill-led, not even speaking each other's languages, present rather to emphasize the power and glory of the Great King than for any serious service expected of them.

This was the array, expecting immediate attack, that Alexander saw when he rode forward on the afternoon of September 30 with a picked body of cavalry. Instead of attacking he went into camp to rest his men after a day's march, to think and to conduct certain incantations after the manner he had been taught by the priests of Egypt. When this private mumbling was over, Parmenio, the old marshal, entered the royal tent to suggest that a night attack would throw so huge a host as the Persian into disorder. Alexander refused, with the recorded reason, "I will not steal a victory." But as with many of his high-flown phrases this indubitably concealed his perfectly rational appreciation of the fact that whatever advantages Macedon had lay in discipline and timing, and these would be lost in a night attack. A little more puzzling is that neither high commander thought about operating against his opponent's communications; the logistics of Darius' big army must have been very difficult, and those of Alexander, so far from his base, precarious. Probably the explanation is that both had a supply problem that could be solved only by victorious battle.

In the morning Alexander drew out his army in an order based on what he had seen the afternoon before, quite confident that the Persian force was too cumbersome for any real alteration. The whole of his right wing consisted of the Companion cavalry, with half the Agrianians, archers, and javelin men across the front as a protection against the elephants and scythe-chariots. Left of the Companions were posted the hypaspists; then the phalanx in its solid formation, finally the cavalry of Greece, Thessaly, and Pharsalia. Old Parmenio was in charge of this wing.

The whole line was so short that although Alexander, with the extreme right wing of the Companions, was nearly opposite Darius, the Macedonian left did not even reach out as far as the Persian right. There was thus a huge overlap on both wings, greatest on the Macedonian right, and Alexander could confidently expect to be flanked on both. Against this he pro-

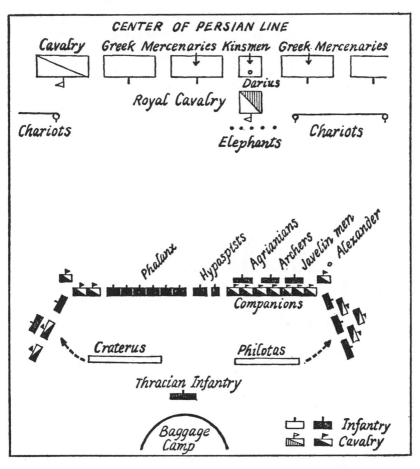

Arbela; Alexander's Order of Battle

vided by setting up two flying wings, for the moment stationed behind the central line of battle. On the right, under an officer named Philotas, were the remainder of the light troops, with a body of light cavalry under Aretes, some Greek mercenary cavalry, and a regiment of veteran mercenary infantry for stiffening. On the left, under Craterus, were formations of Odryssian and Greek allied cavalry, with another regiment of mercenaries and some Thracian infantry. Both these flying wings were very flexible and were instructed to face as occasion dictated, take in the flank any forces attempting the flank of the main battle line, or wheel right around against anything coming from the rear. In charge of the entrenched camp were left some Thracian infantry, hillmen who often swung two swords, not well drilled in precision movements. Alexander's order of battle is very important; it explains everything that happened.

Instead of moving straight forward Alexander obliqued to his right, the Persian left, the heavy cavalry under his own hand

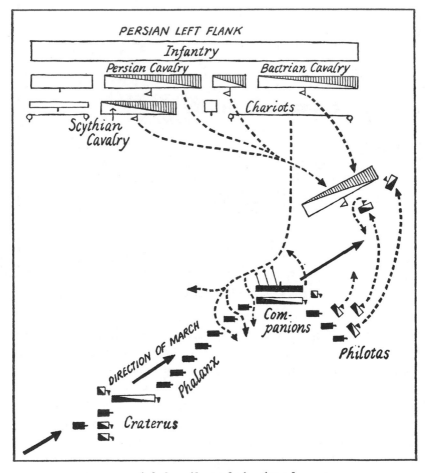

Arbela; Alexander's Attack

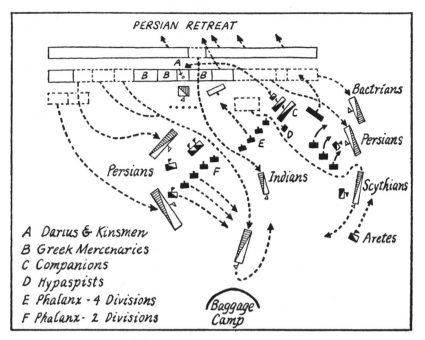

A Darius & Kinsmen
B Greek Mercenaries
C Companions
D Hypaspists
E Phalanx - 4 Divisions
F Phalanx - 2 Divisions

Arbela; the Persian Line Broken

moving fastest. Darius, perceiving that they were reaching the limits of the cleared ground where the scythe-chariots would be effective, ordered the cavalry of his left to halt this movement. Alexander replied by putting in the Greek mercenary cavalry of Philotas' command; they were driven back, but as the light cavalry of Aretes followed them, Bessus turned loose the Bactrian and Scythian horse. There was a violent cavalry fight, involving some of the Companions, in dust that rose so thick it was hard to see anything. The Bactrians had better armor, and for a time the Macedonian losses were heavy; but Alexander's men were trained to give hard, repeated shocks in tight squadrons while the Asiatics fought in a confused mass. They could make nothing whatever of the infantry support on this wing and gradually were driven back.

While this was going on, Darius launched his scythe-chariots against the phalanx, which had been gradually carried out in front of the Companion cavalry by its own continued rightward slant and Alexander's semi-retreat. The light-armed in front shot down the charioteers, flung javelins into horses, and raced along cutting traces and seizing bridles; the few chariots that got away from this swarm of wasps could do nothing but run down the lanes between the taxes of the phalanx to the rear, where they were captured by grooms.

Now the Persian cavalry on the left of Darius' infantry center left its place, with or without orders, to follow Bessus' Bactrians and Scythians around the Macedonian right wing. Alexander ordered Aretes with the light cavalry, recovered from its original shock, to attack them in flank as they did so; he himself formed the Companions into a huge wedge and, swinging out around the right wing of the phalanx, drove them in through the huge gap left by the Persian cavalry, straight toward the Persian infantry center, where Darius stood conspicuous in his high chariot. Both the Companions and the solid ranks of the phalanx took the Greek mercenaries and the apple-bearers at the oblique, and the Persian forces crumpled. Darius' charioteer was killed by his side; he leaped onto a fast horse and fled from the field.

Alexander was just driving the hypaspists into the confused mass of tribal infantry in the rear of Darius' center and making preparations for a pursuit when word reached him that Parmenio and Craterus of the left were in trouble. It was due to the Persian, Indian, and steppe cavalry of the enemy right wing, which launched itself at, and all around, the flying left wing of Craterus, well behind the advancing phalanx. Parmenio had too few mounted men to do more than barely hold head to them on his front; they lapped around his left and through the gap that had unavoidably opened between him and the phalanx. Many of them made for the baggage camp; Parmenio was surrounded by the rest.

However, one taxis of the phalanx, not yet engaged in the center, faced around, formed line with Parmenio's infantry, and fell on the Persians and Indians at the baggage camp from the rear. They could not stand that and all began to drift back just as Alexander fell on their rear with the Companions. Now came the most desperate fighting of the day and Alexander lost sixty of his top 200 Companions before the last fighting formations of the enemy were cut to pieces and utterly routed. Before he camped that night, the army had made a forced march of thirty-five miles in pursuit of the man who was now ex-King of Persia.

V

The decisiveness of Arbela lay not in the fact that it was achieved, but in what Alexander did with it. It was merely on the lowest plane of history that he demolished the menace to Greek culture in the battle and in the campaigns that followed, carrying him beyond the Oxus and to the Indus. It was merely a military event that he had demonstrated, that an army disciplined and armed as his could go anywhere and do anything, that the specific defense mechanism of civilization is in the co-operative and intelligent use of means open for anyone to use.

He did much more, and it was by virtue of his background and constitution that he did that much more. Even from Aristotle he had learned that Greeks were very superior creatures and barbarians hardly human. He went beyond that "and preferred to divide men into good and bad without regard to race."[1] His crowning act was that marriage of 7,000 of his Macedonians to as many Persian women according to Persian rites, at Babylon, following his immense journeys and campaignings. The concept was that the *homonoia*, "the unity in concord," should not apply to the relations between Greek and Greek alone, but those between man and man of any race. His own career hardly allowed him any other process of thinking; the Greeks often denied him the name of Greek and he was always conscious of some Illyrian blood; yet in the interest of Greek culture he had overthrown the enemies of Greece and won the empire of all the world that mattered. Zeus-Ammon

[1] W. W. Tarn

was the sun god; all were entitled to his radiance, and Alexander conceived it his duty to bring it to all.

This concept leads straight to the Pauline "neither Greek nor Jew, circumcision nor uncircumcision, barbarian, Scythian, bond nor free." He spread that concept, with highly practical means of enforcing it and bringing to its support the intelligence of Greece and the arms of Macedon. If his own country ceased to be a great power in the subsequent age, it was chiefly because the best brains in it—and many of those in Greece, for that matter—were siphoned off into the business of Hellenizing the world. Says Ulrich Wilcken, the biographer, "The whole subsequent course of history, the political, economic and cultural life of after times, cannot be understood apart from the career of Alexander."

2. The Red King at Beneventum

I

The ambassador from the northern tribes was a man of the most absurd dignity, with a hook nose and a robe cut too long for him. His Greek was so bad as to be comic, and the people in the agora laughed as he demanded reparations for the four ships their mob had destroyed. They all knew—their orators had told them—that those four ships had no right in their harbor and the mob had merely executed an unofficial act of justice according to law. They laughed, then, and pelted the ambassador with clods. After a while he ceased trying to reason with them, held up the dirtied toga, made some remark in his incorrect Greek to the effect that it would take a good deal to wash it clean, and stalked out.

After he had left, it occurred to the city fathers that those tribesmen were very numerous and could make a good deal of trouble for farmers in the back country. They decided to send an embassy across the Adriatic to ask King Pyrrhus of Epirus to help them in the name of *homonoia*, the union of all Greeks against all barbarians, promising him that he could keep anything he could take from the tribesmen. This was precisely the opportunity for which King Pyrrhus had been waiting. He was now nearly forty and all his life had been something of an adventurer, beginning with the time when, as an infant, he had been carried by night and cloud to take refuge with the Illyrians from those who had usurped his father's throne. Grown to young manhood, he took part as a free-lance in that great Battle of Ipsus, where it was decided that the heritage of Alexander should not remain one, but be split into separate kingdoms. He chose the wrong side, and was carried away a hostage into Egypt.

There he set his cap at Berenice, one of the king's wives, and made such an impression on that forceful woman that she gave him her daughter in marriage and later saw to it that Pyrrhus was furnished with money enough to raise an army and was sent back to his own land. This was also good politics, since King Ptolemy of Egypt was engaged in a struggle with the dynasty that had inherited Macedon, and anything that would weaken the old kingdom was pleasant to him.

Pyrrhus was a collateral relative of the great Alexander, and himself a descendant of Achilles, as proved by the red hair he shared with the son of that Homeric hero. In Epirus he proved himself every bit the man Ptolemy had hoped. Very quickly he raised an army on the Macedonian border and took half of Macedon, which recognized his people as at least as much Greek as themselves. His military skill was prodigious; like Alexander, he was a man who enchanted all hearts, and like Philip, he gave sound administration and honest justice. It was said of his race, the Aecides, that they were more war-strong than wisdom-strong, but in every respect he belied the judgment.

Not that he lacked being war-strong. In his army he had forged an instrument at least equal to that of Philip of Macedon, and over Philip he had the advantage of being in friendly relations with Seleucus Nicator, to whom had fallen the Great East on the breakup of the Alexandrian empire, and that monarch had furnished him with a supply of elephants, one of the most formidable weapons yet discovered. In India they had demonstrated that they could put any cavalry to flight, even Alexander's.

The only trouble was that Pyrrhus, with an ambition as boundless as that of Alexander and a perfectly attuned military instrument, had nowhere to go. The only prospect of war was against another Hellenistic kingdom nearly as well equipped as his own. Experience showed that conquest in this direction would provoke a general alliance against him; it was the custom of these states to pull down the strongest. This was the reason why the appeal from Tarentum, saying she was menaced by barbarian tribes, was so very pleasant. In the barbarian West there ought to be opportunities as wide as Alexander had found in the barbarian East; and the Red King of Epirus responded at once.

In the spring of 280 B.C. he arrived at Tarentum through a storm so violent that it blew some of his ships all the way to Libya. The oracle of Apollo at Delphi had promised him a victory. Cineas, his orator, philosopher, and man of business, had gone on ahead with 3,000 men, and was ready with a report. As to the people of Tarentum, it was not too favorable. They might as well have been Corinthians; luxurious, indolent, and unstable, inclined toward democratic government. In their favor it could be said that they had brought the city of Thurii into alliance; as this place lay on the opposite shore of the Tarentine Gulf, it afforded an excellent base for menacing the rear of the barbarian bands, who were working eastward along the shore.

As to the tribesmen, Cineas said they were reported quite skilled fighters. They had formed one of those confederations which so readily assemble and so readily dissolve among barbarians, and had lately been engaged in war with the Samnites, a strong hill people of the central peninsula, who would probably furnish some auxiliaries. Pyrrhus approved the sending of ambassadors to these Samnites and sat down to wait for the rest of the troops, only 2,000 with two elephants having come with him.

When all were arrived he had 20,000 infantry, 3,000 cavalry, 2,000 archers, 500 slingers, and 20 elephants. The king immediately closed the walks and places of public exercise and prohibited all festivities and drinking parties as unseasonable during a war. This did not endear him to the Tarentines, but they turned out to drill under the eyes of his officers and furnished a contingent of hoplites to the army, probably few more than enough to balance the garrison he left in the citadel.

These arrangements may be conceived as taking a couple of months. When they were complete, Pyrrhus marched out from the town along the Tarentine Gulf with an army that, except for the elephants, was almost a carbon copy of the one Alexander had taken to Asia. Like the Macedonian army, that of Pyrrhus had a solid core of phalangites, thoroughly trained, with hypaspists to link with the cavalry in the wings. His personal bodyguard was less numerous than the Companions, the Epirotes not being so much a horse-riding people, but he had adopted Alexander's practice of brevetting to this corps d'élite the best men he could find anywhere, regardless of origin, and it would grow. Meanwhile the bulk of his horse were Thessalians, very good men. Cineas had arranged with some of the other cities of Italian Greece to send allied contingents of hoplites, but these hardly seemed necessary in dealing with a barbarian force that was reported no greater than his own.

The Red King moved forward at once, then, and, as common courtesy demanded, sent on ahead a herald to offer to arbitrate between Tarentum and the tribesmen. This man presently returned with the proud reply that they neither accepted him as an arbitrator nor feared him as an enemy. Pyrrhus pushed on, and near Heraclea at the river Liris camped at the top of a hill and rode forward to examine the camp of the tribesmen on the opposite slope.

He was looking at a Roman consular army.

II

From where he stood, the king could see the neatly palisaded wall of the Roman camp, the guards posted all in order, the muscular small men filing down to the river for water, with good helmets and mail of iron bands. He turned to one of his generals and friends. "This order of the barbarians is not at all barbarian in character."

He did not have a chance to say much more. No sooner had the Romans sighted his approach than they poured out of their camp and down to the fords, covered with a foam of light-armed. This was an impudence not to be borne, and moreover, for reasons customary and honorific rather than tactical, it was considered at the time desirable to fight on the far slope of a stream after having crossed, as Alexander had done at the Granicus. Pyrrhus dispatched Megacles to draw up and bring on the phalanx, while he himself led the cavalry in a charge to halt this audacious advance.

Instantly he found himself in the fight of his life. The Roman cavalry were not as numerous as he expected, but they were much better fighters than they had any right to be, and behind them he came up against the legionary soldiers, something utterly new in Greek experience. They had big cylinder shields, which they locked together from man to man against attack, short spears, and heavy shortswords. They were formed in little blocks, the maniples, which lined up checkerboardwise instead of in the solid Greek formations, and these maniples displayed an amazing mobility. Attack one of them in the flank and you were promptly flanked by another. Pyrrhus' horse was killed under him, his Companions were rudely thrown back, and he barely reached the shelter of the phalanx before the two main lines came in contact.

The shock was terrific, and as the cavalry filed into the wings, there followed one of the hardest fights of history. The phalanx found it had to tighten up in close order; the gaps in the Roman checkerboard formation tended to split it apart as it advanced into the open spaces, while the Roman soldiers seeped into every interstice, stabbing with their shortswords and using the upper edges of their big shields under the chins of their adversaries. The Romans could not gain against the solid ranks of the phalanx, but neither could it do more than defend itself. Seven times the lines separated and clashed together again. The casualties were terrific; the Roman line, though thinner, was longer than that of Pyrrhus, the hypaspists on the flanks were definitely outmarched, Megacles was killed, and the phalanx itself began to shake when Pyrrhus at last succeeded in bringing the slow-moving elephants around from the rear against the cavalry of the Roman right wing.

No Roman had seen or heard of these huge beasts before, and the horses, as horses always, could not bear them. The Roman cavalry fled and in its flight broke up the legionary formations, Pyrrhus put in the Thessalian horse against the broken line and the battle was won.

It was not an Alexandrian victory. The Romans had lost 7,000 killed and 2,000 prisoners, but Pyrrhus had lost 4,000 men in killed alone, 16 per cent of his total force—a whole forest had to be cut down to burn the dead—and there could be no pursuit. The Romans held their fords and their camp until they were ready to go. On a precedent established by Alexander it had become the custom among the Hellenistic monarchies to offer prisoners service with their captor, and Pyrrhus made the usual offer. To his surprise, it was unanimously refused; he did not get a man.

On top of the battle itself this should have given him a sense that he was dealing with some very peculiar phenomena indeed, and there is evidence that to a certain extent it did, but he continued to apply the accepted formulae. In view of the fact that all the Greek cities of south Italy now enthusiastically joined him, he had every reason for doing so. The way to break up a confederation of barbarians is to strike at its nexus, as Alexander had in Bactria and again in India; the Red King marched straight on Rome.

He received another surprise; the confederation showed no signs of dissolution. Neapolis and Capua refused him admittance, the local people sniped his campfires with arrows from the woods at night, and as he neared the city he found it garrisoned by another consular army, larger than the one he had beaten. The Romans even found resources to reinforce their retreating field force by two additional legions.

Barbarians with such a military organization could clearly

be quite as useful allies as the Thessalians. Moreover, Pyrrhus already had offers that would take him into fabulously rich Sicily, where he could make gains far beyond what he might get out of these tough hillsmen. He sent Cineas to Rome with presents for the leading ladies and political personages and an offer of peace and friendship. He would release his prisoners; the Romans were to pledge autonomy and liberty to the Greek cities, let the Samnites alone in the future and, at least by implication, withdraw the colonies they had placed at Luceria and Venusia in south Italy. That is, there was to be an alliance and a delimitation of boundaries, with the south and west of the Mediterranean open for the empire of Pyrrhus.

The experience of Cineas in Rome, the first nonhostile impact of two utterly different civilizations, has been justly celebrated. The orator's presents were declined with dignity, but he was heard with respect, and voices were raised in the Senate for the acceptance of his offer. At this moment there was led into the hall the aged Appius Claudius, blind and very patrician, who made a fighting speech, the first one we have of Roman record. It was his misfortune, he said, that he was not deaf as well as blind before he heard Romans propose such things; did they not realize that peace with Pyrrhus after a defeat would be an invitation to other invaders from the dynasts, world without end? Rome should make no peace with anyone on her soil.

He convinced them; Cineas was sent back to report that the Romans had already enlisted more new troops than they had lost in the battle. They were not Roman citizens alone, but men from the allies all over central Italy; this business was going to be like fighting the Lernaean hydra, and the Romans had two new generals, P. Sulpicius and Decius Mus, who might be good.

Pyrrhus seems not to have been too deeply impressed. After all, Heracles had found a means of dealing with the hydra, and he himself was conscious of something close to military genius; he had proved it. His direct march on Rome would have been perfectly correct if the assumptions underlying it

47

were true. Now he adopted a more careful strategic approach, retiring to his widespread base in southern Italy, where he picked up important allied contingents, then moved north along the Adriatic coast, with the anti-Roman southern Samnites protecting his communications. Well north of Rome, where he expected to pull in more anti-Roman groups and establish a forward base for direct operations against the city, he turned inland to pass the spine of the Apennines . . .

And encountered a double consular army, about 40,000 men, equal to his own strength, even including the allies he had gathered. There were as many pro-Romans as anti-Romans in those hills, and the consuls had excellent intelligence. The place they chose to stop Pyrrhus was at Asculum, on the Aufidus River, an area rough and wooded, with marshes along the banks of the stream to hinder the operations of Pyrrhus' cavalry and elephants. The Romans got across the stream to set up a parallel order battle with their flanks on marshes, and in April 278 the contest was engaged.

Pyrrhus placed his phalanx in the center and, to avoid the outflanking that had almost ruined him at Heraclea, prolonged its line in both directions with hoplites from the Greek cities and Samnites in semi-manipular formation. The two armies fought a set piece of a battle, with neither side able to make much impression on the other, the usual thing in ancient battles unless one side began to break. At night they drew off by a kind of mutual agreement. At this point it occurred to the Red King that one of the things which made these barbarians so dangerous was the fact that they applied what were essentially cavalry tactics to infantry—charging in intervaled tight shock groups, which withdrew to allow the second line of maniples to charge, then the third. He needed to cramp them, hinder their free movement. He sent forward the light-armed to seize and fortify the flanking marshes for this purpose, at the same time gaining more elbowroom for his own movements. He wanted to use the elephants, but had been unable to find a place to put them in on the first day without opening a fatal gap in his line.

In the morning the Romans attacked him again, and he sent forward the elephants through the low ground, mixed with light-armed. They had provided chariots bearing long sharp spears as a defense against the big beasts, but the ground was too rough for their operation; the elephants broke through. They succeeded in driving off the Roman horse and reaching the legions, but even so, it was a very near thing; the allies on the wings of the phalanx were just giving way, and Pyrrhus himself was badly wounded. The Romans lost 6,000 men, but they held their fords and their camp.

Asculum was the Pyrrhic triumph of the famous quotation, when the king remarked in answer to congratulations, "One more such victory and I am undone." The 3,500 killed on his side included most of his generals and his best friends, the flower of the army; the Companions were practically wiped out, and he was visibly no nearer the end of the war than before Heraclea. The Romans began raising more legions.

III

At this point the Red King began to be conscious of a lack of strategic support. The reinforcements that reached him from across the Adriatic were insufficient to make good his losses, especially in officers, and the troops he could get from the Italian cities were showing an increasing disinclination to fight legionaries. It was therefore with fairly sound strategic logic that he decided to let the Roman war hang while he broadened his base by accepting the offers from Sicily.

These offers were to place him in control of Syracuse, Agrigentum, and Leontini if he would only drive off the Carthaginians, who were threatening to conquer the whole island and already had most of it. For the Carthaginians, Pyrrhus could only have felt the contempt he began by feeling for the Romans. They were un-Hellenized Orientals, not steady in the field. Possession of the main Greek cities of Sicily—and Syracuse was one of the largest in the Hellenistic world—

49

would give him a huge reservoir of manpower, which needed only leadership, drill, discipline, things the Red King could most specifically supply. Moreover, he was sure that the Romans had been hard hit in the two battles. It would take them time to recover, and in that time he would gain faster than they, until he returned with all the resources of Sicily behind him.

He went to Sicily, therefore, and justified his calculation by driving the Carthaginians out of the island, except for the single city of Lilybaeum, in a campaign that lasted a trifle over two years, and whose details need form no part of this narrative. That Sicily did not fully develop into the broad base he expected was due mainly to his lack of the one thing Alexander so abundantly possessed—statesmanship. Or perhaps it was the loss in the Roman battles of his lieutenants and trained administrators—Megacles, Leonnatus, and the rest. There was a gap in the command structure near the top. Sicily remained in his possession, but it was nearing the edge of mutiny when he returned to Italy in the fall of 276. However, he had filled up his ranks, victory in Italy would bring Sicily into line again, and by the spring of 275 he was ready to end the Roman matter.

In the interim Rome had been systematically beating down such tribes as the southern Samnites and Lucanians and conducting a drive against the minor Greek cities. Pyrrhus would not have as many barbarian allies as before, and of the towns only Tarentum and Rhegium were strongly against Rome.

The Red King's opponents were Manius Curius Dentatus and Cornelius Lentulus, consuls for the year. The latter has left no particular mark on history, but Manius Curius was something else. To begin with, he was one of the ugliest men Rome ever saw, his special adornment being a set of buck teeth. He had commanded armies before and had twice been awarded official triumphs, which were considerably more difficult to attain in those days than they became later. When Manius Curius heard that Pyrrhus was again in Italy, he decided that this war was no ordinary contest with Gauls or Samnites, but the real big show. He conducted the yearly enrollment with unexampled strictness, selling at public auction the property of those who failed to report for duty, which shocked contemporaries.

Each consul had an army. That under Lentulus pushed into Lucania to hold the road up central Italy between Tarentum and Rome. Manius Curius, who began by operating against some of the southern Samnite tribes, crossed to the more westerly route at the news of Pyrrhus' approach and went into camp at Beneventum. This was the chief town and market place of the Samnites, and only while Pyrrhus was in Sicily had it fallen into Roman hands. It gave the consul the strategic advantage of holding a nexus, from which he could prevent the Red King from stirring things up in Samnium while the Road to Rome was still held. The lessons of Heraclea and Asculum were not lost on Manius Curius; he chose an area of rough, wooded country, where it would be difficult for cavalry and elephants to operate, with a small stream at the rear of his camp, and out in front a comparatively open, rolling plain, bordered on the right by forest and on the left by timbered ravines.

Pyrrhus' plan seems to have been to crush Manius Curius, then swing around and take Lentulus from along his line of communications. He detached a corps to amuse and contain the latter, something in which it abundantly succeeded, then made a fast march toward Beneventum with 20,000 infantry, 3,000 horse, and always the elephants. The Roman scouting and outpost services were excellent; Manius Curius was fully informed of the king's approach, but the sacrifices (doubtless not without some suggestion from the commander) proved unfavorable, so instead of drawing out for battle as a Roman leader normally would, he stayed in camp, shooting out messengers to summon Lentulus.

Pyrrhus was nearly as well informed about Manius' position as the Roman was about him, and took the Alexandrian view that the boldest course is usually the safest. An attack on one of those square Roman camps, heavily stockaded and ditched, was not normally an operation that would commend itself to a general, but the matter would be considerably handier if he could do it by night and surprise. He set off by a circuit through the woods in the dark, intending to catch the Romans just before dawn.

At this point Pyrrhus' inspiration probably let him down. It is difficult to imagine anything unhandier for progress through a forest in the dark than a twenty-foot sarissa; the men must have split up into files and groups, and the movement was unexpectedly slow. The consequence was that the torches went out, the guides lost their way, and it was already breaking daylight when Pyrrhus' head of column issued into a small open space at the flank of the camp.

Within, the sacrifices instantly became favorable. The Romans poured out like a swarm of hornets and attacked the

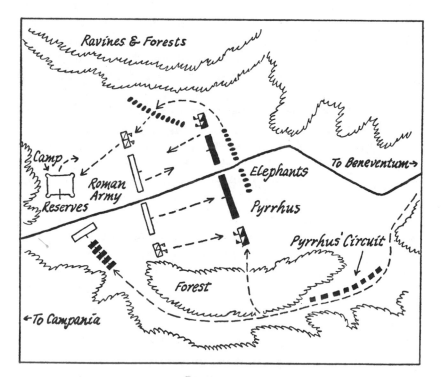

Beneventum

Epirote vanguard at the edge of the trees. This was close-in sword work against opponents who had sacrificed the weight and cohesion that were the specific advantages of Greek armament, and the leading Epirote formations (it is not clear whether they were hypaspists or phalangites) were badly broken, losing a number of prisoners and a couple of the elephants. Pyrrhus was now too deeply involved to disengage and he had no back road; by compulsion rather than choice he had to draw his army through the forest on his right and accept battle in the plain. He performed this difficult maneuver with considerable skill, placing his elephants on the right, with most of the cavalry echeloned behind, and hardly got his formation ready before the lines locked.

At Heraclea, the Romans were dealing with a formation of a type they had never met before; on the second day at Asculum they were cramped into an area which forced them into a more or less solid-block style of fighting, in which the phalanx was at its best. But here they had plenty of elbowroom and the plain was not very plane; that is, it tended to break up the Epirote close order and offered every advantage to the attack-and-withdraw tactics of the maniples. On the Roman right and in the center they carried everything right away before them; Pyrrhus' formations suffered heavily and began to go to pieces.

But on the Roman left, Pyrrhus' right, the elephants produced their usual effect; neither Roman horse nor Roman foot could stand against them. Manius Curius' men were driven right to the walls of their camp. At this point there was revealed something that would have been as much a surprise to any commander of the age as it was to Pyrrhus. Manius Curius had held out a large reserve of legionaries within the camp; as the battle moved down on the stockade, this reserve issued from the side gate and, all in beautiful order, counterattacked the flank of the Epirote movement. The cavalry were cut to pieces by the swarm of Roman javelin spears and driven off; the infantry supports collapsed; the elephants, attacked from flank and rear, were driven into a wooded ravine, where two of them were killed and the remaining eight captured. Rome was victorious all along the line.

Pyrrhus managed to hold some of his taxes together, but after he reached Tarentum and left a small garrison under his general, Milon, there were only 8,000 infantry and 500 cavalry left to take back to Greece. When the Red King was killed three years later by a pisspot thrown by an old woman from a rooftop in Argos, the Tarentum garrison surrendered and Rome owned Italy.

IV

Beneventum decided that the future of the Mediterranean world belonged to Rome and that the transmitting medium for whatever of Greek culture was to survive would be the Roman political system. Or rather Heraclea, Asculum, and Beneventum together achieved this decision. It was gained by the qualities of the Roman soldier and the political organization that produced him. But it could have gone the other way if Rome had not happened to find the buck-toothed Manius Curius at just the right moment.

It would be many years before the decision was written into the records and the long, desperate struggle with Carthage, which was to produce a military genius of its own, lay ahead. But by the time Hannibal arrived, Rome knew all about dealing with geniuses; Pyrrhus had taught them. You tightened your belt, raised another army, and ultimately found a commander who, if not a genius himself, could hold genius in check until the supports were cut from under it by the ceaseless pressure of the Roman system. The essential elements of future were present at Beneventum and the decision was taken there.

That decision was that the Hellenistic states, even when managed by the ablest officers, could not produce a military establishment to overmatch the Roman, even when the latter was headed by quite ordinary men; and when the Romans got generals who were anywhere near as good as the troops they commanded, their superiority was crushing. It was necessary to find that good general—there could have been against Pyrrhus an exhausting series of Asculums if Manius Curius had not appeared—but the point was that the Romans always found their man.

It has been the custom to call Pyrrhus a mere adventurer and to disparage his generalship, but on careful examination it stands up very well indeed. At Heraclea he was certainly surprised by the formidable character of the opposition; but all his information about Romans came from other Greeks, and no one had ever heard of barbarians who could face a civilized army in a pitched battle. At least Pyrrhus realized at once what he was up against and took the right measures. The Asculum campaign was planned to give him the maximum security of communications and the maximum fruits of victory. He very nearly cleared the Carthaginians out of Sicily; and if he had won at Beneventum, he could have had Rome in trouble.

The only thing lacking in the first two battles was pursuit; it was by pursuits that Alexander always turned a victory into a decision. The only thing lacking in the aftermath of Pyrrhus' Roman victories was the surrender of the defeated side and its acceptance into subject alliance; this was the process by which Alexander achieved his empire. But the Romans fought so well that though Pyrrhus could beat them he could never break them; pursuit was impossible against an enemy still having some thousands of men in a heavily fortified camp. And Appius Claudius supplied the answer to the diplomatic question.

That is, the Romans had achieved a military-political system that was incomparably stronger and more resilient than anything Greece or the East could produce. This was obvious at the base, in the method of recruitment, which so surprised Cineas. Philip of Macedon's universal training principle worked very well until it became necessary to keep armies afoot for several years; then it became a question of whom the recruiting agents could persuade or catch. The Roman process of drafts by lot for a campaign kept the ranks full as needed and left a continual reserve of trained manpower. Whether the total system was "better" in a cultural sense or a moral is beside the point. The question of survival, of which system is the more valid, is not decided on moral or cultural grounds; the place of decision is the battlefield and the decision is taken by violence.

It is also worth noting that one of the major factors in the Beneventum decision was political. Nothing so much surprised Cineas, Pyrrhus, and all the Greeks as the fact that after a Roman army had been beaten in battle and the King had marched to the heart of the Roman territory, not a one of Rome's subject allies stirred to join the victor; not even the northern Samnites, who had been subjugated so recently that Pyrrhus was still on the scene when they gave in. In Greek experience there was nothing like this willingness of a conquered people to stay conquered, and through the long range of later Greek literature there has rung down to our own day the idea that somehow Rome enslaved the intellect as well as the body, deprived the nations of their mental as well as their physical freedom.

This is to confound the later Rome with the Rome of Pyrrhus' day and of the Punic Wars. The fact is that in that earlier period the nations were not enslaved, they were not conquered, they were not subjugated; they were taken into the firm. Alexander the Great showed a generosity almost incredible to ancient times in leaving the civil administration of conquered territories in the hands of natives, but there was a Macedonian garrison in every citadel. Ardea, Neapolis, Fregellae, after Rome took them, were not garrisoned by Romans; they were garrisoned by Ardeans, Neapolitans, Fregellans, who had a share, even if a limited one, in directing the affairs of the Roman state of which they became a part, and who believed they could get a better deal within it than under the banner of any foreigner.

That this system was altered and perverted during the process of world expansion should not be allowed to conceal the fact that it was the system which enabled the Apostle Paul to say, *"Civis Romanus sum,"* and thereby force the local magistrate to pronounce that he had no jurisdiction.

3. Fighting in the Streets
and the Future of Order

I

The emperor and one of his subjects slanged each other like fishwives, and everyone in Constantinople heard it, because the debate was chanted by professional *mandators* across the vast space of the Hippodrome. When it was over, the Greens left the place in a body and the trouble had begun.

To understand what kind of trouble and what it meant, a good deal of background is necessary. The Greens were one of the four sectional associations (the others being Blues, Whites, and Reds) which at base were a kind of civic national guard. In case of attack they would have helped to man the walls. To keep them together and active they were organized as sports associations; the chariots in the Hippodrome races bore the colors of Greens, Blues, Reds, or Whites, and rivalry was so intense that it ran over from the field of sports into every other. All the colors maintained groups of "partisans" who enjoyed dressing like Huns, with shaved foreheads, top-knots in back, and baggy sleeves in which they carried daggers, which they had no compunction whatever about using. At this date, which was 532 A.D., the Greens and Blues had become so important that hardly anybody spoke about the Reds or Whites.

In addition to the partisans of the Greens and Blues there was usually around Constantinople another source of turbulence in the form of certain members of the private bodyguards of the great magnates, called "Bucellarians." They were not legal, but licensed, and they became more important as the estates grew larger near the frontiers, where there might be trouble at any time from wild tribesmen and bodyguards were necessary for an establishment. It was perfectly natural that when a magnate went up to the capital for business or fun he would take along some of his bully boys, and it was also natural that sometimes they got into semi-organized rows.

The forces of law and order which had to contend with these unruly elements were represented by two classes of guards—Domestici and Excubitors. The former were the type to be found around any royal or imperial court in a period of general world turmoil—soldiers of fortune of various races who had discovered it was easier to stand to attention behind a well-polished shield than to wander around and fight battles. The Excubitors were something special. They owed their origin to events of nearly a generation before the slanging match, when the Goths were on the verge of taking over the Eastern Empire as they took over that of the West, from the inside. There were so many of these Goths and they were such formidable fighters that no emperor could do without a corps of them or a Gothic commander in chief, or *magister militum*, for his army. One of these officers, named Aspar, fell into the habit of naming emperors, and he set on the throne his steward, a Dacian named Leo. The principal reason Aspar did not take the dignity for himself was that all Goths were Arians, and in spite of martial prowess an Arian heretic could not have maintained himself for a moment against a united empire which regarded his beliefs as no better than pagan.

Besides, the arrangement of having all the real power and practically no responsibility was thoroughly satisfactory to Aspar. However, Leo had not been in office very long before Aspar discovered that the arrangement was not quite as satisfactory as he had imagined. The new emperor proceeded to raise a personal bodyguard of extremely tough hillmen from Isauria in southern Asia Minor—the Excubitors—and began to exhibit signs of independent thought. The Goths knew everything about a campaign in open country but very little about how to handle matters in the capital; when things came to a head, it was Aspar's head that rolled. Ever since that date the Isaurians had been around the palace, a sort of special Goth-prevention guardian.

This was the physical background of the trouble. In addition there was a background of religious deviation. The Byzantines of the fifth and sixth centuries loved to split doctrinal hairs, and every political or personal fission produced a new heresy or something that was called one by somebody. The most significant of these at the moment was that of the Monophysites. Its religious tenets are unimportant and later became so modified by further splinterings that some of them were absolutely indistinguishable from orthodoxy. But the central fact is that Monophysitism was fundamentally a political movement which had taken religious form because most intellectual differences of the age expressed themselves in that way. Although considered a heresy, it was not so dangerous that its adherents could not live with their Catholic cocitizens and take the sacraments from the same priest. It was a Syro-Egyptian nationalism, basically opposed to the growing spiritual power of the Bishop of Rome and even to the temporal power of the Emperor of Constantinople, unless he happened to be a Monophysite.

Anastasius, the last emperor but one before the trouble, had so been. So were the Greens; this also was part of the background. But Anastasius died without leaving any direct issue, and on his death the Byzantine Empire embarked upon its peculiar process of election. The candidates were Anastasius' three nephews, Probus, Pompeius, and Hypatius, with an individual named Theocritus, who was backed by the Grand Chamberlain. Behind the Ivory Gate, which led from the palace to the Hippodrome, the Senate and the leading officials of the Church conferred. In the Hippodrome itself were gathered four groups—the Domestici, the Excubitors, and the armed bands of the Blue and Green gangs. Candidates were being proposed on both sides of the gate; and when a choice was named in the Hippodrome, someone was sent to the Ivory Gate to claim the imperial insignia for him. But no choice could attain a majority on the Hippodrome side; Excubitors, Blues, and Domestici successively put up men who were howled down so loudly, to an accompaniment of broken heads, that the gate remained closed.

Finally it was opened, and a man already dressed in the insignia came out into the imperial box. It was Justin, commander of the Excubitors and at least nominally one of the heads of the Blue party. He was greeted with cheers by all but the Greens and it was an election. The fact that he had been given money by the Grand Chamberlain to promote Theocritus, money which had apparently fallen into the right hands with the wrong instructions, did not invalidate the choice.

Justin was an old soldier, a Macedonian peasant of Latin ancestry, who could not read and needed help in signing his own name, but this does not tell the whole story. When he came to Constantinople to make his fortune a good many years earlier, being childless himself, he brought with him a young nephew named Justinian, and saw to it that the boy received the education he himself had missed. The process was not wasted; as Justinian grew up he displayed an enormous grasp both of minute detail and the large picture of which detail makes the parts; also remarkable gifts of friendliness and self-control, and most especially an incredible capacity for work. No one ever knew when he slept; at any hour he might be writing or conferring. As some of the work inevitably took the form of intrigue in that milieu, it is permissible to hypothesize that he had more than a finger in the election of the Emperor Justin.

This was in 518, and Justinian was about thirty-six years old; he became emperor in fact while old Justin signed the official documents with the aid of a stencil, and made the necessary public appearances. Nine years later, when the old man was failing fast, he associated Justinian with him in his dignities and after four months quietly died. There was no difficulty about the succession.

Justinian's policy was anti-Monophysite. There was no ac-

companiment of violence, as there had been so often in these
religious contests, but Monophysite monasteries were gradually
closed out and Monophysite bishops replaced. Also Justinian
effected a complete reconciliation with the Church of Rome on
terms that left no doubt of his personal orthodoxy, while the
name of Anastasius was erased from the list of emperors as that
of a heretic. But the measures were subtle and gradual; the sect
was too well rooted throughout Syria, Palestine, and Egypt
for Justinian to do anything that might provoke a civil war.
Besides, his wife was a Monophysite.

II

In 526, the year before Justinian took formal charge, the Persians decided to go to war with the empire. Their forces were
considerably in excess of what the new Rome could bring to
bear on the eastern frontier and its line was so long and open
that some nasty raiding could be anticipated. To command in
Persarmenia, Justinian sent out two young men; one was a connection named Sittas, the other an absolutely unknown member of his military household, Belisarius.

This turned out to be a spectacular demonstration of perhaps the most extraordinary of the new emperor's qualities—
his judgment of people. Belisarius was a Thracian peasant,
without a speck of influence, little military experience, and no
money to speak of; the only thing he had was genius. It took
him two campaigns to get his feet under him; then he beat
Persian forces of double his own strength in a great battle at
Daras, a battle which he won not only by leadership, but also
by inspired tactics. He then proceeded to reorganize the army.

By this date it bore practically no resemblance to the Roman
army that fought at Beneventum. The last of the legions had
been destroyed at Adrianople 150 years before, and even if
Belisarius had wished to revive the legionary infantry, he must
have realized that there was insufficient time for training. The
war was in progress; he needed soldiers who could fight to-

morrow morning and it would take years to rear up sound infantry. Moreover, the infantry tradition had been lost since Adrianople; the foot soldiers of the Byzantine army were little better than camp followers. They could be made into fairly good defensive men in a fixed position and had capable archery, but they did not stand up well under persistent cavalry attack and their flanks wanted watching. The striking force of the Roman army, as of all others in the period, lay in the cavalry, and this was of various kinds.

First, there were the Foederati, recruited partly from barbarian tribesmen as individuals, partly from Roman citizens. They were as near a regular force as the empire possessed (unless one counts the Excubitors of the city guard), and while they usually gave an excellent account of themselves in the field, there were never enough of them and recruitment was usually done on a campaign basis, so that the membership was constantly shifting and there was no chance to search out and promote officer material.

Second, there were the Bucellarians, the private posses of the great magnates and the army divisional commanders; there were not many of them, either, and they exhibited a wide variety of equipment and training, both of which were in the hands of the officers who led them. Finally there were the "allies," recruited in tribal groups from the barbarians, and under their tribal chiefs. The best and most numerous of these at the time of Belisarius were the Huns, very good heavy cavalry indeed, and men whose reputation has been traduced. There was usually also a contingent of Heruls, who had a terrific reputation as fighters, and some Saracens for light cavalry.

These tribal contingents were nearly as numerous as the Roman soldiers in any given army, and the leading trouble with them was that they were temperamental. The Huns all regarded themselves as heroes, and could never be persuaded to retreat, even to draw the enemy into a trap. The Heruls insisted on choosing for themselves what spot they would occupy in a battle line, and the Saracens often decided that the amount of plunder was inadequate and went home in the middle of a campaign.

Thus the army Belisarius inherited had no such solidly dedependable body as the phalanx, and its command structure was such that the general in chief often had to accept the strategy and tactics imposed by the prejudices of the "allies" instead of doing his own thinking. Nevertheless, it was with this formless mass that Belisarius met the homogeneous Persians at Daras and brought off a victory in which 8,000 enemy dead were left on the field. It was the only battle in a couple of hundred years in which there were any tactics to speak of; and the idea that men in battle could be maneuvered to make one do the work of two struck contemporaries as so utterly novel that Belisarius' reputation was made at once. After that people listened to him.

He based his reorganization of the Roman army on the concept of the Bucellarians, the private retainers of the great lords. Since he was commanding general, he was entitled to more Bucellarians than anyone else, and he proceeded to raise them into a corps of considerable size. A little after Daras there were 1,500 of them, a large number for the date. They were recruited from all sources—Huns, Goths, Romans, Heruls—and they differed from the Foederati in this: that they were given a standard equipment of full body armor, spear, sword, a stronger bow than any other then in use; and standard training in using the weapons. They were long-term professional soldiers in the fullest sense of the term and they took no oath of allegiance to anyone but Belisarius. He called them his *comitatus*. But it was not the *comitatus* alone that made Belisarius' army so good; it was the fact that possessing it as a core, he could achieve the combination of all arms that had been characteristic of Philip of Macedon, even the degenerate infantry playing a part. The "allies" obeyed orders when they were given by a man who had 1,500 highly skilled fighters at his disposal.

Of course, the matter of the personal oath was a dangerous feature and it was undoubtedly the basis of the series of strains that later arose between the general and his imperial master, strains which appeared only somewhat later. For the present what the emperor wanted was victories and he got them. When the cross-grained old King of Persia died in the fall of 531, Justinian sent his best diplomats to Ctesiphon, recalled Belisarius and his *comitatus* to Constantinople, and saw the general married off to a lady named Antonina.

In this marriage it is possible to see Justinian's first effort to relieve the strain of dealing with a subject who had a more powerful army than he did. Antonina was a close personal friend of the empress, and could be counted upon to keep Belisarius in line if he developed uncomfortable ambitions. She was a lady of somewhat easy virtue (which was not remarkable in the Constantinople of the period) but she got along well with her husband and had the qualities Justinian wanted in her.

III

But Belisarius had not been ordered to Constantinople merely to get married and neither had an officer named Mundus, who commanded the contingent of Heruls. Everyone knew the real reason. The two officers were preparing for one of the most ambitious projects of an emperor whose undertakings were all of enormous dimensions. Justinian intended nothing else than the reconquest of the Western Empire, beginning with the kingdom of the Vandals in North Africa.

The plan has been described as equivalent to sending an army from Europe around Cape Horn to conquer China and, with relation to the available techniques and means of communication, this is perfectly true. Moreover, it had been tried in recent years by that same Leo who founded the Excubitors and he had been well beaten by the Vandals, though he put an army of 100,000 and a large fleet into the enterprise. Justinian had a poorer empire and a smaller army. He also lacked anything like united support, especially in Constantinople.

The opposition to the emperor's adventure centered in the

Monophysites, and it was basically political, nationalism against imperialism, Syria-Egypt against Constantinople, which as the center of a wider empire would be less responsive to Alexandria. It was also fed by a powerful opposition of self-interest to the procedures of John the Cappadocian, Justinian's prime minister and financial officer, who was coming down on rich tax delinquents with a weight not seen in a generation. For reasons that will presently appear, it is impossible to assign any specific names of participants in this movement, or to describe the steps by which the dissident forces were brought into alignment. But there can be no doubt that there was a concerted underground movement whose objective was the overthrow of Justinian by a mass uprising, or that the thing centered in the senators and great magnates. The method had been tried before in Byzantine history and it had usually succeeded.

This was the background of the slanging match in the Hippodrome and the walkout of the Greens. This took place on Sunday, January 11, 532. That night seven of the Green-Blue partisan gangsters who had been condemned to death for rioting were hanged. Through some blunder two of them escaped alive, one a Green and one a Blue, and took sanctuary in the Church of St. Lawrence. The city prefect, who was the chief of police, threw a cordon around the church, and Monday was a quiet day, while the men in the background made preparations.

Tuesday the thirteenth was gala, with the finals of the races whose opening heats had been run on Sunday, and the Hippodrome was crowded. The temper of the gathering was evident from the beginning; they began appealing to the imperial box for clemency for the two men in St. Lawrence, and as Justinian refused to make any reply, the shouting became more and more vehement. At the twenty-second race someone started to chant, "Long live the humane Blue-Greens!" The whole assembly reacted with such enthusiasm that by the time the last race was run the humane Blue-Greens poured out of the Hippodrome as a mob.

Whoever was stage-managing the affair showed excellent

tactical sense. Instead of marching to the Church of St. Lawrence, as might have been expected, the mob made for the central police station, the Praetorium. There they broke in the doors, released all the prisoners, killed the officials or beat them

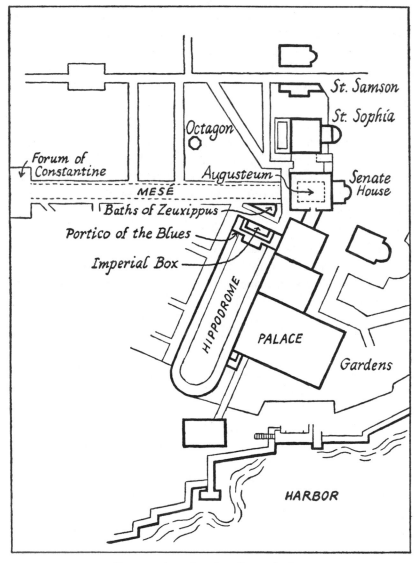

Constantinople; the Central Area

up and drove them into hiding, including the Prefect Eudaimon, then set fire to the place. With the police force scattered and deprived of its command, the mob poured down the main street, the Mesé, growing in numbers and fury. At the terminus they began smashing and burning in the great colonnaded forum known as the Augusteum; the big main entrance to the imperial palace was soon in flames, and so were the Senate House behind the Augusteum and Constantine's Church of St. Sophia.

The fires burned most of the night. In the morning the mob began again, at the Baths of Zeuxippus, in the angle between the Hippodrome and the Augusteum. This structure was nicely alight when word ran through the mob that three of the high officers of state were in the imperial box at the Hippodrome. The crowd poured in; there was a good deal of shouting back and forth between officers and mobsters, in the course of which the latter presented their demands. They were for the dismissal of John of Cappadocia, of the Prefect Eudaimon, and Tribonian, the chief law officer.

Justinian was reported willing to comply; it made not the slightest difference to the mob, which left the Hippodrome only to do some more burning and to hunt out those nephews of Anastasius who had missed the imperial election when old Justin was chosen. The crowd was disappointed to find that two of them, Hypatius and Pompeius, were in the imperial palace with Justinian, so they went to the home of the third brother, Probus, to tell him that he was the new emperor. Probus had had the sense to see this would probably happen and had left for parts unknown, so the mob burned his house as a means of persuasion.

This was Wednesday night, and matters had now so clearly gotten out of hand that no ordinary process would serve to dampen the revolt. Moreover, ordinary process would have included the use of the Domestici and Excubitors to clear the streets, and they had so many friends and relatives in the city that they were more likely to join the rising than to suppress it. But Justinian did have Mundus with his Heruls and Belisarius with his *comitatus*. On the morning of Thursday, January 15, they sallied from the burned gate into the ruins of the Augusteum, and there they encountered something that revealed the origin and animus of the trouble.

They found themselves fighting not a mob with its Blue-Green foam, but thoroughly armed men, Bucellarians, retainers of the great lords. It was merely an incident that in the course of the fighting the clergy tried to stop it by marching in solemn procession between the two parties, and were driven away, passions having now gone beyond that kind of persuasion. There ensued a day of street fighting of the hardest character, work for which Belisarius' men were not particularly well equipped, but with the help of the Heruls, he cleared most of the burned area. He undoubtedly placed strong guard posts around this conquered area and on Friday morning he began again, north of the St. Sophia area. The revolutionists countered by setting fire to the city well to the north, the wind carried the flames through buildings into the faces of Belisarius' men and they destroyed a considerable area, including the Hospital of St. Samson with all its patients.

The base of the revolters appeared to be in the north part of the city, around the Brassmarket. On Saturday the eighteenth Belisarius tried to get at it up a group of streets to the east of his previous line of advance. The insurgents barricaded themselves in a big building called the Octagon and could not be ejected until the soldiers set it ablaze, a fire which spread along most of the main street and cleaned out a good many important buildings.

That night two things happened. Belisarius reported that he was making little progress at anything but burning down Constantinople, and in view of the growing shortage of food and water in the palace area, Justinian sent away everyone who did not have active business there, including a number of senators and the Anastasian nephews, Hypatius and Pompeius. They protested their loyalty and it is just barely possible that the protests were sincere, though Hypatius had been pretty deeply involved in an earlier conspiracy.

But they were packed off, and when the mob found they were available on Sunday morning the nineteenth, it knew what it wanted. Hypatius was carried in triumph through the smoking streets to the Forum of Constantine and crowned with a gold chain, the only object at hand. This proceeding completely ruined Justinian's final effort to quell the revolt with words where more violent methods had failed. He entered the imperial box at the Hippodrome, carrying a copy of the Gospels, and swore to make a faithful peace, with a complete amnesty. He was greeted with shouts of "Perjurer!" and after he had returned to the palace, Hypatius was brought into the box and cheered by the exultant throng. There presently arrived before him a man from the palace named Ephraim, who reported that Justinian and his whole court had fled to Asia and the revolution was a success. A good many of the senators rallied around the box after a private meeting, at which they decided to attack the palace as soon as the celebration for Hypatius was over.

IV

Ephraim was a trifle previous. His informant had left an imperial council just after John the Cappadocian urged flight by sea to Heraclea, and Belisarius agreed with him, in view of the hopelessness of the military situation. The informant had failed to hear the next speaker, who was the Empress Theodora.

About this woman the contemporary historians are very positive. They say she was a prostitute, and she certainly was; she was brought up in that profession. They also agree that she was a comedienne of quite extraordinary gifts, that she was pretty, petite, and vivacious. It takes a little closer reading of the scandalmongers to discover why she was perhaps the most extraordinary example of Justinian's special talent for selecting the right person.

When he first formed an attachment with her, she had given up both the stage and whoring and was a business woman in a small way, with a loom of her own. Doubtless her unquestionable physical charms had something to do with the connection, but they were not the operative factor; Justinian was surrounded by beautiful women, only too willing to be charming to an emperor. It was a union of intelligence, character, and spirit, and it became something more than a marriage.

Justinian gave her one of the largest personal settlements ever received by a woman in an age and place where women commonly turned everything they owned over to their husbands. She managed the property with a skill that excited the admiration of even John of Cappadocia. She could argue theology with a bishop and foreign affairs with a diplomat, and she did both. She took part in every important measure of the government. It was usually in ways not directly traceable because the team of Justinian and Theodora functioned so completely as a unit, with separate but overlapping spheres of authority, but she certainly had a finger in her husband's delicate handling of the Monophysite question.

This was the woman who addressed the palace conference after Ephraim's informant had left. She said, "In a crisis like the present we have not time to argue whether a woman's place is the home, and whether she ought to be meek and modest in the presence of the lords of creation. We have got to get a move on quick. My opinion is that this is not time for flight—not even if it is the easiest course. Everyone who has been born has to die; but it does not follow that everyone who has been made an emperor has to get off his throne. May the day never come when I do! If you want to make yourself safe, Emperor, nothing stops you. There is the sea over there, and boats on it and money to pay your way. But if you go, you may presently very much wish that you had not. As for me, I stand by the old saying, that the best winding sheet is a purple one."[1]

The speech was decisive, and under the influence of his wife's courage Justinian's courage reblossomed. He sent the

[1]No doubt not her exact words, but there is no question that her discussion was very much like this, and the final line was recorded by more than one person. G. P. Baker's translation.

eunuch Narses (who was later to be another of his impossible and monstrously successful choices for military command) with plenty of money to dig out the leaders of the Blues and appeal to them to call off this nonsense on grounds of party loyalty. They now had an emperor of their own faction; were they going to exert themselves further to put a Green in his place? Narses' money was pretty convincing and his words probably quite as much. The rioting had gone on long enough to take most of the fun out of it, and it is probable that the Blue leaders succeeded in getting a good many of their people out of the Hippodrome before the next act.

This was a sufficiently appalling one. At the same time Narses started, Justinian sent Belisarius at the head of the *comitatus* to the imperial box to arrest the new emperor. He could not get in through the passages, and the prospect of fighting a way through heavy doors and guard rooms against Domestici and Excubitors who now considered Hypatius the legal emperor had little appeal. Belisarius therefore went around through the ruined area of the Augusteum and the Baths of Zeuxippus, picking up his guard details as he went, to the colonnaded arcade known as the Portico of the Blues, the main entrance to the Hippodrome. Mundus and his Heruls attacked and broke open a secondary gate, usually barred.

Before them the two groups of steel-clad fighting men had not only the authors of the revolt, but the revolters themselves, caught en masse in a position where they could no longer escape under the cover of burning hospitals. They proceeded methodically to slaughter every one of them. At the very least estimate 30,000 were killed, not all in the massacre, since the street fighting of the previous days had been pretty serious. Hypatius, a rather poor stick of a man, was pulled from his box, and had to be executed with his brother Pompeius to remove any focus for future uprisings, but that was the end of Justinian's vengeance. He banished eighteen men who had escaped the scene in the Hippodrome, but a few months later quietly canceled even these sentences. He could afford to be generous, for his victory was so complete that no other was necessary.

V

It was called the "Nike sedition," but in reality it was a military operation, with a staff, a plan of campaign, and an organized body of troops, the humane Blue-Greens being irregular auxiliaries and the fires a surprise weapon. If Theodora had not talked the council out of their discouragements, if the Justinian-Belisarius team had not acted with lightning efficiency after she did, there would have been a siege as well as a campaign. We do not know who planned the operation, because whoever it was died in the Hippodrome, but it is clear that the planning was good and the campaign came perilously near to success.

Perilously: for the issues involved were far beyond the question of whether the empire should be Monophysite or Catholic, nationalist or imperialist. This issue had its importance, to be sure, and though nothing could have solidified the churches of Rome and Constantinople, they were brought far closer together than if the East had gone fully Monophysite. But it was peculiarly important that the emperor should remain Justinian, the man of wide vision and immense projects. The Nike sedition was directed against only one of these projects, the African invasion; but in a sense it included them all, it was a revolt in favor of provincialism, the narrow view, and fragmentation.

Justinian's conquests in Africa and Italy did not succeed in reuniting the empire, and his military adventures in the West have usually been treated as unproductive acts of aggression. But it is worth looking at what they did accomplish. They destroyed the Vandal kingdom in Africa and fatally crippled the Gothic kingdom in Italy. Sentimental regrets over the downfall of these noble barbarians cannot alter the fact that they were Arians, peculiarly determined to see the triumph of their own sect. Whether they used persecution, like Huneric in Africa, or, like Theodoric in Italy, toleration combined with a firm determination to make all major decisions for a church of which he was not a member, the result was the same. The Arian Church was gaining, it was the official church of the court and upper classes; and it was not a universal church, it had no focus. In a religious sense it was what the Monophysites were in a political: the thing whose greatest effort was turned back by the Justinian-Belisarius-Theodora team in the Nike sedition.

This is not all. It was perhaps not of vital importance that one of Justinian's large projects was the construction of that new Church of St. Sophia, which even yet remains one of the wonders of the world. But it was of the utmost importance that one of the officers whose dismissal was demanded by the mob was Tribonian, and that a dismissal would have been a warrant of execution. For Tribonian was in charge of the most monumental of all Justinian's projects and the most permanent —the codification of the Roman civil law.

The first section, the "Codes," or index of what was to come, had just been published at the date of the Nike sedition and work was just beginning on the more complete classification. It was beginning primarily because Justinian had examined the Codes, decided they were nowhere near good enough or complete enough, and sent Tribonian and his law committee back to start all over. (Nothing was ever good or complete enough for Justinian; his projects were always beyond the human, and partly because they were, what was left of them lasted perdurably.) Some idea of the size of the work done by Tribonian's committee can be gained from the fact that the law had to be extracted from more than 2,000 treatises, comprising 3 million sentences; reconciled, arranged, fused. That law had fallen into inextricable confusion, and it was challenged in various areas by barbarian custom. But after Justinian had sent Tribonian through it, it stood; and the whole of Western civilization was different and better and more just. This was the world that hung in the balance during the Nike sedition.

4. Kadisiyah and the Cost of Conquest

I

The trouble with the second Persian Empire was that it was not an empire. Its rulers bore the Achaemenid title of "king of kings," but the kings to whom the titular ruler acted as chairman of committee were so numerous and had so much individual authority that the head of state hardly dared to promote for ability unless it appeared in one of the lordly houses. There were not only the great feudatories known as "lords of the marches," but also the lesser "lords of the villages" and "knights," who had authority over part of a city or the whole of a smaller town. And in addition there were the Magi, or Mazdean priests, who could always bring a man up for heresy, and any kind of incorrect conduct might turn out to be heretical.

The system was completely interlocked, ironbound; there was no possibility that a change would be made in it at any point. And while the tradition that stood for a constitution required that the king of kings should be a member of the royal house, it was not specific about which member, so that there was usually a war of succession at the end of each reign, and sometimes one in between. On the whole, it is rather surprising that the general political talent which seems endemic in the Indo-European race should have been able to overcome such handicaps and produce an administration that was reasonably orderly and a system of taxation that was reasonably fair. It also produced a military organization that was one of the most effective of the early Middle Ages. The nobility down to and including the knights was a nobility of service, specifically military service. The Achaemenid tradition that a noble need only know how to ride, shoot, and speak the truth had been thoroughly revived, like so many traditions of the pre-Alexander empire, and even improved upon. The nobles knew nothing but war, though not in a way to be confounded with the feudalism that sprang up later in the West. The military caste of the Sassanid empire were not domiciled in isolated castles, and their allegiance was not transmitted by stages through a series of terraced lordships, but went directly to the king of kings.

Professionally also they differed from the Western knights and from any predecessors. They were all cavalry, of course; the decline of infantry already pronounced at the time of Justinian and Belisarius had reached its nadir, and the only footmen who accompanied a Sassanid army were troops of the baggage train, armed with a small spear and a wicker shield covered with hide. The horsemen were a development of the *comitatus* of Justinian's time. They had scale armor, steel caps, and light shields, and carried almost every conceivable kind of weapon— a six-foot spear, a bow, a short straight sword, a mace, a hand ax, and two ropes, which together made a kind of lasso and was used for pulling an opponent off his horse. In view of the amount of training necessary to obtain dexterity with all these weapons, it is not surprising that they had to make a profession of war. At moving in close-knit formations for heavy shock to the sound of the trumpet they were good; they employed many barbarian auxiliaries of the usual desert light cavalry type and had picked up a considerable amount of siegecraft from the Byzantines. Their armies usually employed armored elephants, but only as a reserve. The Westerners had worked out a battlefield technique for dealing with these animals, and refused to be borne down or panicked.

Two institutions of the Persian army were unique and of

75

some importance in the psychological warfare department. It always carried a huge throne, which was set up in the center of the battle line and occupied during action by the shah or the general acting for him. It was surrounded by the picked body-guard, called "the Immortals," as they had been in the days of the old empire, nearly a thousand years before, with an outer circle of foot archers. Before it there was always borne the other institution, the *Diraish-i-kaviyani*, theoretically the leather apron of the heroic smith who had founded the state back in legendary times by leading a revolt against the ruling Semites. It had become a banner of fifteen feet by twenty-two, and was all one crust of precious stones, since it was regarded as holy and each successive king added new decorations to it with the help and approval of the Mazdean priests. When a Persian army was defeated, the first care was always the preservation of the sacred standard; men gave their lives for it.

The greatest weakness of this army was the lack of control by the high command during the frequent struggles for succession. But as no one could remain king of kings very long without making himself thoroughly feared, this was not usually a difficulty. About the turn of the sixth into the seventh century, Chosroes, second of the name, got his war of succession under control and began to think about other things. In a state organized like Sassanid Persia there was only one line intellection could follow; the strong, rigid system permitted no major activity but war. An able grandfather had pushed Chosroes' eastern frontier up to the Oxus and the Himalayas, and there was not much point in proceeding farther in that direction. The only thing the new king of kings could do was take up the war against the Byzantine Empire that had been running off and on for nearly a hundred years, or ever since his great-grandfather attacked Justinian.

The usual thematic material of this war was a series of battles and sieges in Mesopotamia and Armenia, with Persian raids into Syria and Byzantine counterraids into Persian Iraq. Just at this juncture the Byzantine Empire was experiencing some dynastic troubles of its own, the Balkan provinces were pulverized by a huge incursion of Slavic Avars, and the Persians were lucky enough to turn up a couple of highly competent generals besides Chosroes himself. He introduced a variation into the pattern, so effective that it gained him the name of Chosroes Parvez, "Chosroes the Conqueror," and he deserved it. Armenia was so thoroughly subdued that its church split from that of Constantinople; Cilicia and Cappadocia were subdued. Jerusalem was taken in 614, with 57,000 killed and 35,000 more carried away as prisoners. Damascus, Tarsus, Antioch were occupied. Alexandria was captured and all northern Egypt passed into Persian hands. Persian armies cruised at will through Asia Minor and an attempt was made on Constantinople itself.

All this was the work of some years, but by 619 it would have struck a contemporary news chronicler that the Byzantine Empire was done for. The loss of Egypt had cut off the usual grain supply and there were famine and pestilence in the capital. There was no money and no taxes were coming in. Even outside the cities, where the Persians were only too glad to see the Greeks quarreling among themselves, administration had collapsed to the edge of anarchy. The armies had been beaten and broken up in the field. And with Illyria in the hands of the Avars, Armenia, Anatolia, and the mountain districts of southern Asia Minor in those of the Persians, the recruiting grounds where new forces could be raised were no longer available.

However, there remained intact the African province Belisarius had conquered for Justinian after the suppression of the Nike sedition, the conquest which the sedition was started to prevent. The Emperor Heraclius himself was from that province, and to it he turned for men. Its very existence had made it necessary for the empire to keep up a navy; what was left of Byzantium held the sea and the communications it offered. For money Heraclius appealed to the Church, and in view of the fact that the Magians had conducted some fairly intolerant persecutions and encouraged the Jews to join them in massacring the Christians at Jerusalem, the cash was willingly given. The various generals had all proved failures or tried to seize the decaying empire for themselves. In spite of the fact that it was contrary to usage and tradition, and he was warned that only ruin could come of it, Heraclius held a solemn communion, then called a great meeting of Senate, officials, and people in the Hippodrome, placed the empire in charge of the Patriarch Sergius, and took the field in person.

The date was April 5, 622; five months later an Arab who had been making a nuisance of himself by preaching that he was a prophet in the important desert commercial center of Mecca was forced to leave town.

I I

The surviving records about Heraclius and his campaigns are not very satisfactory, nor are the details important, but it is clear that in the tactical field he recovered part of the lost art of infantry, and in strategy he was something like a master. He maneuvered the Persians out of Asia Minor, beat them in a battle in which the enemy army was almost destroyed and, instead of trying to recover the lost places in the south, drove northeast into the country at the foot of the Caucasus. During the next six years the destruction in the West was repaid with doubly compound interest. Every time the Persians sent an army against Heraclius he broke it, usually with heavy loss, and every time he came to a city he sacked it. He reached the Caspian and swung southward; he inflicted a deadly blow to Persian morale by taking and destroying the greatest fire temple in the country; and his ambassadors succeeded in calling in the Khazar tribes of the steppes to do some more damage. In 628 it became evident to the Persians that Chosroes the Conqueror was losing his grip. One of his sons had him thrown into the "Well of Darkness" and then murdered.

The son got a peace out of Heraclius but he did not get much else; that year the Tigris and Euphrates produced a flood of Noahan proportions and the new king of kings died in the ensuing pestilence. His only son was an infant, and as might be expected, there was a chain reaction of wars of succession, in which the various candidates were backed by groups of magnates. It is probable that losses in defeats by Heraclius had weakened the lords, both intellectually and physically. During four years no less than twelve persons, two of them women, wore the mountainous royal tiara, and none of them kept it more than a year, or could get recognition from enough of the country to bring the rest into line. At last the supply of eligible princes began to run low, even for a royal house so prolific as the Persian; in 632 it was generally agreed that a child named Yezdigird III was the real article. A general named Rustam became what we would call regent.

During the next year there was a raid of Arabs against Hira on the border of Iraq; the town was ransomed for the absurdly small sum of 60,000 dirhams, and Rustam followed by a raid into Arab territory to remind the tribes they must not do this sort of thing.

III

Historians of an exclamatory temperament often voice surprise over "the explosion of the Saracens." This is because they have been taken in by Moslem chroniclers, who refer to the period before Mohammed as "the time of ignorance," with the implication that the Prophet was a civilizer as well as a religious leader. It also completely overlooks the nature of the material that exploded. Actually, there was throughout the Arabian peninsula at the time something which, if not meeting all the demands of a civilization, was considerably above barbarism. There were tribes grouped in clans, yes, and feuds among them; a good part of the population were nomads. But the arts flourished, especially poetry (which may be considered a barbaric art), commerce was reasonably secure (Mecca owed its importance to the fact that it was a trading town which had become sacred to business, so no violence was allowed in the area), and the position of women was higher than in most of contemporary Western Europe, a very good index. There was no little agriculture, partly based on peaches and pomegranates, which did not ship well, but partly also on dates and aromatics, which did ship and were in wide demand.

At the time of Mohammed this nascent civilization was suffering from a malaise. There were two basic causes. One was a persistent overproduction of children in spite of the common practice of female infanticide. The consequence was emigration by seepage; Arab stocks had heavily infiltrated the whole of Syria, Palestine, and even Egypt, where they readily mingled with kindred stems that had no basic differences even in language. By the sixth century these emigrant Arabs even had two kingdoms of their own, Ghassan at the northwestern edge of the desert and Hira on the northeast. Ghassan was subdued and broken up into districts by the Byzantines while Hira became a Persian dukedom. But the key fact was that throughout most of Syria, Iraq, and Mesopotamia the bulk of the population was strongly Arabic, with blood and clan connections back in the homeland.

The second difficulty was economic; both on the Red Sea and the Persian Gulf shipping had become efficient as a common carrier. As water transport is always cheaper and easier than that by land, the old caravan routes that had provided a way of life for so many Arabs fell into decline. That is, there was unemployment in the overpopulated peninsula, and almost anything would have touched off some kind of explosion.

That the energies of the explosion were directed outward and not inward was due to several causes. One was the nature of the Prophet's teaching, which contained several features unique to an area where prophets were not uncommon. It made positive virtues out of several things that were necessities of life in the desert—abstemiousness, the avoidance of luxury, the laws of hospitality. This made it very easy to be a Moslem. It forbade the infanticide which is contrary to every human instinct and offered a viable substitute in polygamy. It turned fighting and plunder into profoundly religious acts, provided they were directed against unbelievers; and it provided a com-

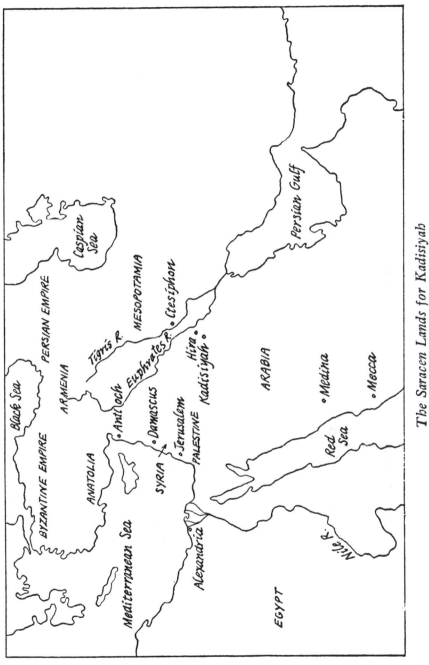

The Saracen Lands for Kadisiyah

mon ground on which every Arab could meet every other Arab, without distinction of tribe or clan. The appeal of Mohammedanism on a purely spiritual basis is not to be neglected; but it is worth noting that if the faith had been put forward in the most cold-blooded rationalism as a solution to the problems of place and date, it could hardly have been better conceived.

In the second place, Mohammed had the good fortune to number among his earliest converts an extremely able administrator, Omar, and a general far beyond the ordinary, Khalid ibn al-Walid. The Prophet himself was certainly an administrator of the highest skill, but as a military commander he was energetic rather than able. The special merit of Khalid as an officer was that he managed to convert a tactical doctrine into a strategic system. The Saracens were naturally light cavalry, bow- and spearmen, and in view of the shortage of natural materials their bows cannot have been much better than those of the Persians, which were not as good as the Byzantine bow. The tactics of this kind of light horse are dictated by their equipment; they are skirmishers. What Khalid did was skirmish the enemy to death. In the period following the death of the Prophet, when many of the desert converts seceded and half a dozen new prophets claiming divine inspiration appeared, Khalid did fight some semi-formal battles which were decided by his own furious energy; but later, when he came up against the Byzantines, a typical "battle" lasted for days, and in one case weeks.

The problem faced by all commanders down to the equalization imposed by firearms was that of using a military tool developed in and intended for one kind of country in a region of quite different physiographical characteristics. The irresistible horsemen of the Tartars were quite helpless when they tried to attack the Japanese by sea, and they had to turn back from an utterly inferior military establishment in the jungles of Burma. The armored knights who ruled Western Europe had terrible trouble when they met pikemen in the Swiss valleys. Khalid turned the skirmishing tactic into something that could be used anywhere. He brought his army into the presence of the enemy and waited; not passively, for he attacked every-thing and anything that moved outside a tight array. But all the same he waited until the battle became one made up exclusively of small skirmishes, his kind of battle. Superior mobility and superior logistics helped him greatly; his men could maneuver around any formation, they needed nothing but a bag of dates and access to water, while his opponents had to have provision convoys.

With this technique he conquered the whole of Syria and Palestine within four years after the death of the Prophet. He was considerably aided by racial and religious forces. The Arabs of Ghassan and, above all, those of southern Palestine, who might have formed a buffer state, had become Christians. But just at the juncture of Khalid's appearance the Emperor Heraclius had been forced to discontinue the customary subsidies to the Palestinian Arabs because, the Persian danger being exorcised, the Church wanted its money back from him in a hurry. Moreover, throughout Syria and Egypt, Christianity retained a strong Monophysite strain. Heraclius and his patriarch sought a compromise formula, the Monothelite, but the men they placed in charge of propagating it turned out to be persecutors instead of persuaders, and the whole area was unhappy over something that meant a great deal to it.

When Khalid and his Arabs appeared, they were welcomed as deliverers by people of their own race, many of whom wished and were allowed to accept the new faith. Christians of non-Semitic stock and Jews found they were allowed to practice their religion in any form they chose, provided they paid a head tax far less than what Constantinople demanded in other forms of contribution. The Bishop of Damascus helped arrange his city's surrender and only the thoroughly Greek cities of Jerusalem and Caesarea held out for any time in hope of relief.

The relief never came. Heraclius was now too old to take the field himself, and after two of the armies he had entrusted to generals who could make nothing of Khalid's tactic were wiped out, he was unable to raise a third. Everything from Antioch and Edessa southward became permanently Moslem. The Prophet's old friend Omar, now caliph, or "successor," Commander of the Faithful, began preparations for the invasion of Egypt. Conditions there were much the same as in Syria.

I V

Hira, like Ghassan, was a state of Arab blood, ruled by non-Arabs. The marshes of the lower Euphrates separated it from an area occupied by a nomadic clan called the Bakr. The head of this clan, one Muthanna, waited on Khalid during his march to Syria, and although the Bakr had not accepted Islam and had no current intention of doing so, suggested a joint raid on Hira as a highly profitable enterprise. Khalid agreed; this was the 60,000 dirham raid of 633, which provoked Rustam to countermeasures. The preparations for these measures were no secret, and as Muthanna did not like the prospect of dealing with a major Persian army unaided, he appealed to Omar at Medina for help. He may also have thrown out some hint about joining the new religion.

It is necessary to note that at this stage Mohammedanism, in spite of the Prophet's statements of universality, was a racial movement. The policy of Medina was to take in only pagan, Christian, and Jewish Arabs (of the last there were a great many), leaving non-Arabs as payers of the head tax. In Syria no effort was made to push beyond the ethnic limit. Muthanna was within that limit and thus entitled to help, regardless of his religion. But at the date of his appeal the Syrian campaign was at its height, Khalid was facing the first of the major Byzantine armies with the issue undecided, and Omar was mobilizing every possible resource in support. The caliph was not interested in fighting Persia. Unlike the sprawling empire, it was a well-knit unit of non-Arabic people, which already claimed some vague suzerainty over the peninsula, and there was not much sense in stirring up such a sleeping lion. The help sent to Muthanna was therefore a small, purely defensive force.

It was not well led, and in the Battle of the Bridge, November 26, 634, was crushingly defeated, mainly as a result of a charge of elephants which the Arab horses refused to face. Muthanna had difficulty in pulling a third of his force out of the wreck, and Abu Obayd, the captain from Medina, was taken and trampled to death by a huge white elephant.

At this date Rustam was only about as much interested in Arabia as Omar was in him; he still had some internal difficulties to settle and undertook nothing beyond a minor raid for the next year and a half. But by the fall of 636 the whole strategic situation had changed: the last of the great Byzantine armies had been wiped out in Syria; Damascus and Antioch were in the hands of the Saracens, Jerusalem and Caesarea were under siege. Rustam assembled an army to put an end to this menace.

As usual, the news crossed the frontier before the troops did, and Omar set about gathering a force to defend not merely fellow Arabs this time, but also the line of communications to the new possessions in Syria. Command was given to an old companion of the Prophet, Sa'ad ibn Abu Wakkas, a man afflicted with boils. Shortly after his arrival in the area Muthanna died and, in accordance with Arab custom, Sa'ad secured the allegiance of the Bakr by marrying his widow. Making up the army was not so easy; word had run through the peninsula that the fertile fields of Syria were something like paradise, and the first great wave of immigration was washing into the corridors. It was doubtless a high religious duty to smite the infidel in the name of the Prophet, but a man had to look out for his family; that also was in the Koran. Sa'ad probably had not collected above 6,000 men (in spite of enormous figures given in the chronicles) when Rustam crossed the Euphrates and encamped just north of the marshes on the border of the cultivated zone, at Kadisiyah. It was May or June 637.

The Arab tale is that the Moslems sent fourteen ambassadors who reached King Yezdigerd himself with a demand that the Persians either adopt their religion or pay a head tax. The people of Ctesiphon jeered at the tattered homely garments of the emissaries. Yezdigerd told them that if they were not ambassadors he would have had them beheaded, and spoke feelingly about Arab customs.

The head of the embassy said, "The prince speaks truly. Whatever you have said regarding the former condition of the Arabs is true. Their food was green lizards; they buried their infant daughters alive. But God in His Mercy has sent us a holy Prophet, a holy volume which teaches us the true faith. Now the Arabs have sent us to ask you either to adopt our religion or fight with us."

The Persian gave them one sack of dirt per man to carry away; they laid the burdens before Sa'ad as an omen: "for earth is the key to empire."

Rustam had considerably more men than the Arabs, and Sa'ad appears to have been unwilling to fight until the arrival of some reinforcements promised from Syria. But the Saracens began to run short of provisions, and when they sent out a foraging corps to collect some fish from the river, the Persians attacked and Sa'ad felt compelled to draw up in battle formation. The ball was opened by a number of Persian knights riding out of the ranks, shouting, "Man to man!" as their custom was, challenging the Moslems to single combat. As it suited the Khalid tactical system to fight this way, they got plenty of customers, but the result of these personal encounters was usually in favor of the better-armed Persians. But as skirmishing went on all along the line Rustam perceived he was not going to get the close general action he wanted and, with the memory of the Battle of the Bridge in mind, ordered up the elephants. Once again the Arab horses would not stand; in fighting that lasted till evening Sa'ad's forces were driven back, much scattered, and saved from destruction only by some foot archers who slowed down the elephants.

An army not inspired by Moslem fanaticism might have broken up then and there, but Sa'ad managed to pull his men together during the night, doubtless not without assuring them that help was on the way from Syria. It began to come toward morning; the Arabs again took the field in their loose formations, and all day long there was one of the typical skirmishing battles of the Khalid system. Light cavalry had rather the better of it that day over heavy; the Persian losses are stated at five to one of the Moslem, but neither army showed any real sign of breaking when night shut down on the second day.

There was anxiety in both camps that night. Sa'ad was so troubled by his boils that he had barely been able to stay on his horse during the day, and in an Arab army, where personal leadership means everything, was unable to provide that indispensable quality. The main body of the Syrians had not arrived and until they did the enemy would be in superior force. There was a grave conference; Sa'ad turned over his field command for the following day to Kakaa ibn Amru, the captain of the Syrians—and one must picture messengers going from campsite to campsite through the dark informing everybody of the change.

In the Persian camp Rustam was still hopeful of victory, but considerably disturbed by his inability to fix on any solid tactical plan in this formless desert fighting. The enemy had no real camp to attack or communications to cut. He received some reinforcements during the night, and doubtless as a result of his report on the first day's fighting, it included additional elephants. In the morning they were to be the main reliance in dealing with the sinuous Saracen formations; they were placed front and center when the Persians drew out toward where the Moslems were advancing in clouds of dust.

But the Persians were not now dealing exclusively with desert Arabs who had never seen an elephant; they now had on their hands the Syrian troops, many of whom had previously served the Byzantine Empire and knew all about elephant fighting. They galled the big animals frightfully with bowshot and javelin and even had the nerve to attack them on foot with spear and sword, jabbing at eyes and cutting off trunks. The elephant was always a two-edged weapon; now these stampeded through the Persian ranks, doing frightful damage, and into the gaps they made, Kakaa poured his formations.

The Persians did not give up easily. Rustam left his official throne to mount a horse and personally rally his lines. They were driven back to a wide canal, where the battle hung for a time, but it did not end even with darkness, since the Arabs, now confident of victory, kept pressing on in small groups, at one point or another. It was called the "Night of Clangor" or "Night of Delirium," "because each one caught the other's beard," and it must have been a wild scene in almost complete darkness, but in this confused close combat most of the Persian advantages in armament were canceled and the gains were all on the side of the Saracens.

With daybreak came a sandstorm, and it blew in the faces of the Persians. Rustam took refuge from it among the baggage camels; a sack of money fell from one of them, injuring his back, and he plunged into the canal to swim to safety. At that moment there appeared an Arab named Hillal ibn Alkama. He hauled the Persian generalissimo from the canal by one foot and cut off his head, then ran to the official throne, by this time in Moslem hands, and mounted it, shouting, "By the Lord, I have slain Rustam!"

It was the final blow; what was left of the Persian army panicked. But there was no place left for them to go; hundreds in their heavy armor were drowned in the canal and thousands were cut down along its banks in utterly open country by Arabs who had no reason for giving quarter and no intention of giving it.

V

The booty was immense, since a Persian knight carried most of his portable wealth on his back, and Rustam's army chest was considerable. When accounts of what had been gained, and still more when some of the tangible booty began to reach Medina, Omar and his advisers decided there was something in this Persian business. Sa'ad, who was resting his army after its victory, was directed to form a military colony at Kufa, near the scene of the battle, and push on later.

Hira town surrendered readily enough, and when the Moslems got into the blackland country between the Tigris and Euphrates they found conditions basically similar to those in Syria—a population composed of Aramaic peasants, who had been under both economic and religious pressure from Aryan overlords, and who were glad to see invaders of their own race. All Iraq fell into the hands of the conquerors without further contest; they pushed on to the Tigris, and when Yezdigerd offered to accept the line of this river as a boundary and was refused, he evacuated his capital at Ctesiphon and fell back into the mountains.

For the second Persian Empire was done. The lost commander's throne could be replaced, but the sacred Diraish-i-Kaviyani, which had been sent to Medina to be cut up in pieces, could not. With its loss the national morale sustained a blow hardly less paralyzing than the one that resulted from Heraclius' destruction of the great fire temple, the more so because one topped the other. Nor could the fighting men lost at Kadisiyah be replaced in any important quantity, and their loss, like that of the symbolic banner, had to be added to those sustained in the war with the empire and the civil troubles that followed it. The Persian upper class was even more seriously crippled than the English was to be in the War of the Roses, and the organization of the state was such that there was no yeomanry underneath, out of which a new upper class could grow.

Yezdigerd, who was now old enough to be considered not to need a regent, managed to assemble a force which met the Moslems again at Jalula, the entrance to the mountains, but not long after Sa'ad took Ctesiphon it was heavily beaten. Four years later the last army of the Persian Empire was destroyed at Nihawand and Persia became a Saracen province.

It took the full four years to reach this point, because the advance into Persia proper represented something completely new, strange, and changed in Saracen policy. Soon after Jalula, Mesopotamia fell into their hands, but like the rest of the early conquests, it was largely Semitic with tribal connections southward and its subjection involved no more than the capture of a few garrison towns. But Persia proper was different; it was inhabited by an alien race, one that already had a strong religion of its own. They heavily outnumbered any Saracen governing class that could be placed in possession.

This was at least dimly visible at the time and was one of the reasons for the delay in completing the work of Kadisiyah. But the results of the battle, including the capture of Ctesiphon, made the prospect irresistible. For if the booty of Rustam's camp was immense, that of the Persian capital was beyond all counting in terms of purchasing power. It was one of the richest cities in the world and it was taken under conditions that made plunder rather than occupation practically obligatory. Arabs who had been living on dates and camel's milk suddenly found themselves with jewels that represented the income of several lifetimes.

Persia thus became a promised land, where wealth could be had for the taking, and a wave of Arabian emigration followed the armies thither. But quite aside from the effects of sudden wealth, which are pretty much the same everywhere, the capture of Persia introduced new factors into the Moslem polity —factors not covered by any revelation to the Prophet.

It has already been noted that the policy of the early caliphs was to let non-Arab Christians and Jews keep their religion and make them a source of revenue by means of the capitation tax. They were so small a minority as hardly to be an irritant; the oyster of the Arab state could readily convert them to pearl. But the classic method clearly would not do in dealing with the Magian fireworshipers. There was no element in their religion on which a Moslem could find agreement with his own as a basis for toleration; they had no Solomon or Moses or Jesus, who have honored places in the Moslem pantheon. But more importantly, as soon as the Arab state had engulfed Persia, it found itself in possession of a huge racially and religiously alien bloc, violently different in customs and culture.

The Western peoples later developed systems of colonial administration for dealing with this type of situation. But the seventh-century Saracens had no long tradition of politics and administration behind them, and no experience with any kind of administration except the patriarchal, with an overlay of the politico-religious control from Medina. In their view the only means of assuring political control over the new conquest was through religious control; the Persians had to be converted under the sword and the Magian religion wiped out, or Islam could never control Iran.

The effectiveness of religious persecutions is often underestimated. Mazdaism was wiped out in a practical sense; but it took a good deal of doing, and the detestation with which fire-worshipers are mentioned in *The Arabian Nights* shows that the issue was not wholly dead a couple of hundred years later. In the meanwhile the forced conversion of Persia completely changed Islam itself. It ceased to be a racial movement; it necessarily became more militant, more willing to expand the frontiers in every direction. If so large a mass as Persia could be digested and become a source of new sinews, there was no reason why other and even larger entities could not be absorbed, and the command of the Prophet to convert or slay was not a figure of speech, but something deserving of literal obedience.

The attempt at complete absorption, of course, was only a partial success. There were too many Persians and they had too much political experience. In the end, under the Abassid caliphs, the Moslem Persians came into command of the whole movement. They swept away the patriarchal system Mohammed had known and designed for his polity in favor of a new, monarchial, conquering system, which completely forgot the democracy that was one of the Prophet's most basic doctrines.

5. Las Navas de Tolosa and

Why the Americas Were Conquered

I

At the beginning of the eleventh century the Christians of Spain began to come up for air. There had never been much danger that the Moslems would get the whole peninsula under their formal jurisdiction. Despite an endless series of forays and several invasions intended to be permanent, the Mohammedans never succeeded in establishing a stable state much north of the line below which the olive grows—a matter which should engage the attention of some economic historian, though there is no visible correlation. The major northward drive, of course, was the one turned back by Charles the Hammer at Tours in 732, and it is just barely possible that a Moorish victory in that struggle would have resulted in the establishment of a Moslem France. But it is no more than barely possible; the absorptive power of the Arabs and their religion found an easier field in the East, which is to say that there were insufficient reserves behind the 732 invasion wave, while the Franks were tough-minded as well as tough fighters, not good subjects for conversion.

Neither were the Visigoths of Spain, for that matter, and there was no compelling reason why they had to be, as in the case of Persia. The Moslem occupation forces were more adequate, and the religion readily found converts among the old Romanized population of the peninsula, who under the Visigoths had become serfs. They formed a reserve which gave the Moslems the necessary numerical superiority over the old Visigothic aristocracy, who adapted to Saracen rule by becoming Mozarabs, Saracen in dress and social customs, but by religion still Christian, having their own courts and magistrates.

The Moslem Spain that stabilized south of the line of the olive after the failure in Gaul had certain internal pressures. These rooted in the unwillingness of genuine Arabs to recognize Persians and Berbers as belonging to the same level of humanity, Moslem though they were, the quarrels of the various tribes, and the personal ambition of the emirs who were their heads. As long as the dynasty of the Omayyad (strictly Spanish) caliphs lasted, these stresses were easily held in check. The caliphs always had available the powerful corps of the Slaves (with a capital), serf soldiers, a typical Mohammedan institution, which was to reappear in the Janissaries of Turkey and the Mamelukes of Egypt. The Slaves were strong enough to overawe or overcome any loose alliance of divisive forces. Also the caliphs enjoyed an unusual range of authority. They were not only civil and military leaders, but also the heads of religion, the only true interpreters of the word of God. It was as though the Pope were also absolute monarch of France and field commander of its armies. Finally, the Omayyads were greatly beloved by their subjects; even the Mozarabs found no objection to living under their rule.

The result was that Spain under the Omayyad caliphs was immune to whatever exterior pressure could be applied by the tiny Christian states of the north. It developed the most solid and brilliant civilization in the Europe of the period, with achievements in science, the arts, and literature far beyond anything the nascent northern or Italian states could offer, or even the decadent Byzantines. It was no earthly paradise, but it was a system that worked. The rulers of Galicia, Leon, Castile, Navarre, Aragon, the county of Barcelona, could make no headway against the unified strength of the caliphate or the willingness of its subjects to remain subjects. While the Christian kingdoms squabbled among themselves, they were forced to pay tribute to Cordova, where the caliph had his capital. This state of affairs began to come to an end with the death of 'Abd-ar Rahman III, the great caliph. He was succeeded by Hakam II, who was too much interested in literature to fulfill his combined duties as Pope, chief justice, and general. Most of the work was turned over to a vizier named Abd-'amir, known historically as Almanzor, from a title he assumed, meaning "Victorious with the help of God." Almanzor reorganized the army by importing Berbers from Africa and bringing in paid soldiers from the Christian states, and he conducted the endemic war with the Christians so vigorously that he was able to storm Barcelona and destroy the city of Leon, all but one tower, which he left as a monument.

Not even the death of Hakam mattered. Almanzor consigned the successor, Hisham II, to an even more cloistered existence than his predecessor, gained favor with the religious leaders by burning Hakam's secular library, and was in a fair way to breaking the boundary of the olive line when he died in 1002. What followed was as typical of a Moslem state as anything in the *Thousand and One Nights*. Almanzor had been arbitrary; the son who succeeded him as vizier was not only cruel in addition, but far from orthodox and utterly incapable of controlling the tribal leaders, who had no taste for Almanzor's army reorganization program. There was a confused series of sectarian and personal revolutions, in the course of which Hisham II disappeared, and after several nominal caliphs of various provenances had failed to consolidate the government, a council of state declared the caliphate abolished in 1031.

At once everything fell into inextricable confusion and the solid, civilized state that had seemed certain to gobble up the peninsula and even to extend beyond dissolved into a fair imitation of England under the Saxons. In every city, in every district, there arose petty kings, the kings of the *taifas* (from the Arabic "tribe"), each of whom was chiefly ambitious to restore the fallen caliphate under his own authority. The institution of slave soldiers, which had been so valuable a cement in a united caliphate, disappeared after a brief period in

which they played kingmakers; there was insufficient conti-
nuity at the head of state to keep them going. Moslem Spain
was ready to be taken over by the Christians.

But the Christians were not ready to take it over. In the tiny
northwest corner never conquered, in the pockets along the
Pyrenees out of which the new kingdoms grew, the tradition
was invincibly Visigothic, that is, Gothic, and the Gothic tradition was one of an equal division of inheritance. Time and
again the kings of Leon, Castile, Aragon, and Navarre succeeded by force or marriage in pulling together dominions of
respectable size, only to dissipate them by dividing the heritage
among sons and daughters. Helped by the Spanish geography
of relatively small and fertile valleys surrounded by mountains
through which the communications were poor, and still further
encouraged by very real differences in custom, method of life,
and even language induced by that geography, the process of
fraction continued wearisomely and interminably. Galicia and
Leon looked out on Biscay and their contacts were across it;
Castile had little commerce except with the Moorish states;
Navarre straddled the Pyrenees and faced obstinately north;
Aragon and Catalonia were Mediterranean powers. The whole
of the central plateau, where these forces might have achieved
union, was still in Moorish hands at the fall of the caliphate.

The result was that the irregularly periodic divisions of the
Spanish kingdoms following a new succession were invariably
succeeded by wars among the successors, each anxious to obtain the entire patrimony. Inevitably one of the successors
would call in the help of the single great power to the south;
and as soon as that broke up, the *taifa* kings as persistently
sought help from the north in their efforts to reunite the caliphate.

Thus the eleventh century in Spain was occupied by an endless chain of small wars and civil wars, Christian against Christian, Moslem against Moslem, with contingents from both
parties fighting indifferently on either side. Ruy Diaz de Vivar,
the Cid Campeador, was held the perfect knight and champion
of his nation and religion; but he spent more of his active ca-

reer fighting for Mohammedan princes than he did for Christian, which, if it made excellent literature, did not make much sense.

II

In this period of pointless minor wars the character of military operations in the peninsula became fixed along lines that diverged considerably from those operative elsewhere in medieval Europe or Asia, and which in turn deeply affected the life of the communities, as military operations do in a land where the main business is war. As elsewhere, the cross-raiding system developed as soon as the militant units became so small that major operations for the capture of cities were difficult; as elsewhere, the defense against cross raiding became the castle.

The difference lay in the intensity with which both were applied. The raids in Spain were more frequent and became more of an object in themselves; it was always both legal and moral to increase resources by taking them away from the party of the other religion, and if the Christian King of Aragon had some Moslems in his pay, the Christian King of Castile could always attack them as Moslems rather than Aragonese. Peasant serfs were a major item in the booty of these raids; they could be settled on one's own soil and become a source of honor and profit. To protect them the castles were much more numerous than in the rest of Europe, and even the villages were in some sense fortresses, closely packed small stone buildings from which the tillers of the soil went forth in the morning and to which they returned at twilight.

Tendencies present elsewhere were also intensified among the military forces which took part in these constant raids. Infantry moved too slowly, and in a country where the only middle classes were in the industrial and mercantile groups of the cities, there was little material for recruiting this arm. The normal and decisive weapon was cavalry, in a proportion of about four to one. A technical non-development also helped keep infantry in its place; the crossbow was only being rein-vented in Italy and Denmark, still was excessively rare and not well made in Spain. The country provides few woods from which decent longbows can be made. The usual type was the Turkish horn bow, a short wooden weapon backed with leather, a horseman's arm for use at close range. That is, the infantry had no missile weapon that could make cavalry keep its distance, and they were neither trained well enough nor equipped to stand on the defensive with pikes. The usual battle formation, when things came to a battle, was for the spear-armed infantry to form a front line, kneeling on the left knee, with archers just behind to conduct the preliminaries. When the arrows were exhausted or the moment became propitious, these footmen got out of the way and the cavalry began the real business of fighting.

Since Spain is a rough country, a large proportion of this cavalry was mounted on mules, especially among the Moslems. Mostly spear- and swordmen, the tactics of the cavaliers were considerably influenced by the skirmishing methods descended from Khalid. Since the deficiencies of the available bows were widely felt, there developed a peculiarly Spanish form of light horse called *genetes*. They wore a heavily quilted form of gam-beson in lieu of armor and carried javelins, about three feet long, with a seven-inch metal head, whose accurate balance has been much admired by military archaeologists. They were very accurate and deadly.

Through the complex of raidings and battles of the minor dynasts there appeared a tendency in favor of the Christian powers. It was observable in small details; with their firmer industrial base, extending back into France, the Christians were the better armored; their opponents held fast to traditional ways and ideas, such as that a shield covered with the hide of the Atlas antelope could not be penetrated by anything. Chris-tian siege engines were better, and better used. The tribal or-ganization of the Moslem armies was less efficient than the knight-and-retainer system of the Christians, who could take in anyone on the basis of efficiency instead of being forced to accept armies recruited by the lottery of birth. And in spite of usurpations and family quarrels there was more permanence of tenure, more orderly succession, and more established administration among the Christian nations than the Moslem, where every officer of state could aspire to become the state itself.

By the end of the century Castile had crossed the olive line and taken Toledo. Saracen Seville and most of the southeast were paying tribute, while Raymond-Berenger, Count of Barcelona, had practically reached the Ebro. The situation had become so serious from the Moslem point of view that the petty kings of the *taifas* took a strictly exceptional step; they banded together, and an embassy from the federated rulers of Badajoz, Seville, Granada, and Cordova went to ask the help of their coreligionists in Africa.

III

It was admittedly a dangerous thing to do. While the Spanish Mohammedans were splitting into fractions of fractions, the Murabitin Berbers, or Almoravides, had built a powerful united empire with overtones of religious revival in western Africa. It extended from Senegal to Algeria, and as usual in Moslem countries, religious revival was accompanied by an outburst of both military ambition and military strength. For the moment the empire of the Almoravides was the most powerful Moslem state of the world, and the invitation from Spain was a heaven-sent opportunity for the use of its energies.

The Berbers came, then, under their Emperor Yusuf ibn Tashfin and, with the help of the kings of the *taifas*, defeated Alfonso of Castile in a great battle near Badajoz, with such loss that the Christian advance was stopped and some parts of the line turned back. Then the petty Saracen kings discovered that they had imported more than military assistance. In the train of Ibn Tashfin came a considerable group of *faqihs*, who may be homologated to religious revivalists or Puritan preachers,

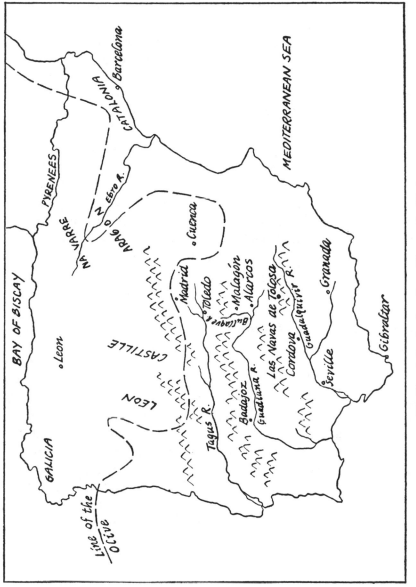

Medieval Spain for Las Navas de Tolosa

and who were by no means pleased with the liberty of religion accorded to Christians and Jews by the Spanish Moslems. At the same time Ibn Tashfin's Berber hillmen were very much pleased indeed with the wealth and luxury they found in Spain, and proceeded to help themselves. By 1111, under Ibn Tashfin's successor, 'Ali, the *taifa* kingdoms had been wiped out except in the northeast and Moslem Spain was a part of the Almoravide state, with Cordova as its capital.

The wars went on, but as border wars of the usual cross-raiding type; the Aragonese succeeded in reducing Saragossa, and the Castilians were not ejected from Toledo. But there things hung; through all the middle years of the twelfth century the Christian kingdoms were racked by a distracting series of dynastic troubles that reduced them to black anarchy, while on the Moorish side of the line the Almoravides were exchanging military habits for the pleasures of civilization. They won most of the battles along the frontiers, but gained little territory, and at home the new luxury lost them the support of the orthodox. The Almoravide empire became subject to a group of independence movements that tore it to pieces. The *taifas* were back, and north and south the pattern was repeating.

It was repeating in another sense also. While the later Almoravides were wrangling among themselves in Spain, there appeared in the Atlas a young man named Abu Mohammed ibn Tumari, son of a lamplighter, who began preaching against luxury and the relaxation of the laws of the holy Koran. He claimed prophetic revelations, led mob attacks on wineshops, and started riots in which overdressed individuals got themselves hurt. Ascetic fanaticism is easily aroused in people of his race and background, and like Mohammed the original, he was lucky enough to find early a convert who had considerable qualities as an administrator and soldier, Abd-el-Mumin. When Mohammed ibn Tumari retired to a monastery to pray, Abd-el-Mumin took over. For two years after the prophet's actual death revelations continued to come from his retreat, all favorable to Abd-el-Mumin, and the movement spread like a current in an ocean through the whole of North African life. By 1149,

Abd-el-Mumin was Emir of Morocco, and when he died in 1163 his territories were already coterminous with those that had belonged to the Almoravides and were reaching beyond.

The imperializing sectarians were the Almohades or "Unitarians." Son and grandson of Abd-el-Mumin were both able and fanatical. Their outriders reached Spain in 1146, at the instance of one of the reformist, independence-movement chiefs, and by 1172 they had swallowed the whole of the Mohammedan territory.

There were these differences between them and the Almoravides they replaced; they kept the capital in the Atlas Mountains of their origin and thus did not so readily succumb to pleasures forbidden by the Koran, and they came down hard on Jews and Mozarabs, who emigrated to the Christian kingdoms by the thousands.

In all this there was little to promise any real change in the repeating pattern of periods of anarchy and recovery on both sides of the border—or if change was indicated, it was in favor of the Moslems. By 1195 they had succeeded in maintaining a stable union of Spain and Africa through three generations and developing to the full the inherent military qualities of religious fanaticism. In that year Ya'cub, the Almohade emperor, for the first time threw the full strength of the combined African-Spanish military establishment against the northern border.

IV

His objective was the Castile of King Alfonso VIII, remarkable man, about whom perhaps the most remarkable thing was his good fortune. He was lucky to be a king at all. His grandfather had united the crowns of Castile and Leon, but when he died it was found that his will made the usual split, Alfonso's father died within a year, leaving that young man an infant king, whether of one and a half or three years is still a matter of dispute. The accession of a baby in that age was an invitation; Leon and Navarre promptly began taking Castilian castles and cities, while the members of the great families challenged each other in private wars whose objective was obtaining the regency.

The normal thing in such cases is for the baby to get lost in the shuffle; Alfonso not only escaped, but even achieved an unusually good education. The latter was probably due to the Lara, one of the imperially minded families, who for a long time had the lead in the struggle for custody of the crown over the rival family of Castro. The king was still in his early teens when he got away from the Lara, but at once there coalesced around him one of those outbursts of unselfish patriotic loyalty which only Spain can produce. It seemed that practically every grandee in the country had only been waiting for Alfonso's appearance to get rid of the Castros and Lara. Surrounded by a cavalcade which grew in numbers and importance at every moment, he made a tour of the communes to accept their allegiance personally (something very important in that part of the Middle Ages) and got the capital of Toledo back from the Lara by surprise.

It took a matter of years for the young king to get things firmly into his own hands, and Alfonso's luck arranged it that these should be the years when the Almohades were extremely busy in the south with the kings of the *taifas*. He was also lucky in having a daughter very early in the game and marrying her to another Alfonso, second of the name to rule in Aragon. Aragon was the one Spanish kingdom that had no particular ambitions in the peninsula at the moment; to it had fallen the heritage of the counts of Barcelona, whose interests lay mainly beyond the Pyrenees. The marriage alliance with Castile thus worked out a good deal better than most such alliances; the lucky Alfonso of Castile got abundant help in recovering what had been lost to Leon and Navarre. By 1175 he was strong enough so that the Christian kingdoms were agreed that more could be gained by fighting the Moors than by fighting each other and the advance toward the south was resumed.

By this date a new element had entered the military situation in the formation of the great military monastic orders of Calatrava, Santiago, and Alcántara. For some reason which should interest a social historian as much as the line of the olive should an economist, celibate military communities have been a success from the time of the Mamertines down through the Jomsvikings to the Janissaries, and conditions in Spain were exceptionally favorable for their development. The orders provided the Spanish kings with something they had never had before—a body of disciplined professional soldiers and, moreover, a body whose religious fervor equaled that of the Almohades and who were not interested in quarrels between one Christian kingdom and another, but only in breaking the heads of the infidels.

The result was a canalization of energies toward the Moorish frontier, and between 1175 and 1195, nearly twenty years, the advance from both Castile and Leon was steady. There were no spectacular gains unless Alfonso's capture of Cuenca by siege could be called one, but the chain of posts moved forward. It took time for the movement to become apparent in an age of leisurely communications, but the pressure was there and it brought Ya'cub and the African army into action.

The armies of Ya'cub and Alfonso clashed at Alarcos on July 18, 1196, and the result was a crushing defeat for the Castilian king, who tried to die among the spears and had to be forcibly led away from the field. The chronicles speak of 25,000 Spanish casualties, which seems very high indeed, but medieval chroniclers seldom exaggerated the losses on their own side. Toledo, Alcalá de Hermanes, and Cuenca were besieged, Moslem columns snaked through Castile, and the kings of Leon and Navarre seized the occasion to snatch a few castles in the north. Alfonso was forced to make a humiliating truce with the Moors.

At this point he was saved by two pieces of his usual luck. Ya'cub was a dying man and had to go back to Africa to set his affairs in order, while Alfonso II of Aragon became a dead man and the succession fell to Alfonso the Lucky's grandson, Pedro II. This young man, twenty-two at the date of his succession, has been described as "a marked and curious character."

He was all of that; a genuine knight-errant, right out of some lay of chivalry, and placed in many of them by the troubadours, with whom he was a great favorite. He also had notable accomplishments as a lecher; it is related of him that he once spent the night before a battle in such a manner that he could not stand at Mass and had to be hoisted onto his horse by a squire. His romantic instincts flared up at the tale of his grandfather's misfortunes; he put all the weight Aragon could swing into the scale, and it was his intervention at least as much as Ya'cub's approaching demise that made the truce possible.

On both sides it was rather definitely recognized as a truce instead of a peace and on both it was followed by a slow-paced gathering of forces to carry the struggle to a definitive result. It was 1200 before Alfonso of Castile found himself strong enough to denounce the truce. Ya'cub had been succeeded the year before by his son, Mohammed al Nazir, who had a holy war preached. It was a period more or less of stasis in the Mohammedan Near East; the Seljuq Turks had fragmented, the Byzantine Empire and the crusader kingdom in Palestine had developed enough stability to make Moslem invasion there temporarily unprofitable, and there was unemployment among fighting men. Mohammed was able to recruit an army stated (probably inaccurately) at 600,000 men, all the way from Persia and Nubia.

In the meanwhile the Christians decided that they too could play the holy war game. Archbishop Rodrigo of Toledo, one of the most militant prelates of the Middle Ages, went to Rome, secured the proclamation of a crusade with generous indulgences from Pope Innocent III, and made a tour of the courts of Western Europe, preaching the good cause. The response was excellent; in the spring of 1212 there assembled at Toledo a number of knights set at 60,000, which is as much of an underestimate as the figures for the Moslems are an overestimate, since each knight included in his retinue enough supporters to double or treble the number of fighting men in line.

They did not all stay. A host of this size must have placed a severe burden on the logistic equipment available in a city of no great size, and the French knights speedily became disgusted with the proud ways of the Castilians and the lack of opportunity for profitable forays. When King Alfonso moved south for the test he had with him only the contingents from his own realm, those of the knightly orders, a rather small group led by King Sancho the Strong of Navarre and a rather large one led by the romantic Pedro of Aragon. It was, nevertheless, the largest army ever assembled in Christian Spain, and it was facing the largest Moorish one. There would be a decision.

V

Mohammed al Nazir had a strategy, and his intelligence organization seems to have been better than anyone would have a right to expect. His army was spread out for the siege of various castles. When his forward elements reported contacts with Alfonso's forces at Malagón, Calatrava, Alarcos (the Christians were apparently marching straight down the valley of the Bullaque), the Moslem leader pulled back behind the Sierra Morena chain and placed strong contingents in all the passes. He was perfectly aware that the specific weaknesses of a medieval knightly force were in its lack of cohesion and inability to solve the supply problem during a long campaign. He intended to make his opponents fight for the passes at considerable disadvantage or (what was infinitely more probable) break up and go home. He was near his own base, had provided magazines of food in the cities, and even remount depots on islands in the Guadalquivir. In the reflex movement he could win back all he had left behind in the valley of the Guadiana and carry on deep into Castile.

Alfonso's army tested the mountain barrier at various points and found the passes too strongly held for penetration. There was a council of war, at which both Sancho of Navarre and Pedro of Aragon advised retreat and a campaign against the by-passed castles still held by the Moslems, while the Archbishop of Toledo was the only one who supported the king in his desire to press on. At this moment there appeared a shepherd, miraculously according to Spanish legend, who offered to show the army a defile by which the passes could be turned. The offer was accepted; the army filed southward through an area where the difficulties were considerable, but purely of a geographic order, and on the heights exhibited themselves to the Moslems.

At this point there is a rather curious gap in the story. Why did not Alfonso attack at once? Mohammed certainly could not have had his full strength at hand and the absent elements would be among the mounted men who were his best armed. There was no question of fighting anywhere but in that place. The Moslems were across the only good road to the valley of the Guadalquivir; to the Christian left were ragged and wooded mountains; any attempt to slide rightward would have brought the Moslems down on flank and rear. The fact remains that, for reasons we do not know, the Spaniards spent two whole days in prayers and conferences before deciding to attack.

During those two days the Moors set up their position on the south bank of a small stream called the Campana Ronegadero, which runs from west to east across the valley just north of the modern town of La Carolina. The area is known as Las Navas de Tolosa, and a *nava* is a small plain among hills; there were several of these along the valley and one can picture the Moors formed across them, with heavily wooded rocky slopes at their backs. They are reported as having 100,000 mounted men in line, which may not be far from correct, with a considerable number of infantry. In the center of the line Mohammed placed himself, behind a palisade bound with heavy iron chains, a Koran in one hand, a sword in the other, surrounded by warriors on foot, while an attendant held over his head the official parasol which was the banner of the army.

His forces formed a single solid mass; the Christians were in the customary three "battles" of a medieval army, King Alfonso in the center with the Archbishop Rodrigo and the knights of Santiago and Calatrava, Pedro of Aragon on the left,

Sancho the Strong on the right. Before the archbishop there was borne an enormous red cross with a shield at its base, the emblem of the day. It was July 16, 1212.

The Christians attacked. There were probably the usual preliminary skirmishings and challenges to single combat before the fronts actually locked. This phase was followed by violent fighting all along the line, not so much of the character of knightly charges as of single combats interlocking, one man falling back as another came forward. The chess game feature of war was utterly absent and it is impossible to speak of tactics. On the wings the Christians gradually forced the Moors back, and the farther they pushed them the worse it became for the Moslems, for they were being driven into trees and rocks, where their individual mobility was lost and the heavier armor and swords of the knights had every advantage. It must, nevertheless, have entailed some fairly obstinate fighting, for this went on most of the day. In the center, where an inevitable concentration of Moslem power had taken place, things were different. The knights of Calatrava were nearly wiped out and the Christians driven back.

Alfonso cried, "Archbishop, it is here we ought to die!" Rodrigo replied, "No, sire, it is here we should live and conquer!" He had a better eye than the king, or he had observed that the Moslem counterstroke in the center had come up against Christian spearmen on foot, stiffened by the knights of Santiago; for once medieval infantry did not give way. The banner of the cross was borne forward; there was a furious new attack against the spur where Mohammed held his ground and at the same time Sancho the Strong personally cut his way through the chained stockade from the right. The emperor's bodyguard began to go; he had the official parasol lowered and the loss of that symbol of leadership produced the usual effect on an Oriental army. The rest became a massacre. The chronicles speak of 185,000 Moslems slain; it is too many, but not by a great deal.

VI

There was no immediacy to the results. After the battle the Christian army took a couple of towns and then broke up, as Mohammed al Nazir had foreseen that it would. Two years later Alfonso VIII died and his issue became involved in a series of obscure rows that seemed to repeat the ancient pattern. The year after the battle Pedro of Aragon was killed in the fight where he had to be hoisted onto his horse, and his successors looked eastward, to the Balearics and Sicily. In the south the empire of the Almohades collapsed into another group of anarchic petty states.

That is, Las Navas de Tolosa appeared to decide nothing. In reality it decided practically everything. It is unnecessary to believe the figures of the chroniclers to realize that the flower of the Moorish army had been wiped out, the point blunted, the edge dulled. Within fifty years the Almohade dynasty became extinct, and there was no replacement. There were no more Moorish raids into Christian territory, only the gradual erosion of Moslem provinces and cities, a process which reached its end with the conquest of the final corner of Granada, which had long been tributary to the Christian kings. As a matter of speculation, one may assume that the Almohades would ultimately have succumbed to the same forces that brought down the Almoravides, but as a matter of historical fact, they did not. Their fighting aristocracy was destroyed on the battlefield. The reserves behind Moslem conquests were always very thin; the Mohammedans depended upon continual success, on the acquisition of recruits to make war feed war, and when the leadership was thus decisively wiped out, the whole structure that it held together went to pieces.

This was the more important because of two factors, one spiritual and the other tactical and technical. The overthrow at Las Navas was not the destruction of an Eastern monarchy already weakened by dry rot; what went down there was a revivalist movement which, if not absolutely at its peak, had been strong enough to attract recruits from across 50 degrees of longitude and 15 of latitude. It was not merely the Almohades, but the Moslem world and Moslem system that were defeated; and the manner of the defeat was quite as important as the fact. A good part of Spain consists of territory so much resembling North Africa that the hit-and-run horse-archer tactics of the Near East were perfectly valid, and the assumption had been that the whole peninsula was subject to such an approach. Las Navas de Tolosa demonstrated on a large scale that this was not a general geographical truth, that a Moorish army was formidable only when fighting under its own conditions, and that it could be forced to fight under conditions which it did not find conformable.

The lesson, never precisely set forth at the time, was by no means lost on the later Christian kings. It helps explain why the erosionary process on the Moorish states went on uninterrupted until they were demolished. The battle, in fact, decided that no part of Europe could remain a part of Africa; that the Western gate was closed to the heirs of the Saracens; that European military organization possessed a flexibility that Africans and Arabs could not rival. The Spaniards could at least hold even with the Moors on the latter's own kind of ground; but when the Europeans could force the choice of the battle area, the Moors were finished.

Much more than this was decided. With the battle of Las Navas, the central plateau of Spain fell into the hands of the Kingdom of Castile and the unification of the peninsula became possible. Before it Spain was a geographical expression, no more a unit than Germany or Italy at the same period, and much less of an entity than England, Denmark, Poland, or even France. The battle placed in the hands of the Castilian kings the headwaters of all the great rivers and the control of the roads that paralleled them. The union of Spain did not become a physical fact for another 250 years, but it had been rendered inevitable by control of communications. When the knot was tied, the expansion of Aragon in the Mediterranean had made her the equal if not the dominant partner, but it was a union and not a conquest for which the foundations were laid at La Navas de Tolosa. It had been demonstrated that control of the central watershed was vital to the possession of Spain—and also that the Spanish kingdoms could work together for a common purpose when that purpose was a crusade.

Centrifugal forces remained and it would be hard to exaggerate their importance, but the remark of one of the Castilian kings when asked to help in the defense of Jerusalem is worth repeating: "We are always on crusade here, and so we do our share." It was in that spirit, with that background, with the desire to smite the infidel everywhere, with the secure knowledge that great things could be achieved if the kingdoms worked together as they had at Las Navas, that the conquest of the Americas was undertaken as soon as the Moors were expelled.

6. Jeanne d'Arc and
the Non-Conquest of England

They met at the bridge of Montereau, where the Aube breaks through the Burgundian highlands to join the Seine. The great duke advanced with a handful of his retainers behind him and knelt at the feet of Charles the Dauphin to show that their resistances were over and there would henceforth be co-operation between them against the English. As Duke Jean lowered his head, a man stepped forward. It was Tanneguy Duchâtel, the dauphin's friend; and before anyone could prevent him or even speak, he hewed at the duke with a battle-ax, striking him just where neck joined shoulder. There was a gush of blood and a shout; someone thrust one of the other Burgundians through the belly with a sword, and the rest of the suite were taken to be thrown in chains.

The date was 19 September, 1419, and the deed inaugurated a series of troubles that tore France to pieces for the next thirty years. Not that the kingdom had lacked evils before the Montereau murder. The weight of the armies of Henry of England, fifth of the name, bore heavily on the land, and he had taken nearly all of Normandy after breaking the French knights at Agincourt. King Charles VI of France was in the habit of going mad every summer; Queen Isabeau had the morals of a slut and took pleasure in informing the dauphin, her son, that he was a bastard. Under Jean the Fearless, Burgundy had been welded into a powerful state, reaching from the Alps to the North Sea, a fit rival for the whole of France, and the Burgundians were currently in possession of king, queen, and Paris.

Dauphin Charles, to be sure, was at liberty and claiming the regency as head of the national cause. But he was weak, slobbering, sensual, sly, and surrounded by the faction of the Armagnacs, who had no qualities but those of capable bandits. They stole the dauphin's money, left his soldiers unpaid, and used their authority so ill that it was the people of Paris themselves who had driven them out and brought the Burgundians in. It was the same elsewhere. When Henry of England besieged Rouen, the people defended themselves bravely, but after the place was forced to surrender, the lords and knights were so disgusted with the dauphin's party that hardly any of them refused to take the oath of allegiance to the conqueror—arrogant and a foreigner, but at least able to keep some order and to administer things with reasonable honesty.

The arrogance might have offered France an avenue of escape. Henry, who had begun the war by asserting the old Plantagenet claim to the whole realm of France, secretly advised Duke Jean of Burgundy that he was willing to settle for the hand of Princess Katherine, with Normandy as her dower. But after Agincourt he raised his sights and said he must have Anjou and the suzerainty of Brittany as well. At this point Tanneguy Duchâtel first came into the picture. It was impossible to keep a secret in any medieval court, and that of Charles the Dauphin was fully advised of Henry's demand. Duchâtel went to Duke Jean with an offer to let him control the royal council if he would take up the good cause against the English.

It was a trap and it was the prelude to the deed on the bridge of Montereau. Charles the Dauphin and his Armagnac friends had no real intention of striking hands with the Burgundians and had now demonstrated it in the most unmistakable manner. It is reasonable to ask whether they were quite aware of what they were doing, for Jean the Fearless had a son named Philip, twenty-three years old (which was ripe maturity for 1419), of approved skill both in council and in war. The answer is probably that Charles never had any mind of his own and the Armagnacs around him had no other idea than revenge for the revolt of Paris against their party. They simply did not care what happened after that.

What did happen was that Philip called a congress of Burgundians and pro-Burgundians at Arras. Subject: how to take counterrevenge on the dauphin for his murderous treachery. The decision of this congress was that peace should be made with Henry of England on any terms acceptable to him in order to make united war on the scoundrel, Charles. Henry's terms now moved higher yet; they now included the hand of the Princess Katherine, recognition of himself as regent for the half-mad king, and succession to the throne of France, to the exclusion of the dauphin, who was described by his own mother as a bastard. The terms were agreed, the alliance was doubled by the marriage of Henry's brother, John, Duke of Bedford, to Burgundy's sister, Anne. The treaty provided that when the crowns of France and England fell into the same hands, it should be a personal union only; the two nations were to preserve their own laws and customs, be ruled by their own nationals, and the Parlement of Paris was to be the supreme authority in France under the king's majesty.

Under this agreement English and Burgundians entered upon the conquest of France. They made progress, since they had a perfectly legitimate King of France on their side and Paris in their possession. The remaining opposition was dumb rather than vocal, passive rather than active, and consisted mainly in a series of holdouts in towns, which turned the war into a procession of sieges. But in the summer of 1422 Henry, called "Henry the Conqueror" in France, fell ill of the conqueror's disease of exhaustion and died within a few weeks. In October mad Charles VI followed him, and an infant less than a year old was proclaimed Henry VI of England and Henri II of France.

II

This hardly seemed to matter. The regent and protector of both realms was John Plantagenet, Duke of Bedford, and even in that able and violent family he had few superiors. He spent most of his time administering the French conquest, leaving England in the hands of his brother Humphrey of Gloucester, who mismanaged things sadly, got into trouble with the bishops and nobles, and had to be bailed out periodically by brother John.

But the main line of the story lies in France. There Bedford was not the equal of Henry the Conqueror, since very few men could have been, but his relations with Burgundy remained excellent and he behaved as though he really were steward of France for the interests of France. He reformed the procedure of the courts of justice and founded a university at Caen. The governors of the great provinces "in the obedience of King Henri" were Frenchmen, and the council of regency was overwhelmingly French. The estates were called regularly, and contemporary chronicles speak of Bedford with genuine enthusiasm. In short, he was succeeding in subduing those parts of France that Henry V had only conquered. Guy de Boutillier, who commanded the defense of Rouen against Henry V, became the loyal provost of Paris for Henri II.

Yet the acceptance of the English was an acceptance at the upper levels of society and beneath it the dumb opposition remained. Bedford's was an enlightened and conciliatory policy, but the men down below who administrated it were neither. They were invaders, aliens, "Goddams," and they behaved like it. When they came to a town they took the eggs and the hen, the milk and the cow, and usually raped any available women. The Burgundians, who at least spoke a kind of French, were not much better; and on those lower levels there was a pronounced tendency toward brawls.

This was not true of the great towns, of course, where the

higher officers could maintain order, but the Anglo-Burgundian occupation came down hard on the countryside. Its weight was accentuated by the conditions of the war. The English occupation of Normandy was fairly solid, and no particular police operation was needed, while in Picardy and northern Champagne, Burgundy was the lawful duke, and the invaders need not put in an appearance as such. But in Maine, Anjou, the Île de France, southern Champagne, there were everywhere little islands of resistance, everywhere towns flaring up, possessors of single châteaux who held for the dauphin. Through this amorphous polity trailed bands of English and Burgundians, looking for enemy holdings with intent to put them down to the accompaniment of plunder, and claiming they had found opposition whether it was there or not.

The Anglo-Burgundians simply did not have men enough to wipe out these islands of resistance systematically. The population of England was just recovering from two bouts with the Black Death and stood at something like 2 million; that of the territory comprised in modern France was about 20 million. Some of these latter were Burgundians, pro-English, or still belonged to the empire, but the proportionate French numerical superiority was still prodigious, and during Bedford's regency the French had the services of a considerable number of Scots.

In themselves numbers were no bar to an ultimate English conquest. England itself had passed under the rule of Normans quite as small proportionately, and Alexander the Great conquered the whole East with not much more than double the number of men Bedford could deploy in France. But weight must be given to local conditions. South of the Loire and all along its length there were bridgeheads in the conquered north, held by a French government which, however despicable, however incompetent, however factional, could claim to be the legitimate government of France. While it remained in possession of a considerable stretch of territory, while it was still able to raise armies and levy taxes, while it had an administrative center, the conquest was incomplete. It had been the lack of any administrative focus for resistance that led to the acceptance of conquerors in Persia and later in England; it was the destruction of such a focus that made Las Navas de Tolosa decisive.

The state of the art of war also had a good deal to do with conditions. Nearly a hundred years before, the Edwards of England had replaced feudal levies by a system of long-term paid professional soldiers and worked out a tactical doctrine that made the most of this material. Basically this consisted of drawing up a solid block of men at arms on foot, using spear, sword, and battle-ax; on the flanks of this formation were thrown forward strong triangles of archers, covered by the sharp stakes they carried. The English then awaited attack. Knightly cavalry piled up under the archer fire; men at arms on foot could not get through it without paralyzing losses. The theme was played in all variations at Crécy, Poitiers, Agincourt, Aljubarita, and in a dozen minor contests. If the enemy refused to attack, the English waited for the operation of the disruptive forces Mohammed al Nazir counted on, then went somewhere else, wherever they pleased. As paid professionals they could afford to make a long campaign. But they usually drew their attack because, aside from other considerations, chivalry forbade their opponents not to attack.

There existed at the time no real method of dealing with this English hedgehog of armed men. No armor would keep out a shaft from an English longbow; it fired so rapidly and had such range that other hand-borne missile weapons could not be brought against it and the archers were so mobile that heavier weapons were useless. To be sure, the longbow required a period of training from childhood up, but this did not matter in a country still largely forested, where the normal method of supplying the cooking pot was by hunting, and in a service of professionals, where archers had nothing to do but be archers. The total result was that an English army in the terrain where it operated was incomparably the best in Europe, and fully aware of the fact.

There were never as many of these English archers as the

commanders wanted, and they had no siegecraft to speak of. Cannon were not yet of a force to deal with strong stone walls nor of a mobility to be taken into the field. The normal method of taking a fortress was by starving it out, since escalade was expensive in manpower when it failed, and manpower was the specific shortage.

Thus the war in France under Bedford's regency was a repetition of Henry V's; a long series of sieges, spotted with occasional battles. The most important of the latter was at Verneuil in 1424, where the French managed to gather a considerable force under the young Duke Jean II d'Alençon, with a large Scottish contingent. The only difference from the classic Anglo-French battle pattern was that Alençon detached a flying wing to attack the English baggage train as a preliminary to falling on the rear of the line of archers and men at arms. Bedford had foreseen this and left a strong archer contingent in charge of the train; they cut the flying wing to pieces and counterattacked so heavily that the French front collapsed. Alençon was taken; Bedford reported over 7,000 French dead or prisoners, which, if true, made Verneuil as great an overthrow as Agincourt.

The old magic thus still held and the war of sieges went on, with the line of the English obedience gradually but inexorably advancing. It advanced only gradually because Bedford had to keep going back to England to unravel the tangles set up by his brother. But by 1427 affairs there were in so much order that Bedford came back to take the general direction of France. The field army, about 5,000 strong, including some Burgundian auxiliaries, was placed under Thomas, Earl of Salisbury, and ordered forward to the siege of Orléans.

This was a sound strategic decision in a war of sieges. Orléans covers the chief passage of the Loire and the one nearest to Paris; it was the largest city remaining in the hands of the dauphin (Bordeaux was English) and the symbol of his dominion. Moreover, there is something almost mystical about the Loire line in French military history. The light of later events says that no less than three times—in 1815, 1871, and

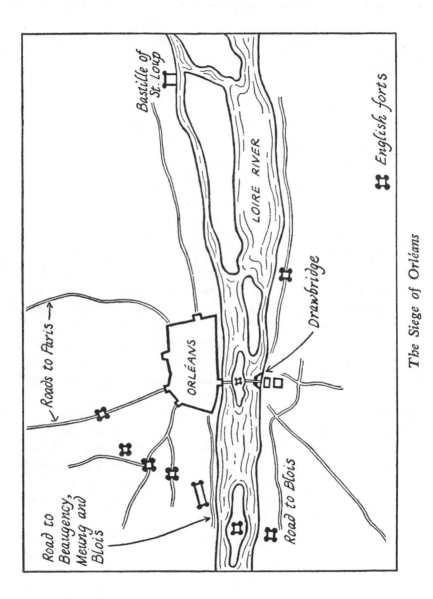

The Siege of Orléans

1940—France has given up after that line was passed; the light of earlier times shows that when the Goths failed to break that line at Châlons from the north and the Moors failed from the south at Tours, France stood.

At this date the city part of Orléans lay north of the river, surrounded by a castellated wall. There is an island in the stream; it held two strong towers, the "Tourelles," connected with the city by a masonry bridge, and with an outwork on the south bank by a drawbridge. Salisbury, who was a reasonably good captain, judged that the key to the place was this southern entrance and threw his weight on it. After several failures he succeeded in storming the outwork and the Tourelles on October 23. From this position his cannon could play on several of the principal streets of the city; and it is worth setting down that in this, the first important siege where guns played a part, they were used exclusively as anti-personnel weapons.

Around the outside of the walls on the north bank a series of six stockaded works were set up, served from the English camps in the rear. Salisbury had not men enough to make a complete line of circumvallation or to guard it. The spaces between his forts were covered by cavalry patrols, which naturally did not stop the passage of messengers and of some small convoys. The river was not fully blocked. Salisbury had every intention of drawing the lines tighter and had begun to work on it when he was killed by a cannon ball on 3 November and was succeeded by his lieutenant, William de la Pole, Duke of Suffolk.

Suffolk would qualify as a first-rate corps commander, but was without the capacity to lead an army. He had served at Agincourt and Verneuil and proved that he could command men in battle; he was also a creditable diplomat, which seems to prove that there was nothing basically wrong with his brain. But somewhere in his faculties there was a gap, a circuit breaker between the fighting man as such and the man who uses his brain for all purposes. It was not in the usual medieval scheme of things for a siege to be pressed around the clock, as Alexander the Great had driven his siege at Tyre, but Suffolk pushed far less than usual. The year turned without any important additions to the siege lines, and as February of 1429 came, with provision beginning to grow short in the town, there was scarcity also in the camps around it.

At this point Bedford dispatched a provision convoy from Paris, consisting largely of barreled herring for Lent, under escort of 1,000 archers and 1,200 Parisian militia. The commander was Sir John Fastolf, who has passed into Shakespeare and legend as Falstaff, the figure of fun, but who was really a very able officer indeed. Someone in the dauphin's circle heard of the expedition, and the Comte de Clermont was sent with a hastily raised body of 4,000 men to intercept. They caught up with Fastolf at Rouvray on February 12, and it was not the conventional French-English battle. Fastolf formed his carts in a circular wagonburg (it is probable that he had heard of the Hussites' doing this sort of thing in Bohemia), with the archers atop the herring barrels and the spearmen operating between the carts and through the wheels. Clermont's men could make nothing of this novel defense; he was beaten, his army broke up, and with it disappeared the last visible French field force.

III

In the early part of the fifteenth century people took their religion personally. Good angels and bad angels, who took the most intimate interest in their charges, were of common acceptance, and the great Henry the Conqueror quite seriously accused his stepmother of practicing sorcery to the detriment of her husband with the aid of an evil spirit. It is therefore not surprising that when Jeanne d'Arc, the daughter of a well-to-do peasant of Domrémy on the border of Lorraine, began to hear voices and see visions she should attribute them to angelic sources, or that when she confided in others they should believe her.

The voices were those of St. Michael, St. Margaret, and St. Catherine, and they came to her oftenest when she heard the churchbells sounding for prayer, a ceremony which she performed assiduously and with genuine devotion. Her family were dauphinists, who at least once had been forced to take refuge in a castle to escape marauding Anglo-Burgundian bands. When the news of the siege of Orléans arrived, the voices became specific and insistent. They told her that she must leave her home, for she was the instrument divinely chosen to drive the English from the sieged city and to see that the dauphin was anointed at Rheims as legitimate King of France. At this date Jeanne was eighteen, a tall, strong girl with black hair, not particularly good-looking.

When she informed her parents of her mission they were first angry, then sad; they would rather see her drowned than in the life of a camp, being perfectly acquainted with what that life meant for an eighteen-year-old girl. Anger and pleas were alike fruitless; finally an uncle took her to the Sieur de Baudricourt at Vaucouleurs, the dauphinist leader in that area. It is possible to imagine a certain amount of skepticism at Vaucouleurs when Jeanne informed them that she had a divine mission to assume the arms of a knight and save France, but this eroded away rapidly under the influence of her peculiarly earnest and vehement method of expression, the fact that she performed all the duties of the Church with unquestionable piety and sincerity, and the other background fact that friars had been traveling all through the country preaching that deliverance from the Anglo-Burgundian oppressors must be sought from heaven. There was nothing at all incredible about the idea that this maid might be heaven's instrument; all of Vaucouleurs contributed to buy her a horse and armor, and De Baudricourt supplied an escort to take her to Chinon, where the dauphin was in residence.

There she encountered higher levels of skepticism. The first incident that shook it was that of the identification. She was led into a hall where three hundred-odd people were gathered, among them Charles, dressed rather simply, while many of the courtiers were elaborately turned out. She walked straight up to the dauphin and said, "God give you life, noble King."

"I am not the king," said Charles.

Jeanne said, "In God's name, sire, you are the king and no other. Give me troops wherewith to succor Orléans and guard you to Rheims to be crowned. It is the will of God."

Charles was impressed enough to take her aside privately and ask her for a sign. He got it. She told him about his doubts as to his own legitimacy, fostered by his harridan of a mother, and about his prayers for reassurance; and she added that his fears were groundless.

This was enough for the dauphin; he assigned to her a chaplain and an old knight, Jean d'Aulnon, under whom she studied the management of horse and sword. The sign was not enough, however, for many of the other courtiers and particularly Archbishop Renault de Chartres, primate of France. The churchman was perfectly willing to admit that Jeanne was supernaturally inspired; his doubt was whether the inspiration was divine or demoniac, and he had her taken to Poitiers for examination by the doctors of the university there. The combination of unmistakable sincerity and piety with correctness on doctrinal points added them to her list of converts.

Six weeks had gone by since Jeanne had arrived at Chinon and she was in a fever of impatience to complete her mission, saying that her voices told her she had "only a year and a little more." Charles sent her to Blois, where a small army had been collected to cover a large convoy of provisions for Orléans, with the best captains available—the young Duke d'Alençon, ransomed from his Verneuil captivity, La Hire, Xaintrailles.

She made a striking figure in the camp, always clad in white armor and riding a big black horse, which she managed with a dexterity that excited admiration, carrying a white banner embroidered with the lilies of France and a representation of Christ in his glory. In an age when all news passed by word of mouth and lost nothing in the passing, it was natural that tales should gather around the figure of the Maid (as everyone was now calling her), but at least some of them must have had foundation. The matter of the sword, for instance. When they offered her one she said no, the sword destined for her would be found at the shrine of St. Catherine of Fierbois, in a coffer long unopened, and it would be engraved with five crosses. The sword was unearthed at the named spot; it was the one she ever afterward carried. There was also the tale of the soldier at the gate of Chinon, who swore when crowded as she entered the castle with her escort.

"In the name of God, do you swear," said Jeanne, "and you so near death?" He fell into the moat an hour later and was drowned.

That is, the men of the little army at Blois were convinced that they were led by a miraculously inspired virgin, and the tale of her spread. The impression was deepened by the Maid's behavior in her capacity as a commander of the army. She left matters of maneuver to the captains without much interference, but she allowed no oaths, she drove whores from the camp with the flat of her sword, she compelled regular attendance at Mass and confessionals; and she was vigorous on points of strategy. Under her guidance it was unquestionably the most moral army of the Middle Ages, and it was glad to be so, for she had given it the thrilling assurance of victory.

On April 25 she marched from Blois. She wished to move by the north bank of the Loire, declaring that the English would neither sally from their "bastilles," the forts around the city, nor from the towns of Beaugency and Meung, which lay along the road. The captains insisted on the south bank as more secure. They were probably wrong; the medieval news service of gossip had functioned very thoroughly during Jeanne's delay at Chinon, the English knew all about her and were worried. Not that there was any admission that she was inspired by God or angels. The official English view was that she was a witch, a sorceress; but this made her more dangerous rather than less. Not many men of that period cared to tamper with black magic.

She came up the south bank, then, and outside the town met Jean, Comte Dunois, commandant of Orléans, an illegitimate son of Charles VI's brother. This man, already one of the most distinguished soldiers of France, was impressed at once. Then came the incident of the barges, hardest of all to explain, however one may designate the stories of the sword and the swearing soldier as magnified tales. The provision convoy was following by boat and Dunois pointed out that with the prevailing east winds it would be impossible for the barges to get past the English forts at the river's banks.

Jeanne said, "You are deceived. Better succor do I bring you than ever yet came to town or men at arms, for it is the aid of the king of heaven."

Half an hour later the east wind dropped; an unseasonable, improper, utterly impossible west wind blew up with the fall of night, bearing a storm of thunder and rain, so strong that the sailing barges could tow those without masts, and Orléans had its provision. For the rest of his life Dunois never forgot it.

The news of this success of the sorceress did not do much for English morale and the subsequent proceedings did still less. Jeanne rode into the town during the storm that night, made a solemn procession through the crowded streets the next morning, went to the principal church, where a *Te Deum* was chanted, and returned to the quarters provided for her, refusing to attend a banquet. The next day she went to the walls and by trumpet and word of mouth repeated a summons she had sent by heralds, bidding the English to go home lest they suffer sorrow and shame. Sir William Gladsdale, who commanded the Tourelles and the south bank outpost, called her "the Armagnac whore"; she wept and made ready for battle.

It is of some importance that although this girl of a little over eighteen had now established her moral ascendancy among the troops she had never been in a fight. That afternoon, while she was lying asleep, Dunois believed he saw a weakness in the easternmost, upriver English post, called St. Loup, and made a sally. It failed; the troops were flowing back when Jeanne, roused by a sound which she afterward identified as one of her voices, came riding into the reflux, carrying her banner and shouting, "Hari! Go boldly in among the English!"

Wild with recovered enthusiasm, they followed her; St. Loup was taken and all its garrison put to the sword, except some few spared at the insistence of the Maid. It was now the judgment of Dunois, d'Alençon and company, that they had moral and material forces sufficient to attempt something more serious than a single fort and, moreover, that they had better do so because it was altogether likely that the regent, Bedford, would be down on them with reinforcements. Jeanne told them calmly that the siege would be raised in five days. Whether it was she or another who suggested the idea that the new enterprise would be an attack on the southern bridgehead and the Tourelles, it was accepted at once. As much of the garrison as could be spared were taken in boats to the southern bank to join the men the Maid had brought with her and the command was forward.

The date was May 7, and it was a desperate business, being scaling-ladder work against strong walls. As Jeanne mounted one of the ladders, an arrow went right through her armor between neck and shoulder; she was carried to the rear, weeping with pain and shock. The wound was dressed and she had begun to pray with her confessor when word arrived that it was a repulse and Dunois had given orders for a retreat to be sounded.

Jeanne sent for the commandant. "By my God," she said, "you shall soon enter in there. Do not doubt it. When you see my banner wave against the wall, to your arms again. The fort is yours. For the present rest a little, and take some food and drink."

She was now recovered from the shock of the wound, but could not carry her banner, which was borne by a soldier. As it went forward and touched against the wall, all the French made a concerted rush up the ladders, while in the rear the Orléannais laid planks across the broken bridge and sallied. The French went up, over, into the outpost, and swept right into the Tourelles when Gladsdale was killed by a cannon ball that took out the drawbridge under his feet. Of the garrison 300 were killed and 200 taken.

The next day was Sunday; the Orléannais woke to see the English forts north of the river in flames, but their troops drawn up for battle before the city. Dunois was eager to go out and give them a fight, but Jeanne said no. "In the name of God, let them depart, and let us return thanks to God." Her view (which was the soundest tactical sense, since one did not attack an English army in the field with good chances) prevailed; instead of a battle, it was a solemn procession around the walls, with services of thanksgiving. Orléans was relieved.

I V

The event was not in itself decisive; there had been sieges and reliefs all through the war, and although English morale had been badly shaken by "that disciple and limb of the fiend called Pucelle, that uses false enchantments and sorcery," they still had strong forces in the field. There was Suffolk's former besieging army and a new one concentrated from various points by Bedford, under Fastolf and John, Lord Talbot, already on the march into the Loire country. Jeanne was in favor of neglecting both for a progress to Rheims and the immediate coronation of Charles in fulfillment of her mission, but the captains persuaded her that the English field forces must first be dealt with.

At this point the gap between Suffolk the fighting man and Suffolk the strategist becomes apparent. Instead of falling back to rally on the Fastolf-Talbot force, he parceled his small army out among the Loire towns—Jargeau, Meung, Beaugency. Jeanne moved on Jargeau first and on June 12 took the place by assault when the defenders flinched from the wall in the face of her black magic. Suffolk the fighting man bravely tried to make a stand in the streets and was taken with whatever men he had left. On the fifteenth Jeanne and her people forced the bridge at Meung and took that place too; next day they were around Beaugency. It was a town of considerable strength and held the largest of Suffolk's detachments, but whether from utterly depleted morale or because there had been no time to assemble provision, it surrendered on terms after only three days of siege.

Talbot learned of this on the day following and began to fall back toward Paris. The region through which he moved was much cut up by hedgerows and small clumps of forest, and it was not the custom of the age to put out flank guards, but near Patay the English commander learned that the French were close, without being able to see too much of them. Instead of accepting advice to continue the retreat, Talbot cried, "By God and St. George, I will attack!" and ordered out the archers to form wings along the hedgerows, while the remainder of his forces filed into position behind them.

He did not realize how close the French were, or that they would be driven by the urgency of the Maid, La Hire, and Alençon. The two armies seem to have been moving along courses roughly parallel, with the French even less aware than their opponents of the enemy's presence, when a stag was started and the English archers, just beginning to fix their stakes along the hedge, raised a view halloo. Jeanne instantly wheeled everything round with all the vehemence she could impart to such a movement, crying that the men at arms should not wait to form line but go straight in.

The archers were scattered before they could shoot, and Talbot's Burgundian and Picard auxiliaries, caught in column, were borne down and away under weight of numbers and momentum in a dusty, clanging, whirlwind melee. Baggage train and artillery, which had been the head of the column, made a brief stand under their archer guard; then they also went. Fastolf with the English knights came up just in time to face the whole French force and then got out as best he could, his men panicking. He was afterward accused of cowardice, and though the charge was justly dismissed, enough of the tar stuck to make the Shakespearean character. Talbot was captured; more than a third of his army was destroyed and the rest pretty well dispersed.

This now was decisive. Charles marched on Rheims and was duly anointed on July 17, while Jeanne threw herself weeping at his feet, her mission accomplished. In a strategic sense it did not matter that she was persuaded by the courtiers to remain in the field, that she failed in an attack on Paris in September, or that in the following spring she was taken by the Burgundians and sold to the English to be cruelly burned at the stake in Rouen.

Patay was locally decisive because it completed the wiping out of two English armies. It is evident that Bedford must have stripped his garrisons down thin to make up the Talbot force; when Jeanne and Charles appeared after the battle, town after town went over to the royal arms—Troyes, Châlons, Rheims, Soissons, Laon. The Regent of England did manage to get together a field force with which he operated all the following summer, but it kept costing him more towns and the English domination of France slid slowly downhill to complete ruin.

It slid because, beyond the local decisions at Orléans and Patay, an answer had at last been found to that English system of war which enabled the smaller nation to bring France to the edge of national collapse. Most obviously the solution lay in the release of moral forces. *In hoc signo vinces* can be quite as useful a military weapon as a sword or a cannon, as Sa'ad's Saracens had earlier demonstrated. Moral forces also ended the effects of the good government with which Bedford was gradually securing northern France. It was not that Charles could offer any better government; practically everything was in the hands of his wretched court favorites, justice was at a minimum, taxes at their peak. It was not even that one government was English and the other French, for Bedford's administration was nearly all French. But Charles had been given the direct support of the king of heaven through the Maid, and he was God's anointed; duty to him had become religious as well as political.

This invalidated the Anglo-Burgundian method of conquering the country by holding the towns, a method which rested on small garrisons and acquiescence. It also had its effect on the morale of the always outnumbered English professional soldiers, whether in towns or in the field. The fall of Jargeau, the surrender of Beaugency are evidential. But the fact that

Jeanne released and channeled moral forces in an atmosphere of mysticism and religious fervor has been allowed to conceal something quite as important—namely, that she and not the captains had found a method of dealing with the strategy and tactics of the English hedgehog.

This method was so simple that no one had been able to think of it before; Jeanne simply refrained from attacking the hedgehog. It has been suggested that her furious out-of-hand assault at Patay was due to no more than a desire to come to handgrips with the enemy as soon as possible. But she had an excellent opportunity to close with the English on the morning after they burned their forts at Orléans, with the moral factors heavily on her side, and she did nothing of the kind; they were in formation. During the campaign that followed the coronation, she had other opportunities to attack English formations, and she made no such attacks. The weight of the evidence says that at Patay the charge was made in a hurry precisely to keep the English from setting up their invincible defense.

Moral authority here reached over into the tactical field. D'Alençon at Verneuil, like other French captains before him, was involved in the concept of chivalry; if he failed to attack, he would have been guilty of unknightly conduct and part of the base on which his ability to command rested would have been taken from under him. The fact that in all the battles of the Hundred Years' War the French had a numerical superiority was plainly visible; the facts that they were opposing one arm to the combined arms, that they were amateurs fighting professionals made no difference to chivalry. But Jeanne had a moral authority that could override chivalry and let her do what the tactics and strategy of the situation plainly demanded.

Dunois, La Hire, the other leaders caught up the lesson, and that they learned it was one of the main reasons why the English were driven from France. They did not attack hedgehogs, they waited to be attacked, and the defect of the English formation stood revealed. It could not move.

It is probably fortunate that they lost in the long run. The conquest of France on the lines begun by Henry V and carried on by Bedford could hardly have resulted in anything but a kind of French conquest of England. Henry VI was half French by blood, he must inevitably have placed the center of gravity of the dual crown in the larger kingdom and set its interests first. This, of course, leaves out of account the character of that unimpressive monarch, or the lack of it. He would very likely have made out as badly in France as he ended by doing in England. But the advisers, the great feudatories, the men reaching for power would have been French and not English, they would have set up a sort of second Norman conquest. The total possible results defy speculation, but there were no such results. Jeanne d'Arc took care of that.

7. Vienna and the Failure to Complete the Crescent

I

In the early part of the sixteenth century there developed a nexus of decision in Western Europe. It centered around five men—two of them kings, one an emperor, one a religious leader, and one a politician wearing the clothes of a religious leader. Though all of them took advice and occasionally changed the details of their policy, they were so consistent that it is possible to deal with them in general terms.

One of the kings was Henry VIII of England; his policy looked inward to England and outward across the Atlantic, and although his support was eagerly sought by other members of the power group and that seeking influenced many of their actions, he was always so unwilling to do anything practical about affairs on the Continent that he may be dismissed with the remark that he raised tides like the moon and remained about the same distance.

The second king was Francis I of France, who thought of himself as a knight-errant like Pedro of Aragon, and behaved like a bandit. He inherited a realm which had become the first modern unified state of Europe under Louis XI, Charles VII's son, with the great feudatories broken down, and a military system based on a combination of artillery with heavy cavalry, especially designed to deal with English armies of static archers and men at arms. In Francis' very first year of 1515 ambition took him to Italy, where he encountered the Swiss pikemen and halberdiers, the terror of Central Europe, at Marignano. It was one of the most gigantic battles of the age. Two days of desperate fighting proved that the new French system was quite as useful against pikemen as against archers. "The drunken Swiss" were driven from the field; France won the duchy of Milan and made with Switzerland a "perpetual peace" that really turned out to be perpetual.

The war in which this took place was really part of the long duel between the royal house of France and the ducal house of Burgundy, which in Jeanne d'Arc's time so nearly missed ending in the completion of Henry V's conquest. But the ducal house of Burgundy had ceased being merely the greatest of the French feudatories. By one of those marriages which caused a rival king to ejaculate, *"Tu, felix Austria, nube,"* its possessions had fallen in with those of the Hapsburg Empire. By another, with Joanna, the heiress of Spain (who, like all queens named Joanna, ultimately went mad), that peninsula and its immense overseas empire were added to the Hapsburg heritage. In 1519 the third protagonist of this story, Charles V, attained the united thrones.

He inherited more than dominions that encircled France on every side and a tradition of implacable hostility toward her. Charles also acquired the Spanish military establishment, based on solid blocks of heavily armored, thoroughly disciplined pikemen, with little knots of arquebusiers at the corners, the *tercias*. At Pavia in 1525 this establishment clashed with Francis and the combination of fire power and push proved so far superior to what France could put in the field, even with Swiss help, that the French army was destroyed and Francis himself taken prisoner.

The event decided the fate of Italy, which in a practical sense became a Spanish possession for two generations, but it did not make things much easier for Charles, because of the politician in the power complex. This was Pope Clement VII, who could never forget that before his election he had been Giulio de' Medici, a member of the former ruling house of Florence.

Neither in this capacity nor as an Italian temporal potentate was he anxious to be helpful to Charles, and in fact was so unhelpful that strains built up to that sack of Rome, which is usually taken as the most convenient date point for the end of the Italian Renaissance.

Quite as importantly the Holy Father procrastinated about calling a general council of the Church, which Charles deeply desired as a means of dealing with one of his leading problems, the fifth member of the combination, Martin Luther. It is by no means certain that a council would have extricated Charles from his difficulties with the Reformers, for when the matter came to a head, Luther had already pronounced his conviction of the fallibility of councils to Charles' face at Worms. By this date the movement had taken on a certain nationalistic aspect in addition to the religious. But the refusal of Clement to call a council made it very certain that Charles would not easily get out of this particular trouble.

These were the forces. They produced a long series of French-Imperial wars that left everybody poor, without any significant territorial changes after Pavia. These wars had the technical characteristic of being largely conducted through siege operations. After Pavia nobody quite dared to meet the Spanish infantry in the field, and in any case, the plunder of a town at reasonable intervals was one of the best methods of keeping mercenary *Landsknechts* and terciaries to the line of discipline.

By 1528 the situation of Western Europe had become not too dissimilar from that in the Middle East at the date when the Persian and Byzantine empires had exhausted each other just in time to clear the track for the coming of the Saracens. Here also there was a sprawling empire, short of financial resources, with part of its population in a state of religious disaffection, engaged in a great struggle with another entity.

The Moslems were at hand to take advantage of the situation here also.

I I

They were no longer the penniless Saracens of the desert, with the drive supplied by a religion which had united a race, but a closely organized and modern, if non-Western state—the Ottoman Turks. They were a clan which appeared in Asia Minor in 1227, nomads from the steppes and relatives of the Seljuq Turks. The Seljuqs assigned them some territory around Ankara as a reward for military services. The Seljuqs themselves had reached Asia Minor earlier, as servants and fighting men for the later and more luxurious caliphs, and soon owned everything; but they had no gift of political organization, and as the clan system tended to fragment where they were in permanent residence, they became a group of quarreling independent principalities about the time the Ottomans arrived on the scene.

These Ottomans had two stupendous pieces of luck. One was in their royal family; in the course of nearly 300 years, down to the point at which this narrative begins, that family produced an unbroken succession of no less than nine extremely able rulers—energetic, adventurous, cruel, just, and intelligent. Conquest was their peculiar pleasure. No other family strain in all history can show such a record.

The second piece of luck was Ala ed-Din, one of the members of this family and elder son of Othman, the first sultan. He was a philosopher and a theoretician, who willingly left the throne to his younger brother Orkhan, and devoted himself to working out a military and administrative system that would make the most of what the Ottoman Turks had.

There were never very many of them, but they were all soldiers, and being of nomad origin, soldiers who fought on horseback. When a district was overrun, it was cut up into fiefs, each of which was to supply a horseman. These fiefs were combined into districts and the districts into larger counties under the authority of a *beylerbey*. Thus far the system was feudal. There was a provision that a fief did not necessarily fall from father to son, each man must prove his own right by valor and service, but there were similar statutes in early European feudalisms also, and the Turkish setup might have taken similar lines of development but for the unique additive supplied by Ala ed-Din.

This was the institution of the *yeni cheri*, Europeanized as Janissaries. Their background was that the later caliphs of Egypt had set up a body of slave soldiers called the Mamelukes; at the same time in all Moslem countries the religious duty of exacting tribute from non-Moslems endured. Ala ed-Din combined the two institutions by taking his tribute in the form of male children. They were brought up in Islam, forbidden to marry or to engage in trade, held under the strictest discipline and, except for those who showed administrative talent, they were confined to the camp from the age of twenty-five. They were infantry.

The Ottoman sultans thus had a celibate military community within the body of their state, one whose only devotion was to them and to Islam, and one whose every member was trained from childhood in the sole business of war. With such an instrument in the hands of the head of state, and with such heads of state as the Ottoman line provided, the feudal lords never had a chance to develop into great feudatories, as in the West. They remained a body of first-class cavalry and a rather loose aristocratic class, since only the son of a feudal tenant could hold a fief.

The military organization thus combined a standing army of elite infantry, whose cavalry wings could be increased in an emergency. It was infinitely superior to anything in the West, and the Ottomans proceeded to prove it, beginning with what was left of the dying Greek Empire, since they were not too interested in subduing other Turks. By 1355 what was left of the Byzantines in Asia Minor had been wiped out; in 1361 Murad I crossed the straits, took Adrianople, made it his capital, and began working on the Balkans. Serbia, Bulgaria, Albania, Montenegro, Wallachia celebrate national heroes for their resistance to the flood from the East, but it always ended the same way, in another nation or district being added to the Ottoman Empire. With each addition the number of available fiefs and of children to be made into robot Janissaries grew, a snowballing process without visible limit.

It was not even interrupted by an incursion of Mongols who captured Sultan Bayezid I and kept him in an iron cage till he died; nor by the fact that each succeeding sultan usually found it necessary to have his brothers and cousins poisoned or strangled. The supply of good blood in the Othmanli line seemed inexhaustible. By the middle of the fifteenth century the whole of the Balkans and Greece were Turkish and their fleets began to dominate the eastern Mediterranean.

One of the specific excellences of that Ottoman line was its ability to learn. It is not certain when and where they first encountered cannon—probably in the hands of Venetian sailors —but it did not take them long to discover that this invention covered the one technical weakness of an army essentially no-madic by habit and thought, its inability to handle siege opera-tions. The new device was adopted with enthusiasm, and under the influence of the Turkish penchant for magnificence the Ottoman heavy artillery speedily became the best in the world. When Mohammed II reached the throne in 1451 he at once began casting enormous guns that could throw stone balls up to twenty-five inches in diameter; two years later he turned them on the greatest city in the world and Constantinople be-came Istanbul.

It was a shock to Christianity, but all efforts to raise a crusade encountered the fact that Christianity was thinking about other things. Moreover, Mohammed failed to take Rhodes from the Knights of St. John, his successor, Bayezid II, kept peace in Europe except with the Hungarians, whom everyone regarded as little better than the Turks, and *his* successor, Selim the Grim, became involved in a series of wars in the East, in support of Moslem orthodoxy against the Shi'ite heretics of Persia. It is worth noting that his artillery won the wars for him and also enabled him to take over Syria and Egypt.

In 1520 he died, and his son Suleiman, known to Turks as

Suleiman the Lawgiver and to Europe as Suleiman the Magnificent, became the tenth sultan.

III

To contemporaries this seemed good news rather than bad. The communications of the West with the Turkish court through Venice were excellent, and people knew all about the new ruler—about twenty-five years old, tall for a Turk, somewhat sallow of countenance, with Tartar blood from his mother; very quick, both of mind and body, delighting in romantic tales and the Moslem type of chivalry, a linguist who could converse with his officers in most of the Balkan dialects, knew Italian, was a master of Persian and Arabic, and wrote poetry in his own language so well that even if he had not been a ruler he would have ranked as one of his country's leading poets. His interests were thoroughly Western; he had been governor of European Turkey while his father was campaigning in the south and east, and he cared nothing for Selim's crusade against the Shi'ite heretics. A despot, but an enlightened despot, on the familiar model of Francis I and Charles V; Europe considered it entirely possible to do business with a man like that. Finally, his grand vizier and alter ego was a Greek turned Moslem, a man named Ibrahim, of infinite charm and accommodation.

Europe overlooked two factors, not very surprisingly, since they were buried in Moslem law and tradition. One was the fact that just before his death, the late Grim Selim had become Caliph of all Islam, Commander of the Faithful. In the theory of Moslem law this office should be in the hands of a member of the Prophet's clan, the Koreish. The last caliph of the blood was a shadowy creature, who held a phantom court at Cairo; when Selim acquired Egypt, the office was resigned to the sultan without much urging. Suleiman thus inherited the position of the early caliphs as combined emperor, Pope, and commander-in-chief of the armies of a Moslem world that had abruptly become very nearly united, thanks to his father's overthrow of the heretical units and the expulsion from Spain of the last remnants of the Almohades.

The second factor overlooked in the West was the compilation of a code of Moslem law, which took in not only the Koran, but also the sayings of the Prophet recorded from oral tradition and the decisions of the early caliphs. The code was not complete when Suleiman reached the throne, but there was enough of it, added to previous codes, to establish the main line, and one point in it was absolutely clear: it was the plain religious duty of Moslems to conquer the unbeliever, convert him to Islam, or impose tribute upon him. It is not recorded that Suleiman was particularly devout, but many of his officers were, and the Janissaries, who were beginning to realize themselves as an influential guild, were not at all happy unless there was a war on.

The sum of these forces was that Suleiman's interest in the West became an interest in conquering the West, and he began with a demand on young King Lajos (or Louis) of Hungary for tribute. Young King Lajos had the ambassadors killed, which would have been a fairly good cause of war even if nobody were trying to provoke one. Suleiman set the troops in motion, and without difficulty captured the two great border fortresses of Szabács and Belgrade. They were, in fact, taken almost too easily; not only did Suleiman wish to shine, but also the vizier, Ibrahim, pointed out to him that the realm had expanded so rapidly to east and south that some labor of consolidation in those directions would be necessary. The shining part of the program was temporarily accomplished by an attack on the Knights of St. John of Rhodes, who were forced to surrender after a tremendous defense. Suleiman was still engaged in distributing fiefs, putting down local troubles, and organizing administration in Egypt and Kurdistan when he received a letter from the King of France.

It was written from Madrid, whither Francis had been taken as a prisoner after Pavia, and it urged the sultan to press on against Hungary and the empire for glory and booty; France would do her part by keeping Charles V occupied in a two-front war. The embassy acted as a detonating charge; Suleiman dropped his administrative details into the hands of subordinates and turned in the direction to which ambition, religion, and the demands of the Janissaries all urged him—Hungary.

That state was particularly ill-prepared to meet attack. Throughout the turn-of-the-century period Hungary had presented the curious spectacle of social evolution backward. The great nobles cased themselves in semi-barbaric luxury and jewels, even wearing their coronets to bed; the burden of taxation fell ever more heavily on the peasantry until they staged a fierce revolt, fiercely repressed in 1514. It was followed by the "Savage Diet," which enacted laws that placed the entire laboring population in actual, not virtual, slavery to "their natural lords," annulled any charters the towns had, permitted nobles to engage in trade tax-free, and came down so hard on the minor gentry that thousands of them preferred to cross the Turkish border, live under Mohammed, and pay tribute rather than be part of such a regime. King Lajos himself was often short of clothes and food.

When Suleiman came through Belgrade with 100,000 men, Lajos could assemble less than 30,000, feudal cavalry, with a group of forced-to-fight peasant infantry. Lajos had hoped and asked for help from Charles V, doubly his brother-in-law, but Francis of France, faithful to his engagement with the Turks, pushed an army into Italy, and the emperor could spare nothing. Young King Lajos led against the Turks at Mohács; on August 28, 1526, he was killed with both archbishops of the realm, five bishops, and 24,000 men, and Hungary ceased to exist as a nation. The plunder of Buda furnished the bazaars of the Near East with wares for years afterward, and Suleiman had John Zápolya, the voivode of Transylvania, elected to the vacant throne as a tributary king.

He was not the only claimant. The emperor's brother Ferdinand called himself King of Hungary in the right of his wife, sister of the late King Lajos, and assembled enough of the magnates to make up something called a Diet, which went through a form of election. "Tell him I will see him at Mohács," said Suleiman when he heard of it, "and if he is not there I will come to Vienna for him."

For the moment the sultan was too busy with affairs in Persia to do anything about Vienna, and with the withdrawal of Turkish troops, Hungary collapsed into an anarchy of roving bands who theoretically held for King Ferdinand or King John, but actually served only themselves. But by the end of 1528, Suleiman had solved out his Persian preoccupations and determined that the next step should be the thorough digestion of Hungary through the fief system, as the Balkans had been digested earlier. A necessary step in this direction was the capture of Vienna and the elimination of any German danger to the new frontier, as the Hungarian danger to the Balkans had been eliminated by Mohács and the capture of Buda.

The strategic plan was to take Vienna in the late summer of 1529, winter there and, drawing in reinforcements, proceed to a spring campaign for the preliminary conquest of Germany. Francis of France could be counted on to keep the empire busy on the opposite flank, the one Charles regarded as vital; Ferdinand, like young King Lajos, would have to depend pretty much on his own resources. Suleiman had observed that these Christian kingdoms lacked such unity of action as was conferred by the combined sultanate-caliphate.

On April 10, 1529, the sultan left Istanbul with more than 200,000 men. The Janissaries were sent up the Danube in boats; King John Zápolya would join with a contingent in Hungary.

IV

Ferdinand, in addition to his title of King of Hungary, was also Archduke of Austria and King of Bohemia. As soon as he heard that Suleiman was on the march, with his ultimate destination the Rhine, meetings of the estates were called in all the dominions where Ferdinand had any authority. The leading limitation on all Central European monarchies of the date was that of weak police power. Austria voted to send every tenth man for the defense of Vienna, but could by no means enforce it, and Bohemia, where the estates valiantly declared in favor of mobilizing every man capable of bearing arms, actually sent only 2,000, and these not till late August. The Diet of the empire, which was assembled at Speyer, voted an assistance of 12,000 foot and 2,000 horse, but tacked on a provision that no troops at all were to move until a deputation had visited Hungary to find out whether this nonsense about a Turkish drive was really true; then went into a series of almost interminable debates as to who should command the imperial forces if it turned out that they were really needed. Charles V was in Italy, very much concerned about what the French were doing there, and Pope Clement VII was intensely occupied in re-establishing the Medici dukedom of Florence in place of the republic.

That is, nobody wished to believe there was any real danger except the men on the spot. Fortunately for Germany and Europe there were a couple of very good men on the spot. The better was a certain Graf Nicolas zu Salm-Reifferscheidt, all his life a soldier of the empire, who had fought at Pavia and personally wounded and been wounded by King Francis. Salm was already sixty-six at that time, and in the year of Suleiman's invasion seventy; a man who had defended the Croat and Slovene lands against the puppet King Zápolya and who knew the country. He was too minor a noble to be named formally as commander; after its endless debate the Diet at Speyer gave this office to Duke Friedrich of the Palatinate.

Graf Nicolas reached Vienna in the early days of September; not long after his arrival word came through that Suleiman had taken Pesth, where the empire had a small garrison, and the Janissaries had slaughtered every man in the place. If any news were needed to stir the Viennese to work on their defenses this was probably it; but down to the coming of Graf Nicolas there had been nobody to take the lead, to tell people what to do. And there was everything to do; the city wall dated from approximately the time when Rudolph of Hapsburg made the place his capital in 1276, was only six feet thick and ruinous, enclosing the strictly limited area now known as "the Ring." The outer palisade beyond the dry ditch was so weak that it bore and deserved the name of "city hedge"—*Städtzaun;* the citadel was an old building of brick and timber; the houses roofed with highly inflammable shingles. There were no magazines.

Graf Nicolas sent details out to scout the countryside for every kind of food, while in and around the city he built and destroyed. All the houses of the suburbs outside the ancient wall were pulled down or burned to deprive the attackers of cover, including the great city hospital, two churches, and three convents. There was no time to build new masonry walls or to extend the old ones; where they were weak, earthwork bastions were thrown up and stoutly palisaded. The bank of the Danube arm that swings past the city was also trenched and fitted with palisades. To avoid the ricochet of shot all the paving stones were taken up and most of them used for a new loose wall inside the old from the Stuben to the Kärnthner Gate—on the east side, along the creek that is called the Wiener Bach, where the old defenses were weakest.

Graf Nicolas conducted a conscientious census, assembling as many of the useless mouths as he could, women, children, old men and ecclesiastics, for dispatch outside the city. On 21 September word came that the Turks were across the river Raab and had taken the outpost of Altenberg; two days later there arrived in the city 700 first-class Spaniards and about 1,000 German troops of the empire under the Pfalzgraf Philip, the second of the two good leaders in the defense. He said that the deputation from the Diet of Speyer had reported that the Turkish danger was indeed serious, and Duke Friedrich had come as far forward as Linz with the imperial contingent but, hearing that Suleiman was in great force, declined to risk ruin by advancing any farther.

That same day there was a skirmish outside the walls between a body of Turks and 500 cuirassiers under Graf Hardegg; the cuirassiers were driven in with the loss of seven prisoners, four of whom were presently sent to Vienna by the sultan, richly dressed, to bear his terms. He expected to breakfast in the city

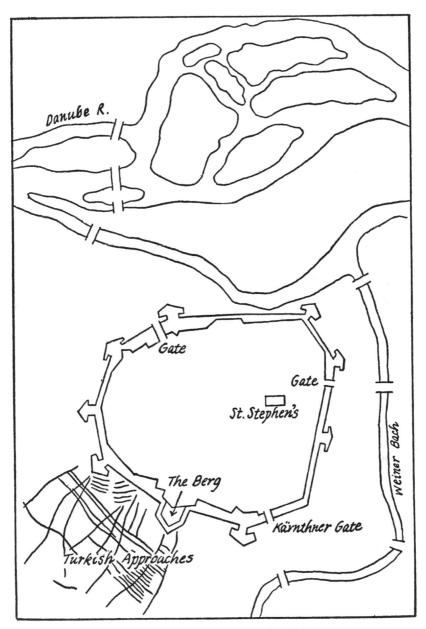

Vienna at the Time of the Siege

on the twenty-ninth; if it would surrender at discretion, none of his people but functionaries should enter and all would be secure; if it held out the place would be so utterly destroyed that no one would know where it had stood, and every living thing in it would be put to the sword. In view of the general proceedings of the Turks one could believe that; the word was that the light troops of their vanguard had come up with a convoy of 5,000 of the useless mouths at Traismauer and massacred every one of them.

Graf Nicolas had four Turkish prisoners dressed as richly as the cuirassier messengers and sent them to Suleiman. They bore no word in return. The garrison numbered 22,000 foot, 2,000 horse, and seventy-two guns of as nearly as many calibers and makes. The cavalry were stationed in the four main squares to rush wherever they were needed; a master gunner was assigned to each of the pieces. Pfalzgraf Philip outranked Salm, but cheerfully waived the fact and only countersigned his orders. There were nearly 350,000 of the attackers.

V

That summer it had rained. It rained with an intensity such as few people in that part of Europe had seen, day after day, one of the most remarkable meteorological events of the century. Suleiman would have thought it beneath him to be impeded by the weather, and in fact he did not allow himself to be. The horsemen who formed the largest numerical proportion of his army were not, and ahead of the main body there moved a corps of 20,000 of them, called by the Turks *akinji*, or "sackmen," whose specific task was to devastate the country and destroy the inhabitants in preparation for Turkish occupation. They were the people who cut off the 5,000 noncombatants at Traismauer, and it is estimated that they got rid of two thirds of the population of the districts through which they moved, which cannot be much of an exaggeration.

The horsemen could thus move, no matter how wet it was.

The camp followers, baggage, and women could move after a fashion in wagons, and it did not matter if they fell behind, because everything they supplied could be had by ravaging the countryside. The Janissary infantry and the light guns moved up the Danube in boats. But there was one force that could not move at all through those perpetual rains in a country largely wooded and with no metalled roads. That was the heavy artillery, the siege guns, which weighed all the way up to twelve tons apiece. Even the Danube flotilla could not carry such monsters, and they were left behind, to the number of 200.

In view of the number of his troops, the fact that he was joined at Mohács by Zápolya, who commanded certain Hungarian loyalties, and the skill of his engineers, this did not seem particularly important to Suleiman. He planned on mining operations if Vienna did not surrender easily, and some thousands of his host were experienced miners from Wallachia and Moldavia. When he arrived opposite the city on September 26 and set up seven great camps around it—tents visible as far as the eye could reach from the tower of St. Stephen, where Salm established his observation post—the first thing he did was to command regular parallels at the southwest side of the city and mining operations against the Kärnthner Gate area on the south side, accompanied by artillery bombardment and a ceaseless storm of arrows.

It was characteristic of Suleiman the Magnificent that while these arrows were so numerous that they made the streets near the walls unsafe, many of them were finished with costly fabrics and even inlaid with pearls. The Janissaries fired most of them from the ruins of the suburban houses. The results from the guns available were notably poor against Salm's emergency earthworks; after the first day target was shifted to the taller buildings, notably St. Stephen's tower, and it says something about the quality of Turkish gunnery practice that they could not even drive Graf Nicolas from his post. The artillery of the defense does not seem to have been much better in the beginning. Many of the embrasures in the old

walls were so narrow that the guns would not traverse properly and there was no fund of experience in mounting pieces
behind earthwork bastions. But Salm, or someone under him,
had a highly judgmatical eye; some of the guns were removed
to the tops of buildings, and for others platforms were built,
after which they really began to hurt, especially in the areas
along the river.

This was to have a highly important result, but in the
meanwhile the main event was a cavalry sally from the
Kärnthner Gate, led by the Austrian Eck von Reischach on
the twenty-ninth, the day Suleiman proposed to breakfast in
Vienna. Von Reischach had spotted numbers of the Turks
spread out among the vineyards on that side, and killed a lot
of them before they could assemble. Through the next day it
was all shooting, and at noon on October 1 the result of the
good artillery practice along the river appeared in the form
of a Turk who came out of the no man's land created by the
guns and said he was of Christian parents, bearing information.

He was turned over to the cavalry commander, Wilhelm
von Roggendorf, who had him tortured a little to make sure
he was telling the truth, and thus learned that the Turks were
driving mines in an utterly unexpected spot—not where their
parallels were, opposite the Berg, but right under the Wiener
Bach, on both sides the Kärnthner Gate. Countermining was
ordered at once; next morning a big mine under the gate tower
was broken into and destroyed in a strange underground battle
by torchlight. General Roggendorf gave the deserter substance
for life; guards were placed in all the cellars, with drums scattered over with dried peas, where activity was suspected.

Suleiman's technique of mining had failed to work by surprise; but there was no other means of getting into the city, so
he turned to making it work by main force and superior
numbers. More mines were dug in the Kärnthner Gate area
and all along under the Wiener Bach. Twice countermines
reached the Turkish powder chambers and as much as eight
tons of explosive was carried off from one of them; three times
in the stormy week between October 4 and October 12 mines

did go off and made breaches in the walls, one of them wide enough for twenty-four men abreast. The always victorious Janissaries assaulted these breaches; but behind them were palisades, and behind the palisades Spanish arquebusiers and German *Landsknechts* with their long swords and huge halberds, quite as rough citizens as the Janissaries, and better armed for the conditions. There were 1,200 bodies in the breach on the afternoon of the twelfth.

Late that night there was a council of war in the Turkish camp. It was still raining, the food situation in the huge army had become distinctly serious, since provision convoys could not move. The losses had not been intolerable in numerical terms —the figures ran between 14,000 and 20,000—but their incidence was alarming, most of them falling on the aristocratic horsemen and the Janissaries. The latter proud troops were depressed and doing something they had never done before, complaining that their lives were being sacrificed uselessly. The vizier, Ibrahim, remarked that the law of the Koran had been satisfied by three main assaults, each three times renewed. But Suleiman the Magnificent was not satisfied. Three more great mines, one on each side of the Kärnthner Gate, one directly under the Berg, were just ready, and he wanted a really grand attack, the whole force of the army, supported by all its guns. He promised the Janissaries a donative of 1,000 aspers per man for this attack, with 30,000 aspers and promotion to the highest military rank for the first man inside the city.

On the morning of the fourteenth everything was ready. At nine the order to explode the mines was given and the sacred horsetails borne forward. The thing miscarried from the start. The mine at the Berg never went off at all (the Austrians had countermined it and robbed it of its powder) and though the Kärnthner Gate mines made a breach 130 feet across, the rubble fell outward, and the defense had a trench inside with new palisades, behind which waited the same nasty Spaniards and Germans with their long spits. From the walls the Turkish officers, including the vizier himself, could be seen trying to drive the men forward with whips and sabers. It was no use; for the first time in Turkish history an army refused to advance any farther, almost en masse.

Graf Salm was hit in the hip by the splinters of a stone ball during the attack, a wound from which he never recovered, but that night Vienna was kept awake by the light of fires, as the Janissaries burned everything not portable, and the screams as they threw their prisoners into the fire. Next morning they were gone. It snowed.

In the deserted camps the Austrians found some curious-looking brown beans. They boiled them; the beans themselves were not very good, but the soup that came from them proved quite potable. It was the first coffee in Europe.

VI

Various causes add up to the Turkish defeat at Vienna, one of the main ones undoubtedly Suleiman's lack of those heavy guns that had battered holes in besieged places from Constantinople to Rhodes to Belgrade. The rains deprived him of the guns and also of the time to take the city without them, and the miners were not a particularly efficient substitute. They produced gaps in the walls, but their very operations allowed new defenses to be set up behind the gaps, and mass attacks were powerless against these defenses. Yet the breaking of the siege had a positive technical side as well as a negative; those resolute Spanish arquebusiers and German *Landsknechts* were something the Janissaries had not encountered before; and the West had at last developed a tactical force that could meet the standing army of the Turkish Empire on equal terms.

Yet it was the effects rather than the causes that made Vienna decisive. The unbeatable Janissaries had been beaten, and not only beaten, but broken in morale. They were only human after all, and now they knew it. Not only that; a main line of the story lies in that donative of 1,000 aspers per man to make them undertake an attack they would normally have urged upon their sultan. Vienna, in fact, marked the end of the Janissaries as the tribute-children fanatics founded by Ala ed-Din. They began by taking in their own children and making it a privilege to be a Janissary with the disabilities that accompany any hereditary caste, and there was eventually nothing left of them but the savagery that made them throw prisoners into the fire.

This development did not reach its peak at once, to be sure. The Janissaries were to turn into unruly Praetorian guards, who made and unmade sultans, and this was perhaps inevitable. But even determinism must admit that Vienna started them down the long slide. After they had been defeated there and were paid extra for being defeated, their basic morale broke and they were never the same. The marvelous Turkish military instrument had a crack in it.

So did the marvelous Turkish family of the Othmanli sultans. Suleiman had a son, Mustapha, universally and probably correctly reported as not inferior in ability to any in the line. He was reasonably friendly with the vizier, Ibrahim, but after his birth there had been brought to Suleiman the Russian girl known historically as Roxelana. After the defeat at Vienna she became for Suleiman something rare in Oriental history, a devouring passion which nothing could slake. She bore him two sons and a daughter, and it was elementary that she should want one of her sons to be the heir of empire. There were two barriers; and in spite of the fact that Turkish sultans usually kept their private and public lives separate, the defeat at Vienna made it quite easy for Roxelana to destroy the major hindrance, Suleiman's friend, the almost genius, Ibrahim. He was executed for inefficiency, Roxelana married her daughter to a man whom she had no difficulty in getting promoted to the viziership, and started a deliberate campaign against Mustapha. One afternoon when he called on his father he was met by the seven mutes with their bowstrings, whom Suleiman watched at their work, urging them to hurry.

That was the end of the great line. Roxelana's son Selim became sultan, but he was correctly known as Selim the Sot, and down to the time Kemal Ataturk overthrew the remains of the dynasty, the Othmanli never produced another able man. For some years the Turks made faces and horrible noises in Eastern Europe, but always on a declining scale, always steps going down. They even worked up to another siege of Vienna in 1683, but it was a matter of local politics and brought on them the combined forces of Venice, Poland, Austria, and Russia, and the end of it was that they lost most of Hungary and all of the Crimea. The real Turkish danger to Europe was ended for good on the morning of October 14, 1529.

And this was not all that was ended. When Martin Luther heard of the advance of Suleiman against the Hungarians, he declared it was a visitation from God in punishment for the sins of the Pope and his bishops; but after Suleiman started for the Rhine by way of Vienna, he rapidly changed stance and declared it the duty of every Christian to oppose the Turk. This had a double effect; for Charles the Emperor, already involved in a two-front war against France in Italy and the Netherlands, could not neglect the help of the north German Protestants. He therefore tolerated internal religious disorder for the sake of keeping out the external, and not a few of the stern halberdiers of Vienna were Lutherans. By the time Charles was ready to turn against the Protestants, they were too solidly established for even an emperor to cut them down.

8. Leyden and the Foundation of Sea Power

"We may regard the Prince as a dead man; he has neither influence nor credit." Thus wrote Fernando Álvarez de Toledo, Duke of Alva, to his master, King Philip II of Spain and the Netherlands, Emperor of America and the Indies. The date was 1568 and the prince referred to was William of Orange, called "the Silent" because, although he talked a great deal, he so seldom said the wrong thing.

There was some justification for Alva's statement; he had been captain-general in the Netherlands for barely a year, but already those turbulent estates were well in hand, their revolt was over. Of the great Catholic nobles who led it, Hoogstraeten had died of a wound, Egmont and Hoorn had lost their heads on the scaffold. Only Orange was left, and he was wandering from place to place, pursued by creditors, while his wife lived as she pleased in Cologne and pleased to live in a fashion referred to as "irregular." "We may regard the Prince as a dead man"; the army he had gathered by selling everything he owned had dissolved at a touch from Alva and in a manner that brought an imputation of personal cowardice on Orange himself.

Nor was it likely that any other army Orange could raise would have better luck. The best he could get were mercenaries, Walloon and German *Landsknechts*, farily good men, but lacking in cohesion, while Alva led the "invincible terciaries" of Spain, infantry such as the world had hardly seen since Roman days. They had training and morale, a consciousness that nothing could break or shake them; they had proved it a hundred times under every conceivable battle condition. Alva gave them iron discipline; saving always the right of sack when a town was taken, they behaved. When his army marched from Italy to the uneasy Netherlands, even the 2,000 prostitutes who came with it were organized in battalions and companies and under military command.

There was something of the iron, of the perpetual struggle against adversaries who could only be overcome by crusade in everything Alva said or did. "I have tamed men of iron in my day," he remarked on taking up the mission to Brussels. "I shall know how to deal with these men of butter." He began that dealing by placing a garrison of the metallic terciaries in every town that had any importance; he prosecuted it by setting up a trial court, or "Council of Troubles," which soon and more accurately became known as the "Council of Blood," for its verdict was always guilty and the sentence always death. Nobody knows how many thousands besides Egmont and Hoorn passed through its hands to stake, sword, or gibbet during the year before Alva decided to regard the prince as a dead man. On Ash Wednesday morning alone, when people would be found in their beds after the carnival, 1,500 were taken. "I have ordered them all to be executed," wrote Alva.

Basically he was acting as agent of the perpetual crusade, as the right arm of Philip of Spain, who had publicly prayed never to be allowed to be called king over those who rejected God (as recognized by the Catholic confession) as their Lord, and who had said he would sacrifice 100,000 lives rather. But there was also a constitutional question involved, and Alva was acute enough to perceive that he could never extirpate the Protestant heresy without first getting rid of those councils which, all through the Netherlands, had cognizance of juridical and financial matters under a complex system of charters, grants, and privileges, one for each town or province. In the eyes of the perpetual crusaders these councils had failed to do their plain duty. They had not put down heresy; they had winked at Calvinist conventicles openly held; they had visited no punishment on the vandals who sacked and plundered churches during the great wave of iconoclasm in 1566.

It was therefore upon the great Catholic nobles who maintained the integrity of the charters that Alva first bore down, then on the minor clergy, who resented their revenues being taken away for new bishops from Spain, and finally upon the magistrates of the big cities, Catholic every man. Of course, Protestants stood automatically condemned; but the main first movement, the necessary step, was to get rid of local authority, or rather to place above it an authority that would enforce obedience to orders from Spain.

This Alva had achieved. Egmont, Hoorn, Hoogstraeten were dead and their estates forfeit; Orange could be regarded as dead and his estates were also forfeit so far as they lay within Philip's dominion. To a disposition to resistance there had succeeded such utter apathy that hardly a man joined Prince William when he brought his mercenaries over the French border. The Inquisition was proceeding famously with its job of eliminating heretics when there occurred a key event. The pay chest for Alva's terciaries, 450,000 ducats, was aboard five ships forced by a gale to put into Plymouth, and Elizabeth of England, that untrustworthy woman who so seldom neglected any opportunity to lay her hands on money, seized both vessels and cash.

Trying to get the money back was a matter for diplomacy, but even if diplomacy succeeded far better than it usually did in extracting ducats from Elizabeth, the process would take time and the emergency was immediate. The invincible terciaries were deeply in arrears for their pay, they were grumbling about it, and they possessed a monopoly of military force within the Netherlands. If they chose to take what they wanted, there was no power that could stop them, and it would not be the first time that unpaid Spanish soldiers had done their own collecting. In thoroughly well-founded apprehension, Alva summoned the States-General of the realm to Brussels in March 1569 and told them they would have to pay taxes to support the soldiers who were protecting them. He proposed a special 1 per cent tax on all real property, once only; a 5 per cent tax on real estate transfers, and a 10 per cent sales tax. He explained to the estates that this was the system of the *alcabala*, which worked very well in Spain.

Perhaps, but the Netherlands was a closely populated commercial area, and the real estate and sales taxes simply meant ruin. The States-General refused them; Alva got part of his 1 per cent tax and that was all. Utrecht refused to pay even this; Alva quartered a regiment there, then declared the city and province guilty of high treason, its charters, privileges, and property confiscated to the crown. Even the Catholic bishops and two members of Alva's Council of Blood joined the protest, and a seep of discontent went through the country like underground water, only waiting for a puncture to bring it to the surface.

II

At this point Alva discovered that William of Orange was not quite as dead as he thought. Back in '66, before the outbreak of the iconoclasts, a not inconsiderable number of the lesser nobility held a meeting in Brussels to protest against the vigor with which the Inquisition was putting down heresy, and submitted a "Request" to the then regent for mitigation. They heard themselves described as "beggars," and adjourned to a hotel, where, with the accompaniment of a good deal of drinking, they enthusiastically accepted the name, adopted the beggar's staff, wallet, and bowl as their emblem, and formed an association in support of the privileges of the Netherlands. One of the charges that sent Egmont and Hoorn to the block was that they had looked in while this festive scene was taking place, though they had retired with cluckings of disapproval.

Alva's repressive measures made it dangerous to wear the

beggar badge, and the movement seemed reasonably well beaten down when the tax dispute arose. William the Silent was perfectly well aware of the state of feeling engendered by that row. One of the things that helped him stay alive was that he ran an extremely good intelligence service, with spies even in the cabinet of Madrid, who tipped him off every time a new assassin was dispatched. Now, in his capacity as a sovereign prince, he issued letters of marque to eighteen ships. His brother, Louis of Nassau, saw to it that the ships were actually equipped at the Huguenot port of La Rochelle in France, and that they put to sea. They became the "Sea Beggars," and their business was plundering and killing Catholics.

By the end of 1569 eighty-four ships were in commission, and they had taken 300; no church or convent along the shore was safe from them. William of Orange tried to keep them in bounds by drawing regulations and appointing an admiral, but he might as well have tried to restrain a rhinoceros. The main leaders of the Sea Beggars were William of Blois, Lord of Treslong, and William de la Marck, a descendant of the famous "Wild Boar of the Ardennes," who was very like his ancestor. Nothing that happened on the Spanish Main went beyond the doings of the Sea Beggars. They were under no civil control and animated by fierce hatreds. Many of them had lost ears or a nose to the executioners of the Inquisition or had been otherwise mutilated, and now was the chance to pay it all out. Priests, nuns, and Catholic magistrates they usually tortured to death, letting everyone know that it stood to the account of Alva.

What the Duke of Alva thought of this is not a matter of record. He had no experience or knowledge of sea power—nobody did at that date—and no naval service. He probably regarded the Sea Beggars as banditti, who could in time be exorcised by the method normal for dealing with such gentry on land: that is, cutting their bases of operation from under them. In this case it took diplomatic action. Queen Elizabeth of England, as might be expected, was allowing the Beggars to use her harbors for victualing and the disposal of plunder, but she was unwilling to push Philip of Spain too far at this particular time, and when protests from Madrid became really stiff, she stopped procrastinating and issued a proclamation closing her harbors to the sea robbers.

This was early in 1572. The German ports were at some distance and not very good markets, and it is likely that discussions in the Beggar fleet about what to do were still going on when an unseasonable westerly gale blew up on April 1 and drove twenty-eight Beggar ships under Treslong into the estuary of the Scheldt. They anchored off Brill on the island of Walcheren, and the word from the town was that its Spanish garrison had gone to Utrecht to help enforce the edict of high treason.

Treslong instantly conceived the idea of taking the town; the Beggars set fire to the north gate and beat it in with the stump of a mast. They treated the Catholic churches and religious houses as usual, but the people well, and were about to leave when it occurred to Treslong that here was the answer to the base problem. Instead of pulling out he landed some guns and raised the flag of the Prince of Orange.

The news of this mad exploit produced a chain reaction. Jean de Henin-Liétard, Comte Bossu, the governor of Holland province, came down with a strong force to repossess the place. There were not over 300 of the Beggars in Brill, but the townspeople helped in the defense, someone cut a sluice gate and flooded the Spaniards onto a dike, where the ships cannonaded them. Most of the boats in which they came were taken. Bossu just barely got away; his force was practically wiped out.

When Orange heard of it, he was inclined to treat the whole episode as just one more caprice of the ungovernable Sea Beggars. But the water table had been breached; it stood demonstrated that there was one thing against which the terciaries were not invincible—water. Flushing rose against its garrison, the Sea Beggars sent help, and Alva's chief engineer, hastily rushed in to strengthen the citadel, was hanged from its gate. All Walcheren island except Middelburg fell into the hands of the revolters, and from Walcheren the movement spread to the mainland. Everywhere in Zeeland, Holland, Gelderland, Overyssel, Utrecht, and Friesland the Orange flag was hoisted; in these provinces only Amsterdam and a few minor places failed to kill their garrisons and were held for the king. At this precise moment Louis of Nassau succeeded in raising an army in France, which pushed in to take Mons, and the revolters received the spiritual lift of one of the great war songs of history, "Wilhelmus van Nassouwen," still the Dutch national anthem. On the wave of excitement money contributions flowed in that enabled Prince William to raise an army of mercenaries and march over the German border.

Any popular revolt carries things with a dash in the beginning, but unless the upper authority is quite swept away, as in the French Revolution, this period is succeeded by one in which the contending parties shake down to the forces that will actually be employed during the struggle. In the Netherlands revolt Alva lost only a comparatively small number of men from his garrisons, and was by no means swept away. After the first rush the counterrevolutionary elements in the situation began to become manifest. One of them remained in the background, but helped to determine the character of the struggle from that point; the rising was economic as well as religious, and what the burghers wanted was to be let alone in the conduct of their commercial affairs. They did not rush to join the standard and were not very anxious to contribute money; they simply wanted to get rid of the Spanish system of taxation.

Another of the pro-Spanish factors was fortuitous; the Massacre of St. Bartholemew in France took place soon after Louis of Nassau threw himself into Mons, and it cut from under him the support of the French Huguenots, who had planned to join him with 12,000 men. Alva instantly saw and scized the strategic occasion by drawing troops from everywhere to besiege the place.

A third influence was supplied by William of Orange's men. He began a war of sieges and actually took several towns—

Roermond, Tirlemont, Malines, Oudenarde—but in every one his German Protestant mercenaries sacked churches and maltreated churchmen, in spite of the prince's efforts to enforce religious toleration. The southern Netherlands, where he was operating, had grave economic and political complaints against Spanish rule, but they remained predominantly Catholic, and forced converson was no more acceptable to one side than to the other. William found himself treated as an enemy; Louvain closed its gates, and he could make no impression on Brussels, where the citizens joined the small garrison in defense against him. That is, the Low Countries were beginning their ultimate fission along the line of language and religion.

Nevertheless, William pressed on toward the relief of Mons. Alva, with an army that could have destroyed him in battle, made no attempt to fight. He had a lively appreciation of the structural weakness of a mercenary force, which lay in the financial department, and no intention of wasting his manpower resources to achieve a breakup that should come about through natural causes. However, he did help the natural causes along. On the night of September 11, 1572, Orange encamped at the village of Harmignies, a league from Mons. During the dark hours 600 Spanish soldiers under Julian Romero slipped into his camp with white shirts over their armor for identification, and just barely missed taking the prince himself while killing 800 of his men.

The natural causes took effect at once. The army went to pieces, Orange was tagged as a timid and incompetent general, who had not even set guards to provide for his own safety. Louis in Mons surrendered six days later and the war entered a new phase.

III

Instead of sieges by the Orange party it became an affair of Spanish sieges of towns held for Orange. Alva organized two columns, one under his natural son, Don Frederic of Toledo,

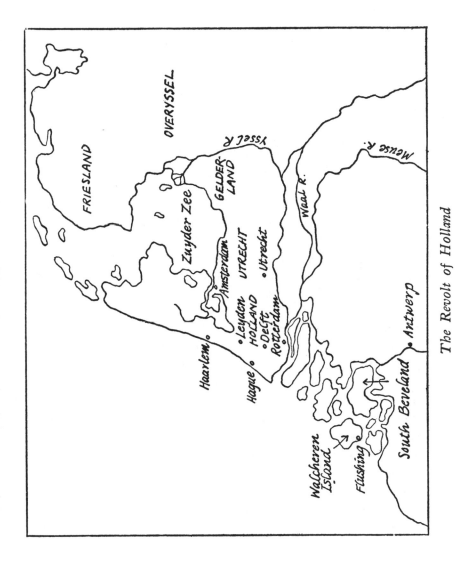

The Revolt of Holland

159

for the province of Holland, the other under General Mondragon for Zeeland. The Mondragon command performed some extraordinary feats, such as assaulting the island of South Beveland by crossing a channel at ebb tide, with water up to the soldiers' breasts, but its operations were off the main line. The decisive command was that of Frederic of Toledo. He took Malines first and, as it was the most important town that had surrendered to Orange, made an example by giving it up to his soldiers for a three-day sack, in which no distinction was made between Catholic and Protestant; all equally raped, robbed, or slaughtered. Zutphen came next; as it was largely Protestant, there was more killing than at Malines. At Naarden the destruction was systematic; the women were publicly raped, then every living thing was put to the sword, just as Suleiman had promised at Vienna.

Don Frederic now pushed through to Amsterdam and, basing there, advanced against Haarlem at the beginning of December 1572. The place was of both symbolic and intrinsic importance, a hotbed of Calvinism and one of the largest cities in the Netherlands. It was also one of the weakest; the garrison of 4,000 was nowhere near enough for the wide circuit of its half-ruinous walls, and Toledo had 30,000 men, Spaniards, Walloons, and Germans. He expected to take the place by assault, and after a bombardment tried it; but Haarlem had heard of Zutphen and Naarden, the burghers joined in the defense, and in fierce fighting the assault was beaten off with heavy loss.

This caused Don Frederic to take stock. On the east the town was protected by a sheet of shallow water, and not approachable; on the north by the estuary of the Y, an arm of the Zuyder Zee, with outlying forts on the estuary; only on the west and south was solid ground. Across this ground Don Frederic began a formal siege approach, and all winter long there were mining and countermining, cannon battering the walls and citizens repairing them by night. The burghers made frequent and violent sallies, cut off the heads of the men they captured and rolled them into the Spanish lines in barrels; the Spaniards hanged their prisoners on gibbets; and the townspeople parodied Catholic religious services in indecent processions along the walls. Toledo tried another assault on January 31; this also was beaten, and he wanted to give up, but Alva threatened to disown him if he did. The siege ran down to a blockade.

The Spanish difficulty was that the blockade could not be made complete. All winter long skaters carried provisions across the frozen lake, and with the coming of spring their place was taken by shallow-draft boats. Don Frederic solved this by setting up a fleet of curiously made ships on the Y under Count Bossu, and on May 28, Bossu engaged and utterly defeated the Dutch inland ships. After this it became merely a question of time. When shoe leather, rats, and weeds had been eaten, Haarlem surrendered on July 11. Don Frederic executed every man of the garrison and the 400 most prominent citizens, but was gracious enough to spare the rest of the town in return for all the money in it.

The cause of the revolt was now in reasonably bad shape. During the siege William of Orange made frantic efforts to get together and three times managed to send forces of three or four thousand men under various commanders for a relief. They were always cut to pieces; the terciaries were still invincible in the field, and free to go on besieging until the Netherlanders ran out of towns. William's efforts to persuade Elizabeth of England to assume a protectorate over the provinces came to nothing, and he was always faced by a grinding shortage of money.

As in any contest, the difficulties were not all on one side. Alva had spent 25 million florins sent from Spain, besides the 5 million he got out of the 1 per cent tax, and his treasury was empty. Don Frederic had lost 12,000 men at Haarlem, whom it would be onerous and expensive to replace. The duke wrote to the king that the only way to suppress this heresy was to burn every Protestant town to the ground and kill everyone in it, and in August he sent Don Frederic to Alkmaar with 16,000 men to make a beginning on this new policy.

Toledo failed. Alkmaar had only 2,000 burghers, but they beat off an assault and, after a seven-week siege, opened the dikes, with a slogan from Prince William: "Better to ruin the land than to lose the land." The water rose around the Spanish camp, an event not necessarily fatal in itself, but which turned into defeat when Count Bossu attempted to bring the Spanish inland fleet up from the Y. It was met in the Zuyder Zee by the Beggars under Admiral Dirkzoon and utterly destroyed, Bossu himself being taken prisoner, and the investment could not be maintained through the waters.

That finished Alva. He asked to be relieved, and at the end of 1573 there arrived to replace him the Grand Commander, Don Luis Requesens. He brought a less savage policy, with some effort at conciliation, but the utmost Philip of Spain would concede was that heretics should have time to sell their property before leaving the country, and the least William of Orange would accept was full freedom of worship; the war went on. Strategically there was no change. Requesens continued Alva's policy of working south through the Holland towns to crack the coastal provinces against the anvil of Flanders. He built a fleet at Antwerp and Bergen op Zoom to clear the Sea Beggars from the Scheldt, and sent an army of 8,000 under General Valdez to besiege Leyden. The Hague was already Spanish, and the coast down to the mouth of the New Meuse; possession of Leyden would cut the whole of Holland province from the sea.

The Spanish fleet, commanded by the same Julian Romero who almost caught William at Harmignies, found the Beggars off Walcheren, now led by Louis de Boisot, Sieur de Ruart. (William de la Marck had been dismissed for torturing a seventy-two-year-old priest who was a friend of Orange, and a couple of years later met a singuarly appropriate death as the result of being bitten by a mad dog.) The battle ended as Spanish attempts to deal with the Sea Beggars usually did, in total defeat. Romero got out of a porthole of his burning flagship and, swimming to the bank where Requesens was watching, climbed out of the water and said, "I told Your Excellency that I was a land fighter, not a sailor." In exchange the Spaniards fell on Louis of Nassau, who had crossed the

Rhine with one of the usual ragtag armies of mercenaries and volunteers, and wiped it out with hardly any loss to themselves, Louis being killed in the process.

The minor pieces had now been swept from the board. William was between Delft and Rotterdam with some 6,000 men, certainly not enough to meet the Spaniards in the field or to raise a siege of Leyden, and if the Spaniards took Leyden, they could take anything.

IV

Valdez originally approached the place in October 1573, but after some rather desultory operations, in which he does not seem even to have established a complete blockade, he had to be recalled because of a mutiny in Antwerp. His second approach was on May 26, 1574, and this time he was thoroughly clear on plan and technique. Leyden lay at the heart of a concentric ring of dikes, with occasional villages along them. These villages Valdez fortified, and where there was no town at the right strategic point, a redoubt was built, making a total of sixty-two strong points in all, mutually supporting. The Spaniard intended to avoid the expensive assaults, battering and mining operations Don Frederic had used at Haarlem and Alkmaar, and let hunger work for him through a pure but very tight blockade. He seems to have been aware that the lazy Netherlanders, deep in their own affairs, had failed to reprovision the place after his first approach, or to strengthen its garrison.

Just before the ring closed, Orange got through a letter telling the townspeople that if they could hold out for three months it would be enough, they would be relieved. But the days passed and the weeks passed; Orange fell ill of a tertian fever, he had no money, and there was no hope of raising an army to break the Valdez ring. The estates of the realm were summoned, and authorized the prince to take the desperate measure of cutting the great dikes along the Meuse and Yssel at Rotterdam, Schiedam, Delfshaven, submerging half of Holland. On August 21 the townspeople got out a message saying they had made good the three months asked; bread was now all gone and malt cake would last only four days more.

Be of good cheer, said the reply from Orange, flown in by carrier pigeon, the water is coming. Burgomaster Van der Werff read the missive from the steps of the town hall and sent musicians through the streets playing "Wilhelmus van Nassouwen." In the Spanish camp there was anxiety, but the "Glippers," as the Medizing Netherlanders were called, told Valdez not to worry, this was not Alkmaar, protected by a single dike system; here the tiers of dikes were so extensive, one behind another, that there was no chance the besiegers would be drowned out. So it proved; the waters spread indeed, but the ruined land was a useless sacrifice, there were only ten inches of sea, the redoubts and fortified villages were still dry. On August 27, Leyden got through another desperate appeal to the estates; the town was eating horses and dogs, all cereal had vanished.

Orange's body was so ill that his life was despaired of, but the affliction had not attacked his brain, and as soon as he got the authorization to cut the dikes, he had determined to make use of the one force in which the Netherlanders had a clear superiority—the sea arm. On September 1, Admiral Boisot and the Sea Beggars arrived at Rotterdam with 200 shallow-draft ships, most of them specially built, carrying about ten light guns apiece and ten to eighteen oars. They included experimental craft like the huge *Ark of Delft*, with shotproof bulwarks and paddle wheels on hand-operated cranks.

With this fleet the Beggars floated through to a huge dike called the *Land Schieding*, Shield of the Land, five miles from Leyden. On Orange's orders Boisot waited till it fell dark on the night of September 10, then warped in and seized a section of the dike. The Spaniards attempted a counterattack from the villages flanking the seized section, but the guns of the ships were too much for them; the dike was cut and Boisot's squadron floated through.

Three quarters of a mile farther was another dike, the Greenway, still a foot above water. Once more Boisot worked the game of a night surprise; once more the dike was cut and the ships passed. But now came a check; beyond the Greenway lay an extensive marsh, the Freshwater Lake, into which the tide spread without rising high enough to float the fleet. A canal led through this marsh, but the Spaniards had fortified both ends; the ships could approach the barrier only one at a time, end on, and so could make no use of their superior artillery. For nearly a week the fleet milled about confusedly, doubtless with tempers growing short; then on September 18 a northwest gale blew up to increase the depth of water, and simultaneously there appeared some refugees who said there was a low dike between the villlages of Zoetermeer and Benthuysen by cutting which the lake could be avoided. Boisot made for it; both villages had been fortified, but the ships carried too many guns, the Spaniards were driven out after a sharp little fight, and the fleet pushed on. Boisot had the houses fired as a signal to Leyden that help was coming.

But was it? Beyond the burning villages stood the strong point of Zoeterwoude, a mile and a quarter from Leyden, heavily fortified, well above the floods, and the wind held steadily and seasonably to light airs from the east, keeping the water level in the operating area at no more than nine inches, while Boisot's ships needed twenty. Even the presence of William of Orange, who had himself brought to the spearhead of the advance on a litter, could not help. Within the town nearly the last edible morsel was gone; people were dying of starvation, and a crowd swarmed around Burgomaster Van der Werff, begging him to surrender and take a chance on what the Spaniards would do to them. "Here is my sword," he cried. "If you will, plunge it into my heart and divide my flesh among you to appease your hunger; but expect no surrender as long as I am alive."

Orange went back to Rotterdam, and the sun rose and set; but on the morning of October 1 a gale rose from the northwest, as unreasonable as Jeanne d'Arc's wind. It switched to southwest, the whole North Sea came piling through the broken dikes, and in a matter of hours Boisot had more than two feet of water. The ships moved to the storm of Zoeterwoude, there was a singular amphibious battle against Spanish picket boats afloat in the dark among treetops and houses and Spanish terciaries on the causeways and patches of emergent ground. The Beggars were the better men at this kind of game; the Spanish ships were all sunk, their men were driven down the causeways by Zeeland fishermen, using gun, harpoon, and pike, and Boisot was through.

But not yet in Leyden. Only 300 yards from the walls were the two strongest fortifications yet, Lammen and Leyderdorp, heavily armed, one of them holding Valdez himself. Boisot moved up toward Lammen, just out of gun range, and spent a day looking it over. The appearance was very formidable indeed; he held off till dark and called a council of his captains.

It was a night full of apocalyptic events, and it is unlikely that anyone slept much. There was some firing through it, where ships approached Leyderdorp on the Dutch right. Toward midnight a terrible crash of unexplained origin came from the direction of the town; then a long series of lights visible from Lammen, the Spaniards engaged in some mysterious activity. But at daybreak a figure was seen wildly gesticulating from the top of Lammen fort; when a ship pulled in, it was a Netherlander, and the fort had been abandoned during the night. The crash had been a section of wall falling, undermined by the waters, and Valdez had left, fearing a sally combined with an attack from the outside, which he lacked the strength to sustain in this curious wet war.

Leyden was relieved. Boisot's ships pulled in and began tossing out bread on all sides to the famished inhabitants. William of Orange offered them a remission of taxes for their heroic endurance, but they said they would rather have a university, and one of the greatest institutions of learning in Europe came into being.

V

The relief was doubly, trebly, quadruply decisive. It was decisive because the jealous States-General said it was: they held a meeting and conferred on William of Orange "absolute power, authority and sovereign command in all concerns of the common land without exception." Henceforth he was no longer a free-lance, helping out as best he could, but stadtholder of the realm. It is true that he and his successors were often hampered by those same States-General; but the new nation had been given a central executive, which could coordinate its activities as never before. A united effort became possible, and united effort was made.

Secondly, while Haarlem had cost the Spaniards 12,000 nearly irreplaceable men, Leyden was nearly as expensive, and they had failed to take the town. As a result, no more great sieges were attempted; the war slid down to minor enterprises and battlings. Neither Requesens nor his successors could get enough money to pay their troops, there were mutinies and a series of confused events lasting for years, but the independence of Holland was substantially achieved when Boisot sailed past Fort Lammen.

It was also decisive for its effect on the Spanish command; for there had been brought into the combination something new in the world's history, something realized at the time rather than comprehended, but acted upon in realization—the influence of sea power. There was nothing in the Spanish system fitted to deal with the Sea Beggars. "I am a land fighter, not a sailor"; the Spaniards never did succeed in finding the latter, and it was to be the ruin of that vast empire whose roots went down to Las Navas de Tolosa. The invocation of sea power at Leyden was more or less accidental on the part of William of Orange; it was the only weapon he had left on the wall. But it was effective and it demonstrated that a city on the water could always be supported from the water. This was one of the reasons why there were no more great sieges.

And much more. The relief of Leyden made it certain that the Catholic reaction would not submerge northwest Europe as it had Bohemia and Poland; that the liberty of conscience, for which William of Orange so earnestly strove, would not be wiped out, at least from this one little corner. That certitude is usually referred to the English defeat of the Spanish Armada, and the English-speaking peoples have taken a justifiable pride in the events of the summer of 1588. But the fighting against the Armada was not only the crowning event in a series; it also contained an element too easily and too often overlooked. When the Duke of Medina Sidonia sailed for the English Channel, his mission was not direct attack on England; it was to clear the way for that most astute of the governors of the Spanish Netherlands, Alexander Farnese, Prince of Parma, who was to cross the Channel at the head of 25,000 men. They were Spanish veterans, and it is not likely that the English levies could have made out any better against them in the field than the successive mercenary armies of Orange and his brothers did.

But Parma never made it, and his failure was not entirely due to the defeat of the Armada. Even in defeat, even before he was defeated, Medina Sidonia had done his part in the combined operation. Every English ship that would bear guns was concentrated in the western mouth of the Channel when the Armada put into Calais, and the duke wrote from there to Parma, urging him to hurry, to cross while there was nothing to oppose his crossing. Parma had his transports ready and his troops; he even had an elaborate equipment of flat-bottomed landing craft.

But he did not move; and the reason he did not move was that there lay in the mouth of the Scheldt the Dutch squadron of Justinian of Nassau, William's natural son. He sat there; and the Spaniards reflected that they were land fighters, not sailors. "The shippes of Holland and Zeeland stood continually in their sight, threatening shot and powder and many inconveniences; for fear of which shippes the Mariners and sea-men secretly withdrew themselves both day and night, lest the Duke of Parma his soldiers should compell them by maine force to goe on board."

So in the chain of causation Queen Elizabeth builded better than she knew when she seized Alva's pay chest and forced him to lay the taxes that provoked the rise of the Dutch republic. For it was those high-pooped, ungainly little ships, rocking gently on the sluggish waves of the Scheldt, the ships that had become a national navy when Leyden was relieved, that kept Parma where he was and rendered the operation against England futile. It was a singularly rich reward for stealing someone's money.

9. Gustavus Adolphus and the
End of the Middle Ages

I

Ten years after the siege of Vienna, in 1539, one Ignatius Loyola founded the Society of Jesus, or Jesuit Order. From the beginning it was conceived of as an army; its head was a general, its training course long, rigorous, and carried out with military precision. Discipline was strict and absolute obedience was demanded. "Let us all think alike and talk in the same manner if possible," the founder once said. The order was as much of a celibate military community within the body politic as the Janissaries, and like them, its purpose was militant, for Loyola conceived that the Church was at war—against those enemies of true religion, the Protestants of the North. The Jesuits produced no great men to speak of, but they did produce the devoted formations which conducted the Catholic Counter Reformation.

Unity of doctrine, action, and purpose made them a most conspicuous success, especially in view of the fact that the Protestants were splintering into all sorts of sects—Lutherans, Calvinists, Bohemian Brothers, Church of England, Anabaptists—some of which went off into pedantry and some into witch burning. Sometime early in the 1580s, while William the Silent was being assassinated and Philip II was building up to that quarrel with Elizabeth of England that issued in the Armada fighting, a group of these Jesuits got hold of a young son of a cadet branch of the house of Hapsburg, a boy named Ferdinand. They brought him up in the right way. There is no sign that they tried to make a Jesuit of him—after all, his destiny was royal and not ecclesiastical—but they trained him so thoroughly that all the rest of his life he behaved as though he were in fact a Jesuit, as though his first and almost his only duty was the service of the Church. In 1590, when he was twelve, his father died, and he became Duke of Styria, which is the southern part of Austria. Six years later he finished his education, made a trip to Rome, and on his return assumed personal control of the province.

The Steiermark was a border country, subject to incursions of Turks; Duke Ferdinand considered keeping them out nowhere near as important as getting rid of the Protestants, who had made considerable headway in the area. One decree prohibited any form of Protestant worship, another offered everyone in Styria a reasonable choice—recant and conform or leave the country. There had been similar instruments of government in various jurisdictions before; the difference this time was that it was enforced with the utmost Jesuit rigor. Nearly one third of the population was driven over the frontiers, and by the twentieth century Styria was still over 98 per cent Catholic. Ferdinand's local Counter Reformation was a success.

At this point something unusual occurred in the dynastic history of the Hapsburgs. None of the sons of the Emperor Maximilian II had any children, and Ferdinand of Styria, the pet of the Jesuits, emerged as the heir apparent of the whole Hapsburg heritage, except for Spain and the Netherlands. This was not particularly pleasant for the Protestants, and the friction point appeared in Bohemia. Like most of the East European states, it was at least theoretically an elective monarchy; and in 1617, when Emperor Matthias, the last of Maximilian's childless sons, was obviously not going to live much longer, the Bohemian estates were persuaded to name Ferdinand of Styria as king-designate.

The Emperor Matthias was principally interested in establishing his personal power and concerned himself very little with religious matters. His predecessor, Rudolph II, had been a gloomy man, chiefly interested in art, who had issued a "Letter of Majesty," giving the Protestants full religious toleration. It stood up; in 1617, at the time of Ferdinand's election, there were more Protestants than Catholics in Bohemia. But now things changed at once; the Jesuits were in control. Peasants who refused to profess Catholicism were driven into exile; the town councils were packed with Catholics, and in at least two places Protestant churches were physically pulled down.

The opposition was at least partly political and dynastic. The whole history of the German lands from the time of Charles the Great is one of efforts on the part of various houses—Wittelsbach, Wettin, Zähringen, Hohenzollern, or toll off any number you please—to establish themselves independently, which subtended resistance to the supremacy of the house of Austria. At this date Hohenzollern was still insignificant, Wettin was in the hands of one of its weakest members and Wittelsbach in those of Maximilian II of Bavaria (not to be confounded with Maximilian II, the emperor), who, like Ferdinand, was a child of the Jesuits, and heartily willing to second his religious projects. In accordance with the thought of the period, the Bohemian Protestants needed a titular head, a royal personage, and they chose Friedrich of the Simmern line, Elector Palatine and husband of Princess Elizabeth of England, which should assure some financial help from that quarter. (It is interesting to note how deeply and over how many years Continental politics have been influenced by the hope or actuality of financial help from England.)

On May 23, 1618, the Protestant estates of Bohemia met in the Hradčany Palace at Prague; denounced the Catholic board of regents that had been running the country in Matthias' name, threw two of them out of the window, and set up a provisional government under thirty "directors." This was the "Defenestration of Prague," and it was the real beginning of the Thirty Years' War. Count Matthias Thurn, the Protestant leader, recognized that he had committed an act of rebellion and at once began to raise troops but, having few financial resources of his own and none being forthcoming from England, got very few men. Ferdinand's forces crossed the Bohemian border that fall and began burning villages, but there was no serious fighting until March 1619, when, the Emperor Matthias having decided to die in a fit, the full Estates of Bohemia met, declared Ferdinand deposed, and elected Friedrich as their king.

II

The news of this proceeding reached Frankfurt am Main just as the election was being held to determine a new emperor in succession to Matthias. In the Holy Roman Empire there were seven voters for the crown. Three of them were the bishops of Mainz, Köln, and Trèves, and these were safely Catholic; three were Protestant, the electors of Brandenburg and Saxony and the Elector Palatine, while the seventh was the Bohemian vote. Thus if Ferdinand were not King of Bohemia, he could not be emperor. It was absolutely necessary for him to conquer Bohemia, and he had little money and hardly any troops. His fellow Jesuit, Maximilian of Bavaria, offered to help him out with both for a price, the same being the transfer of the lucrative Palatine electorate to Bavaria. The ministers of Philip III of Spain, who had no brains to act for himself, sent money and a Spanish army from the Netherlands, in view of the fact that this was a matter of the faith and they had joined Ferdinand in a Catholic League.

It took time to get these forces moving and they did not cross the Bohemian border until July 1620. This march was important; it brought to the center of the stage Johann Tzerclaes Tilly, then sixty-one, a professional soldier from Brabant, who had begun as a simple pikeman and fought his way up to command against the Turks, the French, and anyone else who wanted fighting. He was a past master of the Spanish system of war; of handling those steady blocks of pikemen with musketeers in their corners, guns planted carefully across the front, and cavalry in the wings—the armies that had marched from one end of Europe to the other. In 1610 he entered the service of Maximilian of Bavaria; Maximilian made him general of the Catholic League for the invasion of Bohemia, and on November 8, 1620, he and his troops came up with the Protestants at the White Hill, near Prague.

No details need be supplied. The Protestant army, composed of post-feudal levies, could not stand for a moment against the iron *tercias* of Spain, and was utterly destroyed. At the same time Ambrose Spinola, with the troops from the Spanish Netherlands, overran most of the Palatinate, and Friedrich gained the title of "the Winter King," for the one season he had been allowed in Prague.

This double disaster broke up the Evangelical Union of Protestant Princes, which had been formed to face the Catholic League. Ferdinand proceeded to settle matters in accordance with his state principle of: "Better to rule over a desert than a country full of heretics." The Palatine electorate was transferred to Bavaria, in accordance with the deal, and in Bohemia the punishments began. Only twenty-seven people were executed, but more than 700 nobles and landowners were declared deprived of their estates and sentenced to exile unless they conformed to the Catholic confession. Protestant churches were closed or destroyed; Protestant teachers and professors were given three days to leave the country; the revenues of the University of Prague were turned over to the Jesuits, the rites of any but the Catholic Church were forbidden, and even those who wished to leave the country had to abandon everything they owned. Within less than two years nearly half the landed property in Bohemia belonged to Ferdinand, and he announced his intention of selling the whole business for cash, of which, like all dukes of Austria and Holy Roman emperors, he was forever short.

Substantially this was the economic error Alva made when trying to enforce a similar Catholicization in the Netherlands. Among the escheated noblemen the majority were certainly

Protestants, but there were also a certain number of perfectly good Catholics, who regarded the transfer of the imperial electoral dignity and the proceedings of a king whom they did not even recognize as a violation of charters and rights. So did many people inside the empire but outside Bohemia; for instance, Johann Georg, Elector of Saxony, a Lutheran who detested the Calvinists of Brandenburg and the Palatinate, and who had been mildly pro-Hapsburg up to this point. Ferdinand may have acted from the purest religious motives, but when religious motives pay off so handsomely, there is at least a suspicion that they are tainted by something else. Moreover, even if the motive remained purely religious, the procedure was such as to arouse apprehension. Ferdinand practically wiped out the Bohemian nobility and replaced it with Germans, Spaniards, and Italians. If he could do this in Bohemia, he could do it elsewhere and no one was safe.

Ferdinand proceeded to prove that this was precisely the case. Various Protestant lords and various mercenary soldiers appeared in the Palatinate; Tilly beat them all in a series of battles, and Ferdinand entered upon the same thoroughgoing re-Catholicization as in Bohemia. There and in Austria, where he had promised the nobles freedom of worship, Protestant ministers were expelled, the churches were turned over to the Jesuits and so were the universities, including that of Heidelberg, long the intellectual center of Calvinism. Its famous library, one of the finest in Europe, was carried off to Rome, and little of it was ever seen again.

The result was a reconstitution of the Protestant union on a diplomatic rather than a religious basis. Only Johann Georg of Saxony clung to an impossible neutrality. James I of England promised money which he never delivered, the Estates of Holland promised troops which were actually forthcoming, and which formed the nucleus of an army, placed under command of an able mercenary, Graf Ernst von Mansfeld. In spite of a couple of defeats by Tilly he still ranked high as a soldier; and most important of all, King Christian IV of Denmark entered the combination.

175

This King of Denmark was not to be taken lightly. He had a considerable reputation as a military leader, which he deserved. He had built up the Danish navy to be the first in Europe and set up a strong Danish army. He was head of the largest, most prosperous, and most powerful state in the North. Handling him at the same time as the resuscitated Protestant forces under Mansfeld was a far different proposition for Ferdinand than merely dealing with the disorderly Bohemian levies and the mercenaries who had followed the Elector Palatine. Moreover, Tilly, though technically in the service of the Catholic League, was actually Maximilian of Bavaria's general. Since Elector Max was already claiming pieces of the Palatinate, the price for Tilly's services was apt to be high.

Ferdinand II was thus in something of a dilemma when Mephistopheles stepped from the wings in the person of a Czech named Albrecht Wenzel Eusebius von Waldstein, better known to history as Wallenstein. In 1617 he was already rich (by marriage) and growing richer by raising troops for the Bohemian war. He had made connections with the banking house of De Vito, which had a patent to buy up and remint all the silver in Bohemia; lent the emperor up to a million florins, and was one of the chief beneficiaries of the Protestant confiscations. From these he had assembled a whole principality and received the title of Duke of Friedland. He was tall, dark, implacable, and never laughed; and ruled his subordinates by naked fear. There is no indication that he had a conscience. At one time he was a member of the Protestant sect of Bohemian Brothers but, being possessed of an absolutely infallible gift of foresight, converted in time to ride the rising wave. His actual faith remained astrology, but in military as well as civil matters he attained greatness by a process of the purest intellection without any necessity for training. This was the character who came forward with an offer that Ferdinand could not possibly refuse—to raise an army of 50,000 men in the imperial interest and operate it absolutely without charge if he were allowed to command it.

It was a mercenary army, but not at Wallenstein's expense.

He was engaged in a war of conquest and he made it pay for itself; his troops were well fed and well paid, and the districts through which they moved footed the bill. The men were a completely motley crowd in the beginning, welded into a unit by their commander's discipline of fear and system of reward. In 1626 he had this army in marching condition and moved north to co-operate with Tilly against Mansfeld and King Christian.

Tilly advanced against Christian along the line of the Elbe and beat him badly in battle, while Wallenstein in the Saxon country beat Mansfeld and threw him off in the direction of Silesia. Wallenstein followed hard, broke up Mansfeld's army in December 1626, and forced its leader from the stage. Tilly was meanwhile pursuing Christian into Holstein. Wallenstein turned back to join him, assumed command of both forces as superior officer, beat Christian again, and flooded the whole of Jutland with imperial troops. The Danes took to their ships and Wallenstein to the Baltic provinces. Mecklenburg and Pomerania were overrun, and in March 1628, Ferdinand made his general Duke of Mecklenburg, declaring the Protestant duke deposed. King Christian signed a peace which took him out of the war entirely, and in March 1629, Ferdinand crowned his work by pronouncing the Edict of Restitution.

At this date there remained of the major Protestant states in north Germany only Saxony and Brandenburg, whose electors were a pair of soft-shelled creatures, only desirous of being let alone. There were numerous minor states and free cities belonging to the old Hanseatic League, neither united nor individually capable of resisting the imperial power, as wielded by Wallenstein. The Edict of Restitution required that in all these states and cities anything secularized since 1552 was to be given back to the Church; all archbishops, bishops, and abbots were to receive the return of their sees and full possession of lands lost under the Reformation; all churches that had gone Protestant to be reopened for Catholic worship. Ferdinand was going to re-Catholicize north Germany as he had Styria and Bohemia; and in the face of Wallenstein's 80,000 men there could be no resistance. "There is too much of this local privilege!" cried the new Duke of Mecklenburg. "We want one land, one faith, one monarch, as in other countries!"

But the final steps were to be carried out without Wallenstein's personal supervision. In 1630 the Imperial Diet was held at Regensburg, and even the representatives of the Catholic states became so exercised over the manner in which the Duke of Friedland and Mecklenburg had paid and provisioned his army (which had marched through their lands as well as the Protestant), and over his growing pretensions (which did not seem to fall short of the empire itself), that Ferdinand was forced to dismiss him. Wallenstein retired to a castle in Bohemia; Tilly was appointed to complete the work of re-Catholicization, as general of both empire and Catholic League.

III

This was a process that appeared within the competence of Tilly and the army he headed, since there was no opposition above the local level. But it was a process which attracted the attention of a man with a wide forehead, speculative eyes, sharp mustaches, a pointed beard, and an almost incredible talent for intrigue—Armand Jean du Plessis de Richelieu, first minister of France. He had no objection to re-Catholicization, for he was himself a cardinal; but he had every objection to seeing the princes of Germany placed in the position of state officers who held their possessions only at the emperor's pleasure. An emperor having so vast a territory at his absolute disposal, able to summon an army like Wallenstein's out of the ground, and allied with the Spanish Hapsburgs would not be very long in deciding that France was next on the list. Richelieu had helped Christian of Denmark with money; now he turned to the one remaining power that might accomplish something against this overwhelming empire and agreed to terms the King of Sweden had previously proposed—a lump sum down and 400,000 rixdollars a year, with a truce arranged by France between Sweden and Poland, where there was a quarrel on.

The French diplomatic reports were excellent, but it is unlikely that even Richelieu realized quite what he was buying. Sweden, with her possessions east of the Baltic, had a population of less than a million and a half, one third that of England, less than a tenth that of the Hapsburg crown lands. In that system of predatory states she had been engaged for years in a struggle with immensely stronger Poland, whose Catholic king claimed her throne, as well as having to hold off Muscovy and Denmark. What Richelieu did know about the little nation was that it had furnished reinforcements and naval help to Stralsund, when Wallenstein besieged it in 1628, as part of his policy of reducing the Hanseatic towns, and the help had been effective. Richelieu knew also that the Poles were persuaded to their truce by a stunning defeat at Stuhm. Since the Swedish king had reported it to his own estates in a one-paragraph letter, the cardinal could not have known much more.

He certainly was not aware that he had drawn into the conflict one of the greatest statesmen of the age, Axel Oxenstjerna, and one of the greatest generals of any age, Gustavus II Adolphus, for whom Napoleon could find a comparison only in Alexander the Great. Somewhere between knowledge and ignorance there would be an area of semi-information, in whose technical details it is unlikely that Richelieu was much interested. These technical details were due to Gustavus himself; he was brought up for war and in the expectation of war, but he had to be his own Philip as well as Alexander. The furious energy of the Vasa family, to which he belonged, drove him into almost every available department of human activity (he spoke nine languages with ease, designed buildings, and wrote hymns which are still sung), but it was to war that he mainly devoted himself.

There were never enough troops for Sweden, even though Gustavus' father, Karl IX, had converted the country from something like a feudal state into something like a military monarchy by requiring each district to maintain a certain number of men in the standing army. Lacking numbers, Gustavus turned to technique when he came to the throne in 1611, and gradually hammered out a series of improvements—not all of them personally, but he knew how to state what he wanted, and he knew how to delegate authority, so the reforms were really his.

What he wanted was a force that could deal with those solid blocks of Spanish-trained pikemen, the invincible terciaries. It occurred to him that these masses of humanity would make admirable targets for gunfire if gunfire could be brought against them; and by 1626, Gustavus had discovered the means, by lightening the musket till it no longer had to be fired from a crotch and fitting it with a wheel lock. This made it possible to turn two thirds of the infantry mass into musketeers and to rank them, together with the one third of pikemen who accompanied them, six deep, instead of the sixteen, twenty, thirty of the massive Spanish formations. Nearly all their armor was taken away to let them move.

The cavalry underwent an alteration quite as radical. It had long been considered that no horse could strike home against blocks of pikemen; the custom was for them to trot up to an infantry formation, fire their pistols, file back, and repeat. It struck Gustavus that no law of nature required so ponderous a procedure; he trained his horsemen to ride in at the gallop, loose-reined and bloody-spurred, and to use the sword; moreover, to charge in successive squadrons. It made for violence, but that was precisely what the king wanted.

The greatest change was in the artillery. The usual guns employed in war were so heavy that twenty-four horses apiece was the normal allowance; the pieces were hauled to the field, put in place, and the horses led away to safety, while the guns operated from that spot from then on. In fact, the immobility of artillery was one of the reasons for the relative scarcity of battles; if guns were used, the battle had to come about by a kind of mutual agreement or because one of the commanders was so confident that he was willing to attack an artillery position. With the help of his artillery chief, Von Sigeroth, Gustavus introduced a 4-pounder that could be drawn by a single horse and that used a fixed cartridge; it could be fired eight times while a musketeer was getting off six shots. Two of these light guns were attached to each regiment; slightly heavier two-horse pieces formed an army artillery park. But the main point was that all these guns could be moved on the battlefield and under fire, and they were so moved.

Finally, Gustavus would have nothing to do with Wallenstein's system of living off the country, or Tilly's of occasional plunder. Food, equipment, and clothing were kept in magazines and issued by proper officers; the men were promptly paid (this was Oxenstjerna) and they paid for everything they took, under the severest penalties. This alone was a revolution; no one had ever heard of such a thing before.

When the instrument was thus constituted, Gustavus summoned his Riksraad (Senate) and told them he was going to Germany not only because the cause of Protestantism, of all freedom of thought, was in the scales, but also because Wallenstein, before his dismissal, had been named "Admiral of the Empire." His siege of Stralsund, his attacks on the Hansa towns were specifically aimed at control of the Baltic. The policy was not likely to be discontinued, and it would be better to fight abroad than at home. The Riksraad heartily concurred. On July 4, 1630, Gustavus landed at Peenemünde with 13,000 men. Recruiting agents in Scotland and Denmark were gathering more and the king expected important aid from the German princes, but even so this was an insignificant force to fling in the face of an empire.

Such was the opinion on the other side also. When he heard of the king's advance, Ferdinand remarked lightly, "So we have a new little enemy, do we?" and Wallenstein in his castle spoke of "the Snow King," who would melt in a German summer.

I V

Not a Protestant prince stirred to help, not a heart beat faster. Duke Bogislav of Pomerania only asked the Swedes to go away; to obtain a base Gustavus had to force Stettin to open its gates, and incorporated its garrison into his army by decree. (They turned out to be very good troops.) He held a slender wedge into the Oder valley, completely surrounded by imperial troops and towns with imperial garrisons, and even with Stralsund there was communication only by sea. Of the great Protestant electors, Johann Georg of Saxony wanted no part of the war on any terms and Georg Wilhelm of Brandenburg even refused to allow Swedish troops in his territory and admitted imperial garrisons to his strong places.

The story of the next nine months can be found in most military textbooks and is immensely admired by soldiers and very complicated. Gustavus received acquisitions of force by recruitment and new men from home, and he reduced the imperialists no little by victories in small battles and the capture of towns. He had to do his work by a series of maneuvers as intricate as the passes of an expert fencer, which he accomplished so well that by May 1631 all Pomerania, all Mecklenburg except the single city of Greifswald, had been freed of imperial garrisons and exactions, and the Swedish king had a bastion in northern Germany which could be penetrated only at the cost of fighting a battle.

Tilly was not interested in fighting battles except on the most favorable terms; they were an unnecessary expense. He had adopted and extended the method of Wallenstein, subduing the country bit by bit, burning out everything, killing off everyone, and taking all the goods, so that no hostile army could support a campaign against him. Behind this policy was Ferdinand, and it was based on the idea that each Protestant principality would remain quiet, believing itself safe as long as it remained loyal to the empire. This was usually correct, but in May 1631 there was furnished an impressive demonstration of where the peace-in-our-time policy led Protestants.

The city of Magdeburg had once been the seat of an archbishop who was ejected by the Reformation. Under Ferdinand's Edict of Restitution it must be returned to a prelate, and in April 1631, Tilly appeared before the town with 30,000 men to demand submission. The place had been under a loose siege for several months by Graf Gottfried zu Pappenheim, one of the best imperial cavalry officers, and Gustavus had been making energetic efforts for its relief. But between him and Magdeburg lay Saxon territories, and nothing could move Elector Johann Georg to let him pass. On May 20, Tilly sent a herald into the town to negotiate; while the conversations were going on, Pappenheim threw a body of troops across the wall and the place was taken. The sack that followed became famous even in the seventeenth century; 40,000 people were butchered and every building in Magdeburg except the cathedral was burned.

This, then, was the alternative to submitting to the Edict of Restitution. To Ferdinand the operation was a complete success; it demonstrated that nothing could stand against the army of the League and the empire, and he followed it by a series of demands on west-central Germany. Saxe-Weimar and Hesse-Cassel were to submit to the Edict of Restitution; Johann Georg was to disband his army, except for a contingent which was to join Tilly for further police operations. Tilly was ordered to march at once on Saxe-Weimar and Hesse-Cassel.

The detachment sent against the former caught a Tartar in the young Duke Bernard, who later became one of Gustavus' most trusted officers, but the main events were in Brandenburg and Saxony. The fall of Magdeburg irritated Gustavus to the point where he decided that neutralities in this war were nonsense; he lined up his cannon at the gates of Berlin and told Georg Wilhelm that he must have free passage and the keys to the fortress of Spandau or he would start shooting; and Georg Wilhelm gave in. The Swedes turned southwest toward the dominions of Johann Georg, who found himself compelled to join either the imperialists or his fellow Protestants; and he chose the latter. About 12,000 of his men were added to Gustavus' army, and on September 17, 1631, just north of Leipzig, on the plain of Breitenfeld, Tilly found himself forced to fight a battle.

It was a decisive battle. There were 26,000 Swedes on the field, drawn up separately from the Saxons, who were on their left. Opposite them, the imperialists, huge blocks of terciaries in the center, cannon across the front, on the flanks masses of cavalry, commanded by Pappenheim on one flank, Graf Fürstenberg on the other, 40,000 all told, for a straight parallel order fight. Across the Swedish front were those new light guns under Lennart Torstensson, who would be no little famous as a general one day. He opened a fire so hot that Pappenheim on the imperial left could not take it, and without orders charged the Swedish right, while Fürstenberg, accepting this as a signal for action, went down against the Saxons. The Saxons fled at the first fire, and Johann Georg spurred from the field in terror that did not evaporate until he learned what happened after he left. Fürstenberg turned in on the naked Swedish left while Tilly obliqued his terciaries to the right to follow and roll up their line.

But things were not going so well for the empire on the other flank, where Pappenheim charged with his famous Black Cuirassiers. They found that between his squadrons of horse in that quarter Gustavus had interspersed small blocks of musketeers; these stood their ground, shooting down horse and man, and the Swedish cavalry on their lighter ponies counterattacked so fiercely that Pappenheim was driven from the field. It was the moment; Gustavus placed himself at the head of the cavalry regiments of Vastergotland, Ostergotland, Smaaland, and Finland, hurling them in at the gallop, in a charge such as no man living had seen, on the flank of the imperial guns and Tilly's solid *tercias*.

These *tercias* were already having no easy time in front. They found that the Swedes had held out a reserve; it formed a new line at right angles to the first, and instead of taking a naked flank the imperials were up against another line of those musketeers who shot so fast and, above all, that dreadful quickmoving artillery. They stood it; the cruel Spaniards, Walloons, and Croats were hard-bitten fighting men, veterans who had never known defeat, and they had every confidence in Father Tilly. But they could not gain an inch against the guns, and the merciless horsemen kept cutting them down from behind; toward twilight the stampede began. Seven thousand of the imperialists were dead, 6,000 more were prisoners, and the Snow King had become the Lion of the North. In Ingolstadt they offered public prayer for deliverance from "the Devil, the Swedes and the Finns."

V

It was obvious what the Emperor Ferdinand must do; he now had no choice but to recall the diabolical genius, Wallenstein. But Ferdinand had so lively a sense of what this might cost him that for the time being he merely ordered Tilly to raise a new army in place of that dispersed at Breitenfeld and co-operate with Maximilian of Bavaria.

Gustavus turned west into the Lower Palatinate and the Rhineland. Some critics have blamed him for not marching on Vienna at once; but just as when he was establishing his secure bastion south of the Baltic, he was less interested in the spectacular than in putting things on a really solid basis. In three months he had the whole area under control; the Protestant princes were now ready to help, the Catholics reduced to treaties and impotence, the Jesuits banished. Mainz, which had a Spanish garrison, was taken after a brief siege, the Spaniards driven back into the Netherlands and communications between them and the Austrians broken, while Johann Georg moved his army into Silesia and Bohemia.

During the winter Tilly got his new army on foot; Gustavus turned toward it and Bavaria in the spring, and came up with the old general at the river Lech. On April 15, 1632, the question of forcing a passage across that stream arose. Gustavus answered it by a device which has since become classic, but in his day was as original as his light artillery and galloping cavalry. He selected a bend convex toward his own side, massed artillery all round it, and made the attack under cover of a smoke screen from burning wet straw. It was not the least of his battles or his victories. The imperials lost 4,000 men, including Father Tilly, who had his leg shattered by a cannon ball. Munich fell and there was now absolutely nothing for obstinate Ferdinand to do but turn to Wallenstein.

The genius drove the kind of bargain that might have been expected. He demanded and received unconditional control of the army, control of all confiscated territories, a veto on all orders to be issued by the emperor. That he was promised one of the electorates is also probable; in practice it would have made him sole elector.

One of the reasons for Wallenstein's uncanny prescience was his ability at analysis. In retirement he had not lost touch with events, and he understood perfectly where the weakness of Gustavus' situation lay. It lay in the Saxon alliance, the personality of Johann Georg, and the fact that he was across the Swedish communications for any operation in south Germany. As soon as Wallenstein had recruited a new army, which did not take long, he moved it into Bohemia and easily drove the Saxons out. At the same time he very quietly opened negotiations with Johann Georg and Georg Wilhelm of Brandenburg, suggesting that a major objective on which they could agree was to get the foreign invader out of Germany. If they concurred, concessions on religion would be forthcoming—even the abandonment of the Edict of Restitution. Ferdinand might care for nothing but the true religion; Wallenstein thought in terms of empire.

He now gathered in the Bavarian forces and moved toward Gustavus in the region of Nürnberg, where he set up a wide intrenched camp and waited. He had analyzed Gustavus' military operations quite as shrewdly as the political, and understood that the Swedish tactical system depended on mobility, especially of guns in the field, and the strategic system on fighting battles. Wallenstein had no such speed of maneuver and no such artillery. Very well, he would not fight battles, and see who could stand the deadlock longer. His own amoral method of supplying his troops should make his problem of static maintenance lighter than that of the king.

He calculated accurately. For six weeks the armies faced each other, both going hungry, and decimated by illness. At last, on

September 3–4, Gustavus could stand it no longer and made a desperate attempt to storm Wallenstein's lines on a commanding height. It failed, with the loss of 3,000 men.

The impact of this event was considerable, and it was followed by another indication that genius has an answer for every problem, and Wallenstein's system might be practically superior to that of Gustavus. It was required of the king to show results, to get the imperial forces out of the territory, and Wallenstein was dangerously far north, dangerously close to Protestant lands. To pull him back Gustavus started a drive toward Vienna. Wallenstein simply ignored him, marched into Saxony and took Leipzig, then began to devastate the country around it. Johann Georg sent frantic appeals for protection to the Swedish king, and the cleverness of Wallenstein's political moves became apparent. The imperialists could spare Vienna far better than Gustavus could Dresden, and the Swede was forced to send his columns streaming north.

Difficulties of provisioning and the need for garrisons against imperial raids brought it about that the mobile field force with Gustavus, as he moved up toward Leipzig, was relatively small —about 18,000 men, although this was increased by a contingent under young Duke Bernard of Saxe-Weimar, which presently fell in. Johann Georg had nearly as many men at Torgau, on the other side of Leipzig, but letters begging him to join for battle produced only a reply that they would meet at Magdeburg. Johann Georg had been in one battle and did not wish to see another; besides, he could always get some kind of terms from Wallenstein.

The Czech was at least 33,000 strong; it was already November and he intended to intrench a camp for winter quarters on much the same pattern as his lines at Nürnberg, which would force Gustavus also to be quiet. The place Wallenstein chose was Lützen, southwest of Leipzig. There was no height to work with, as in the Nürnberg position, since this part of Saxony is all one gently rolling plain, but a road with deep ditches on either side runs from Lützen to Leipzig. As a beginning to his intrenched camp, Wallenstein deepened the ditches until they were very effective trenches, filling them with musketeers. On the right of his position was Lützen village, and behind it the only eminence in the neighborhood, Windmill Hill; here the bulk of the artillery was posted. On his left he had the Flossgraben, a fordable stream, but still a military obstacle.

That is, he was locked in, and could fall on the rear of any force that tried to get around him. Moreover, it was a position guaranteed to demobilize Swedish mobility; the causeway road was as near a straight line as it could be, there was no room for the kind of maneuvers that had won for Gustavus at Breitenfeld and the passage of the Lech. When, on November 14, Wallenstein heard that the king was approaching, he hurriedly sent to recall Pappenheim with 8,000 cavalry from Halle, where they had been sent to ease the problem of provision.

Wallenstein's judgment was that when Gustavus came he would fight, regardless of numbers, position, or anything else, and he was perfectly right. Not only did the king intend to attack, but to attack at once, in spite of a plea from Duke Bernard that he at least wait for the arrival of two or three thousand men from Lüneberg. Neither would Gustavus sleep in a wagon; it was a damp, chilly night and his men had to lie on the ground, he would take no better.

All woke to a dawn heavy with fog; the king ranked the troops and led the whole army singing *"Ein feste Burg ist unser Gott,"* Martin Luther's hymn. Wallenstein had fired Lützen village to keep it from being a cover; the smoke and smell of the burning drifted through the murk. In spite of poor visibility Gustavus' intelligence of his enemy's position was good, and in spite of the fact that this must be a straight parallel order battle he had a plan of maneuver. While Duke Bernard with the cavalry of the left attacked Lützen, he himself with a weighted right wing intended to break down the enemy on that flank, having noted that it was a "strategic wing," that is, in prolongation of it lay Wallenstein's line of communication to Leipzig. If it were broken through, the imperialists would have no line of retreat. There were two lines of infantry among the Swedes, as at Breitenfeld; General Niels Brahe led the first, old

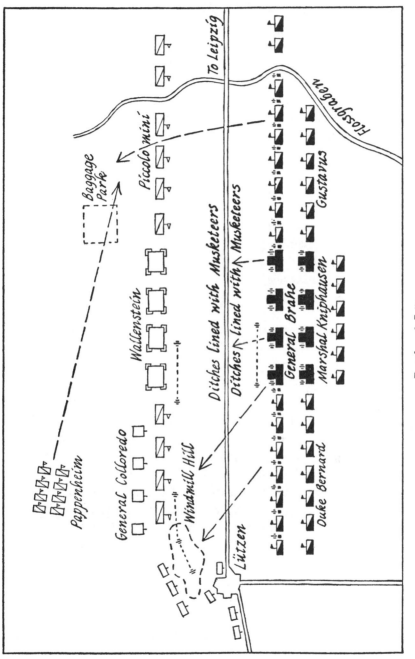

Battle of Lützen

Marshal Kniphausen the second, while Torstensson commanded the artillery all across the front.

In the imperial lines Piccolomini commanded the Austrian and Hungarian cuirassiers; facing the king, General Colloredo some horse and foot supporting the guns around Windmill Hill, while Wallenstein, in a litter because his gout troubled him so sore, was carried back and forth along the solid blocks of pikemen along the center—Spanish or Spanish-trained, the old terciary formation, not trying to move, as at Breitenfeld, but on the defensive this day, where they were best. Through the shrouding mist the guns of both sides boomed.

At ten the fog cleared enough to show the lines to each other, as through a glass darkly. King Gustavus lifted his sword, as it is shown in the painting, uttered a brief prayer, and gave the order for the attack.

VI

Duke Bernard on the Swedish left was overlapped and had a hill to climb. But he was ardent and a hard driver; the early gain he made attracted Wallenstein's attention so that the Czech found it necessary to take charge there personally. In the center the flexible Swedish infantry swept forward to the doubleditched road, Torstensson got some of the light regimental guns up to enfilade the imperial musketeers in the ditches, and the Swedes went right across into the imperial artillery positions, captured the big immobile guns, and spiked them. The big blocks of pikemen behind had been deprived of most of their musketry support in the fighting along the road. Now, under the fire of Gustavus' line, they began to go back, not breaking, but unable to make a forward movement in the face of the rapid-firing Swedish muskets and Torstensson's light cannon. They went back farthest on their own left, the Swedish right; Wallenstein was anchoring the other flank, and he was a good anchor. But even Wallenstein could not hold Windmill Hill against Duke Bernard when some of Brahe's infantry joined the attack; the big battery there was taken.

Yet it was where the king in person led his famous Stalhanske horse on the Swedish right that the key events were taking place, and the key to them all was that (in the words of a wandering Englishman), "As the Battaile was ioyned there fell soe great a miste that we could not see one another, which if it had not bene, I beleave wee had quickly made an ende of them (but all must be as God will have it)." In that murk the Stalhanskes scattered a group of Croat light cavalry at the first shock, then came through it against cuirassiers. They were solider, but the Swedes came on in successive waves; back and down went the imperialists and the battle was all but won.

All *but* won. In the blind groping mist word reached the king that he had somehow pulled too far out to the right, that Wallenstein had brought his pikemen, accompanied by more cavalry, back against the right flank of Brahe's infantry line where it jutted farthest forward. With only four companions Gustavus rode off to rectify matters, in the mist got into a whole party of the enemy, and was instantly killed.

The worst of it was that the tale about the counterattack was perfectly true. Through the fog it fell as a complete surprise on the extreme end of Brahe's line and rolled it up. The Swedes went back to the road, lost one ditch, then the other, and their artillery had no points of aim; the pikes were better in this weather. Just as the Swedish infantry began to retreat, Pappenheim reached the field with his 8,000 fresh cavalry. "Where is the king?" he demanded, burning to revenge the defeat of Breitenfeld, and being told, led on against the Swedish right. The horse that had followed Gustavus nearly to Wallenstein's baggage camp were caught at the standstill and, more than doubly outnumbered, driven back across the causeway. It was five o'clock and the swing of Pappenheim's counterattack should have carried the disordered Swedes right away.

It did not, and there were several reasons why it did not. The mist began to clear, and Torstensson got his guns going again, while the imperial cannon in the center were still spiked. The captured Windmill Hill battery enfiladed their line and discouraged any advance beyond the road; Pappenheim got himself killed.

But the greatest and the ruling reason was what happened when old Marshal Kniphausen sought out Duke Bernard to tell him that Gustavus was dead and the duke was in command of the army; the second line of foot was still undamaged, and the marshal thought he could make good a retreat.

"Retreat!" cried Bernard. "This is not the time to talk of retreat, but of vengeance!" He snatched off his helmet and rode down the line, shouting in a great, booming voice, "Swedes! They have killed the king!"

Kniphausen was a careful, accurate soldier. He used his second line to stay the weak spots of the first at just the right points. But it was not anything that Kniphausen did that now took charge of the battle, it was Bernard of Saxe-Weimar and the incredible fury his words engendered in men who had already been fighting most of the day. They swept forward in such an assault as has rarely been seen on any battlefield; in such a rage that afterward there were found imperialists who had been daggered and even throttled. Brave men, trained men, the terciaries could not stand it. "The soldyers flonge down theire armes and ran awaye, and the officers could by noe means make them longer stande; ffor here Hertike Bernerde charged himself the enimie soe sore."

Wallenstein's army was not so much beaten as destroyed, and "the wilde bores cut off manie of them in theire flyght."

VII

It was more than Wallenstein's army that was destroyed at Lützen; it was also the imperial system and Wallenstein himself. The genius lasted a couple of years longer at his castle of Eger in Bohemia when some bravoes sent by Ferdinand burst into his study and dispatched him. To the imperial mind the only thing that could justify giving any man power so extensive was a success complete enough to make possible the dispo-

sition of the rest of Germany as he had the Duchy of Mecklenburg and the noble estates of Bohemia. When Wallenstein first
came on the scene, the objective was still re-Catholicization.
But Richelieu's intervention and the Battle of Breitenfeld rendered this so clearly unattainable that the emphasis had subtly
shifted, and what had been a means to an end became the end
itself. The war of religion was decided at Breitenfeld; the war
for the absolute empire was decided at Lützen.

Before the Reformation, whatever wars took place, there remained throughout Europe the underlying concept of an essential unity of Christendom, an idea that all states still formed
part of a common body. Even after it, when Charles V came to
an agreement with the Protestantizing princes of the empire in
1555, that idea and ideal remained. It was technically in the
name of this idea, however perverted in expression, that Ferdinand II launched his campaign of re-Catholicization. It was still
in the name of it that Wallenstein laid his grandiose imperial
plans. Lützen destroyed the ideal; the concept as well as the fact
of European unity broke.

Both Reformation and imperialism were decided on military
grounds and by military means. The system of Tilly and Wallenstein was essentially to assemble an army so strong defen-
sively that it was immune to any attack, then march through
the enemy's country, destroying his resources by devastations
—which, incidentally, paid the soldiers. It even provided mercenary recruits. "Whose house doth burn, must soldier turn,"
was a current proverb. Wallenstein developed this system more
thoroughly than Tilly, but only because he was even more
ruthless, and to his predecessor's talent for war he added talents
in intrigue, finance, and diplomacy. Yet even in its highest expression this was no more than a development of the Spanish
system of war and it was fundamentally medieval.

It was this system that Gustavus Adolphus proved invalid.
He proved it invalid tactically at Breitenfeld; proved that a formation based on mere immunity to attack could always be
beaten if the attack moved fast enough and hit hard enough.
The Spanish-Tilly-Wallenstein system was one of establishing

infantry and its guns as a kind of fortress, with the cavalry making sallies; but the trouble with a fortress is that it cannot change shape, and it is always possible for a fast mover to throw overwhelming force against some part of it.

Gustavus also proved the system strategically erroneous. The fact that he failed to dislodge the fortress army near Nürnberg should not be allowed to conceal the other fact that Wallenstein's army suffered badly there from hunger and disease, and the second time Wallenstein tried that trick, he got Lützen. An army has to have communications, supply. The fast-marching Swedes could always threaten communications and force a battle of the kind they wanted to fight by threatening communications, and this is what Gustavus did.

Finally and above all, the king produced his demonstration in the field of morality and morale. The Swedes paid; cities opened their gates and peasants came with their horses to haul supplies, even in the Catholic districts from which men fled away before Wallenstein. This enormously facilitated military operations and assured to Gustavus the widespread support he began to receive as soon as he proved he could win battles and protect his adherents against the exponents of the opposite system.

But in the long run this was perhaps less important than in what the moral values did within the army itself. For the whole of the Spanish-imperialist system was based on men who were fighting for what they could make out of it; when it became obvious that they were not going to make anything, the army dissolved, as on the afternoon after Breitenfeld and through the smoky twilight of Lützen. The Swedish army was recruited from men who were enlisted for the war, not hired for the campaign. They were fighting for something, a ponderable ideal, the concept that a man should be allowed to do his own thinking. When the king died on the field of Lützen, that concept did not; it was the basis of the fury of the Northmen that carried everything away before it that evening and forever ended the Middle Ages.

10. Interlude; the Day of Inadequate Decisions

I

After Lützen the Thirty Years' War became a very inferior affair. On the Swedish side there was no one with Gustavus' prestige to keep the Protestant combination together, and it began to crack at the seams; nor was there anyone with Gustavus' strategic skill to make a victory mean something permanent. There was not even anyone who had the king's tactical ability; the best was Bernard of Saxe-Weimar, and at Nördlingen in 1634 he sustained a defeat that changed the whole aspect of the war, and is therefore entitled to rank as a somewhat decisive battle.

It brought two decisions. Johann Georg of Saxony and a group of small states in alliance with him, having been delivered from the fear of Ferdinand's imperialism at Breitenfeld and from that of Wallenstein's imperialism at Lützen, negotiated a separate peace with the emperor, to whom at last it had become clear that neither imperialism could be made to work, and he would have to go on living in a world from which the concept of European unity had been lost. Nördlingen also brought the whole of southwest Germany under imperial authority, and once more closed around France that Hapsburg ring which Richelieu had been paying the Swedes to break.

The fact was signalized by the unhindered march of a Spanish force from Italy to the Netherlands; and with the Saxon group out of the war, Richelieu felt he could no longer delay in the hope of finding another ally of the stature of Gustavus. France went in, and for thirteen years more the armies marched and fought across the plains and hills of Germany, leaving behind such devastation that the land had still not recovered 200 years later.

This was the only decision really arrived at. Names renowned in military history stalk across the pages of that war—the Swedes Banér, Torstensson, Wrangel, pupils of Gustavus; Turenne, the Great Condé, Montecuculi. Famous battles were fought and campaigns made that have excited the admiration of soldiers; but still no result. The Peace of Westphalia in 1648 was a peace of exhaustion.

Why? Because they were all trying to copy Gustavus, and as usual with military copyists, it was the detail that was imitated, not the ensemble. They copied his six- or three-deep musketeers against the huge blocks of pikemen; they copied the light artillery and the cavalry going in with the cold weapon; they copied his method of provisioning from a previously established set of magazines; and after some time they began to copy his process of recruiting a standing army.

But there was always something a little off key, a little out of drawing about these copies. The guns were never as light as Gustavus had made them, nor could they move as fast. The cavalry made most of its "charges" at a slow trot, except in the hands of the Great Condé. Gustavus had been so successful with cavalry that horse once again became the main arm, as numerous as infantry in most armies, and sometimes more so; and the question of supply became most prominently one of forage. The system of magazines was degraded into becoming an objective in itself; a fortress was the usual magazine, and it was considered very honorable to force an adversary to leave his campaigning ground by capturing such a *point d'appui*. In fact, it became a main purpose; Turenne was considered most inelegant for wishing to fight battles instead of driving the enemy from their positions by maneuver, and he was often favored with a court order to avoid battle.

On the battlefield also the imitation of what was thought to be Gustavus' method became the rule. He had opened the fighting in parallel order, with his infantry in two lines, guns in little groups across the front, and cavalry on the wings. Therefore everybody else adopted this arrangement. They failed to realize that at Breitenfeld and Lützen the king placed his guns across the front in order to get the most out of them against the blocks of pikemen; at the Lech he did nothing of the kind. The diadochi completely overlooked the fact that Breitenfeld and Lützen were only parallel order battles at the very beginning; that the former was decided by battlefield maneuver and in the latter Gustavus concentrated the mailed fist of his greatest weight to smash the enemy from his communications. Particularly, the successors made no real effort to use the three arms in combination and according to opportunity. In their typical battles cavalry fought cavalry, infantry, infantry, and the battle was decided by whose line went back in a piece.

Nor did they pursue after a battle. Gustavus, who had studied the campaigns of Alexander and knew what pursuit was, followed up his minor battles and the passage of the Lech remorselessly, but at Lützen he was not alive to order a pursuit, and at Breitenfeld it was unnecessary. In the latter he had broken a mercenary army in the field, and was perfectly aware that with that breaking the campaign for which the army had enlisted was over and the army would dissolve. But the armies that succeeded Gustavus were in tighter bonds. He had taught them discipline; they did not break up after a defeat, but retreated to the nearest fortress and asked for reinforcements, and they were able to do so because they remained unpursued. The result was that in those showy battles and famous victories the losing side was pushed back rather than destroyed, and the contradance of fortress plucking and maneuver went on again. The whole art of war became as formal as fencing with buttoned foils—and about as decisive.

This was a condition that lasted for a hundred years.

II

There also developed during the later period of the Thirty Years' War a new concept—the concept of the expanding state. It had been latent all the time, and the dissolution of the old basic idea of the unity of Christendom as the result of the Reformation only brought it to the surface. The dominant political idea of the period following the Peace of Westphalia became that of a number of states in fierce competition for power, wealth, territory, everything, and this idea was powerfully pushed forward by colonizations beyond the seas and the things that flowed therefrom. Every state was in competition with every other for the avenues of expansion, and the natural method of competition was war, just as the natural business of a member of the upper class was fighting.

In 1661 there was injected into this complex the personality of Louis XIV, King of France. He was magnificent and very proud, author of the remark that he was not the head of state but the state itself, and at the death of his tutor, the great Cardinal Mazarin, declared he would be his own first minister. It turned out that he was perfectly capable of doing this, for he was industrious, patient and, at least in his early years, chose subordinates with the greatest skill. The idea of the competitive and expanding state formed a part of his basic mental equipment; he would no more have questioned it than he would have doubted the morality of killing cattle for beefsteaks; the only points to be decided were those of execution.

Therefore wars. Wars directed in the beginning at breaking the Hapsburg ring around France, then to placing that country in a position where she would be invulnerable to the ambition of any nation or combination of nations. In the early years Louis was lucky enough to catch England under the self-centered later Stuarts, Spain under Charles II, who was afflicted with fainting fits and indifference to anything that went on outside the cathedral, and the Holy Roman Empire busy with a somewhat revived Turkey. During nearly three decades the French achieved most of their objectives, and achieved them for good—the left bank of the Rhine and that part of the Spanish Netherlands which protected Paris against attack from the north. The plan of these wars, their strategy and tactics, was essentially the same as those of the last half of the Thirty Years' War. There were battles which decided nothing except that the victorious army would be free to besiege another fortress, and since the area of operations was heavily populated and cut up by water courses, the fortresses became more important than ever. The wars were engineers' wars, and the greatest names were those of Vauban of France and Coehorn of Holland.

III

By 1700 changes had developed in both the technological and the political climate. The main technological change was the invention of the socket bayonet, introduced in France in 1687, in most other countries within the following ten years. It made pikemen unnecessary and furnished musketeers with a weapon both for driving home an attack and for defense against cavalry, enormously simplifying the minor tactics of infantry.

The political change was that up through the complex of expanding states there pushed the green shoots of a new idea —the balance of power. If all states were competitive and expanding, then all were in danger when any one became so great in territory and resources that it could do as it pleased. This was in fundamental opposition to Louis XIV's plan of placing France in precisely such a position, and the ideological conflict reached the shooting stage with the death of Charles II of Spain.

He was childless, and his heirs were limited to Louis XIV and Leopold, Holy Roman emperor. Both resigned their claims to younger sons of their issue—Louis to Philip of Anjou, his second grandson, Leopold to Charles of Austria, his second son. Both agreed to some partition of the vast Spanish heritage, which included the southern Netherlands and most of Italy besides the vast empire beyond the seas. But the accession of either would destroy the precious balance of power, for if concentration and administrative efficiency had made France incomparably the strongest nation on the Continent, victories over the Turk had placed Austria in control of all Hungary. Yet it was judged by most of Europe that the French danger was the greater, particularly since the will of Charles II of Spain left his dominions to Philip and the Spaniards accepted this decision. England and the states of the empire joined a Grand Alliance with Holland against France, and the War of the Spanish Succession was on. Bavaria went with France, a key fact, for it became one of Louis' politico-military objectives to drive Leopold from the throne of the empire and substitute a Wittelsbach dynasty, with Munich as its capital.

That war produced some remarkable soldiers, of whom the best was probably Prince Eugene of Savoy, who was unable to find military preferment in France in spite of high birth because of a puny physique; he went to Vienna and, by unusual courage and the ability to exercise responsibility, became a field marshal at the age of twenty-five. A perfect example of the reasons why it was difficult for any officer of the age to attain decisive results was furnished by his campaign against the Turks in 1697. At Zenta on the Theiss he beat them in a battle where they lost 20,000 men—and on returning to Vienna was placed under arrest for having fought without orders.

That is, the prevailing doctrine of maneuver and siege ran all the way back through the echelons to the cabinet level, it was ungentlemanly to fight hard, and even victory might somehow upset the magic balance of power. Of course, this was unexpressed, part of the invisible but universally accepted mental atmosphere, like the concept of the expanding and competitive state. Only a man of something close to genius could shake loose from it sufficiently to form his own ideas— in the large area as well as the limited, the political as well as the military.

Such a man was John Churchill, Duke of Marlborough, who was reliably reported to have got his start by jumping out the king's mistress's window at just the right moment. His talent for war turned out to be quite equal to that for intrigue; in spite of some extremely dubious connections he was made commander of the army of the Grand Alliance in the Netherlands. The campaigns of his first two years there ran according to pattern. His army was at least half Dutch, there were Dutch civilian deputies at his headquarters to see that he performed in line with the wishes of their government, and these wishes were to avoid fighting and take fortresses.

He took them, but in the meanwhile the Grand Alliance was slowly losing the war. Villars, the ablest of the French marshals in the field, drove an army under Prince Louis of Baden into lines at Stolhofen on the middle Rhine, pinned it there with detachments, and linked up with the Elector Maximilian II of Bavaria. The Emperor Leopold had a revolt in Hungary on his hands, and could have made but a very poor defense if the combined Franco-Bavarian forces had moved on Vienna, which Villars wished to do. The Elector Maximilian, however, was in business for a quick profit, and his ideas of profit had the same limitations as all those in the balance-of-power, expanding-state period. Instead of striking boldly for empire, he insisted on spending 1703 in conquering the Tyrol for Bavaria. Villars became so violent with him as to make himself *persona non grata*. For 1704, Louis XIV adopted the old political device of repudiating the man with an unpopular plan but accepting the plan. Villars was recalled; the new marshal, Marsin, was sent out with orders to insist on an offensive into the heart of Austria. He had the means for it.

Prince Eugene had been operating for the empire in Italy with some success; he was called back to command the defense, but his forces were very weak, not over 10,000 troops at the beginning of the campaign against some 50,000 or more of the Franco-Bavarians. He got in touch with Marlborough, or Marlborough with him, and very secretly, to keep the Dutch deputies and the imperial war council from finding out about it, they concerted a campaign. The position was that a major French army was operating in the Netherlands; a secondary one along the Moselle, north of Metz; another in Baden, under Marshal Tallard, besides the troops of Marsin and the Elector Max in Bavaria. When spring broke, the bulk of Eugene's troops, gradually reinforced, shifted westward to watch Tallard in Baden. Marlborough's plan, as announced to the Dutch, was to slip leftward to the Moselle country. He moved then, on May 25, to Coblenz, where the Moselle falls into the Rhine, but instead of turning up the former river crossed the Rhine and kept right on eastward, toward Bavaria and the Danube.

That march, with bad roads and heavy transport, was slow by modern standards, but with relation to the speed of movement and spread of intelligence of the age, it went at rocket speed. On July 3, Marlborough was at Donauwörth on the Danube, an important fortress. He assaulted it and carried it out of hand, with 10,000 loss to the Franco-Bavarians, then began to devastate the Bavarian homeland in a manner that brought anguished howls from the elector and the calling in of Tallard's army from the Baden country. Eugene followed, linked up with Marlborough early in August, and moved forward to where the Franco-Bavarian forces were posted on the bank of the Danube at Blenheim village.

Marsin and Tallard had 60,000 men, strongly arranged behind a marshy brook, the right anchored on Blenheim and the river, the left on the hamlet of Oberglau. They had no expectation of fighting, since Marlborough and Eugene were only 56,000 strong and one simply did not attack a position like that. But on the morning of August 13, 1704, the English and imperialists moved forward as though for reconnaissance and kept right on coming. Tallard had made the mistake of concentrating his infantry in the two villages; while Eugene pinned and virtually besieged part of them in Oberglau, with the help of some uncommonly steady Prussians, Marlborough did the same at Blenheim, then broke through the cavalry of the enemy center. When evening closed across the smoking field, France and Bavaria had lost 38,609 in killed, wounded, and prisoners, and Tallard himself was taken.

This, now, was decisive; but the area of the decision was not extensive and the decision itself was in negative terms. Blenheim decided that Wittelsbach should not replace Hapsburg on the imperial throne, that the empire would remain in the war, and that France should not establish a hegemony in south Germany. But it did not decide the war except in that area, and in 1705, Marlborough was back in the Netherlands, hampered by lack of men and money, maneuvering to protect the frontiers of Holland, while Eugene was in Italy, working in the valley of the Po.

In 1706, Marlborough managed to assemble enough men and permissions to take the offensive, and won another great battle at Ramillies; it decided that the Spanish Netherlands, with Brussels, Dunkirk, Antwerp, and Louvain, should fall into the hands of the allies. Eugene beat the French at Turin and took all Italy from them and the Spaniards. In 1708 the two generals were together again and won a famous battle at Oudenarde; in 1709 they beat the French at Malplaquet, that "very murdering battle," but nothing at all followed except more maneuvering and sieges in Flanders and Brabant and Lorraine, and the war died out in 1713.

The terms of peace gave the Spanish Netherlands and Spanish Italy to the empire, and thus by reflection rendered Ramillies and Turin decisive battles—in the same manner Blenheim was, for a limited area and in terms of denial. The matrix of fortresses, slow-moving armies restrained from fighting battles, consolidated states that could easily make good losses, and apprehension lest the allies of today become the enemies of tomorrow were such that the defensive had become superior to the attack. The balance of power had been struck, the expanding state checked; there were no longer ideas and ideals on the battlefield, only minor decisions among members of the same system, which had to be determined by fighting, but which could be settled without rancor. The military art, which includes everything back to the recruiting stations and powder mills, no longer permitted major issues to be settled in war or by war.

11. Frederick the Great and the Unacceptable Decision

When Friedrich II, later called the Great, came to the throne of Prussia in 1740, he inherited a realm both physically and in population a little larger than Portugal, but sprawled all across northeast Germany in little packages, and without any natural barriers to serve as *points d'appui* for fortresses. An unfortunate heritage of the Thirty Years' War was the fact that the armies of both sides had marched very much where they pleased, regardless of neutralities, except in those few cases where the neutral had an armed force of his own big enough to insure respect. Johann Georg of Saxony was such a neutral until the Emperor Ferdinand forced him to choose sides; Georg Wilhelm of Brandenburg tried to be such a neutral and found he lacked the means. The lesson was not lost on the strong and imperious Hohenzollerns who followed him and turned the Electorate of Brandenburg into the Kingdom of Prussia, and most especially not on Friedrich II's father, Friedrich Wilhelm I, not the least strong or imperious of that remarkable line. In addition, Friedrich Wilhelm was a kind of military connoisseur. In his younger days he had personally fought under Marlborough and Eugene at Malplaquet, and had fully accepted the opinion that one of the leading concerns of a royal personage was war.

There were no wars any more, but Friedrich Wilhelm behaved as though he expected one tomorrow morning. A series of financial and administrative economies, including the maintenance of his own court on a scale hardly more elaborate than that of a country gentleman, gave him one of the fattest treasuries of Europe from one of its poorest countries. He used the money to equip an army of 80,000, almost as large as the imperial forces, and equal to 4 per cent of Prussia's population. In spite of a conscription system and the duty laid on males of noble families to serve in the officer corps from childhood up, little Prussia simply could not furnish that many men. Friedrich Wilhelm's recruiting agents cruised through the whole of Europe in search of what they wanted, and when the candidates did not come willingly, they were kidnaped. This was especially true of very tall men; in one of those evolutionary specializations that made the head of triceratops almost too heavy to carry, the king devoted vast effort to assembling a regiment of giants for his personal guard. His people even sandbagged and carried off an exceptionally tall Italian priest while he was saying Mass.

The armies of the age of the balance of power were the product of a sharply stratified society, seeking everywhere to improve its productive mechanism. Even in soldier-hungry Prussia the fact that a man was an artisan or a trader exempted him from military service. It was the business of the middle class to pay taxes to support the armies, and the men who made them up were drawn from the lower levels—peasants, vagabonds, the tradeless. As a result, discipline everywhere was of the severest sort; but this severity was carried further under Friedrich Wilhelm than anywhere else in Europe. Flogging through the line was the usual punishment for talking back to an officer; a man who struck his superior was simply shot out of hand without trial. With this discipline went unceasing drill in the Prussian army, day in and day out, till the men moved like machines, on reflex and without even thinking.

Also there went with it a reduction in the number of movements required to load and fire a musket, and a new type of iron ramrod, introduced by Friedrich Wilhelm's friend and officer, Prince Leopold of Anhalt-Dessau. In other armies the ramrods were wood.

The rest of Europe regarded these antics with amusement; the regiment of giants was funny, and an army that drilled all the time but never did any fighting was an agreeable royal idiosyncrasy, like a collection of cameos, and about as useful. Indeed, an official report to the Holy Roman emperor said that the Prussian soldiers had been flogged so much that they would infallibly desert at the first fire.

But on October 20, 1740, the Holy Roman emperor died.

II

King Friedrich II was twenty-seven at the time of his accession, known for his liberalizing tendencies, his addiction to the arts and sciences, and what was generally considered to be a levity of temper. He abolished torture, proclaimed the freedom of the press and absolute religious toleration, and began writing all over Europe to tempt Voltaire, Maupertuis, anyone with a reputation, to come to Berlin and help set up an academy. He discontinued the regiment of giants, gave orders that in view of a prospective poor harvest the army magazines should be opened and grain sold at low rates. European editorial opinion was that he would reduce the army and maintain one of those German courts shining with reflected French cultural glitter.

All this was before the death of the emperor, Charles VI. He had produced only daughters, but before his death he spent a great deal of time and effort hurrying about Europe to get everybody to sign a document called the Pragmatic Sanction, guaranteeing the Hapsburg succession to the eldest girl, Maria Theresa, who was married to Francis, titular Duke of Lorraine. Everybody did sign, probably most of them with mental reservations, for there were two women with better hereditary claims, the daughters of Charles' elder brother, Joseph. One was the wife of Charles Albert, Elector of Bavaria, and the Wittelsbach house had never abandoned its hope of becoming imperial; the other was the wife of Augustus, Elector of Saxony and King of Poland, who did not want the whole heritage, but only a part of it. Spain and Sardinia also had claims of a vague sort; and in the background there was always France, ready to promote anything that would keep the empire weak and divided.

These complications added up to the fact that the Hapsburg empire, made up of a collection of possessions under varying rules of inheritance, was surrounded by expanding states, which saw an opportunity to chip off pieces. But the balance of power and the futility of war to attain decisions had become so well established that nobody did anything practical about it until December 16, two months after Charles VI's death.

On that date Friedrich marched across the border of the duchy of Silesia at the head of 30,000 men, claiming it as his own.

Legally the claim was of the flimsiest sort. It was rested on a document of 1537, in which the Duke of Liegnitz and the then Markgraf of Brandenburg mutually agreed that if the male heirs of either line ran out the other should inherit. Actually, as everyone recognized at the time, it was a straight case of expanding state, and, moreover, expansion by war. The effect was a transvaluation of values, not instantaneously, but as soon as Friedrich had demonstrated that something important could be accomplished by such means.

The demonstration was furnished at Mollwitz on 10 April, 1741, on a field blanketed with snow. Friedrich had been masking and besieging fortresses throughout Silesia and his strategy left a great deal to be desired, but he managed to get some 20,000 men to Mollwitz to oppose an approximately equal number of Austrians under Marshal Neipperg. There were several peculiarities about that battle. Although the total forces were nearly equal, the Austrian cavalry outnumbered the Prussian slightly more than two to one, which meant that Austria was similarly deficient in infantry; and the Prussians had sixty field guns against eighteen. King Friedrich, in imitation of Gustavus, took his station with the cavalry of the right wing. In the deployment there was not quite enough room for all the infantry on that wing, so that some of it had to be drawn back at an angle, *en potence;* and the ground was such that this wing was much forward, nearer the enemy.

The battle was opened by the guns; they galled the horse of the Austrian left so sore that these charged without orders and carried the Prussian cavalry right away—including the king, who took no further part in the proceedings that day. But when the Austrians tried to finish things by turning in on the infantary flank, they found themselves up against something much tougher than they could have imagined. Friedrich Wilhelm's foot, drilled to the likeness of machines, did not break, but stood in their ranks and shot the horsemen down. Five times Austria tried against that angle of the Prussian right wing, five times the cavalry went back; at the last charge broken, just as the infantry lines came into contact. The battalions *en potence* swung forward, they overlapped the Austrian left, and with the mechanical Prussians firing five shots with their iron ramrods for every two of their opponents, with the overplus of Prussian artillery cutting holes in the Austrian front, Neipperg's men could not stand it. They melted away into a wintry twilight, their line collapsing from left to right.

Mollwitz decided Silesia for the time being, and also made in Europe a noise almost as loud as Breitenfeld, for it was the defeat of a mighty empire by a power almost as little regarded as Sicily. The required demonstration was furnished; namely, that the military strength of a state is not necessarily proportionate to its size, and that it was still possible to accomplish something by military means. Forthwith, Charles Albert of Bavaria claimed the whole imperial heritage, Augustus of Saxony-Poland claimed part of it, and their alliance was backed by France with force of arms. This made it practically obligatory for England, already locked with France in a struggle for overseas dominion, to support Austria, and the War of the Austrian Succession began.

But these were only the publicly, immediately decisive

events that flowed from Mollwitz. The privately decisive matters, which became the more important in the long run, were that Friedrich, who deserves to rank as a great man, if only because he learned something from every blunder and accident with humility unequaled in history, meditated long and hard over what happened in battle. His infantry had withstood the best cavalry in Europe; very well, infantry trained in the school of Friedrich Wilhelm could turn back any cavalry. His Marshal Schwerin had urged him to leave the field after the first cavalry charge, and then won the battle; very well, he would never leave a battlefield again and Schwerin was in disfavor. Most important of all was the train of accidents that resulted in a heavily weighted Prussian right wing striking the Austrian left at an oblique angle. Friedrich studied military history very hard and had the memory of an elephant; it reminded him of Epaminondas of Thebes, and he never forgot it.

III

If you had spoken to an expanding-state dignitary about anything like consent of the governed or plebiscites, he would have thought you out of your mind; but the million or more Silesians conquered by Friedrich at Mollwitz or in the sieges were well content to be Prussian. They were predominantly Protestant, and the Austrian Catholic officials, while not actually oppressing them, made things difficult. Moreover, Prussian administration was more efficient than Austrian; more precise, with a better sense of essential justice. Friedrich had not only made a conquest, he had secured the reconciliation of the conquered.

But there was one person who would never be reconciled to Prussia in Silesia, and that was Maria Theresa, empress and queen. She regarded Friedrich as the most wicked and dangerous man in Europe, and she said so; a reaction not merely of personal pique, but of an underlying sense that his success threatened the whole system of which she formed a part. This opinion was implemented through a long series of diplomatic and military maneuvers. In 1742, at the urging of her British friends, Maria Theresa signed a peace which turned out to be an armistice. It gave Friedrich his Silesia and allowed her to turn on the Bavarians and French. In 1743 the French were disastrously defeated in Bohemia and on the Rhine; Bavaria fell entirely into Austrian hands and Friedrich re-entered the war as the ally of France, more or less to keep the revived Hapsburg power from being turned on him alone. In 1744 he invaded Bohemia and captured Prague, but got himself maneuvered out by attacks on his communications. In 1745 the Austrians, now with Saxony as an ally, counterinvaded Silesia and were well beaten at Hohenfriedberg and Sohr, so that the peace finally signed only confirmed the verdict of Mollwitz.

In every series of campaigns certain features establish themselves on a semi-permanent basis as part of the frame of reference. In the War of the Austrian Succession one of these features was the operations of the Hungarian irregular light cavalry, pandours, who hung in clouds across the front and flanks of every Austrian army. They were barbarians who used to burn towns, raid camps, and cut the wounded to pieces when they found them, but they made communications a problem for every army opposing the Austrian, and they forced the king to fight for his intelligence of enemy movements. As a result he developed his own cavalry service on lines parallel to those given the infantry by Friedrich Wilhelm—careful training, perfect co-ordination, precision of movement—and reared up a group of remarkable cavalry officers, Ziethen, Seydlitz, Rothenbourg. This was not so much a true light cavalry, like the pandours, but an instrument for combat intelligence and battle purposes, and it was the first of its kind.

The infantry did not need improving, only an intensification of its previous status. Friedrich had discovered that his foot could not only fire twice as fast as its opponents, but also that it could maneuver much faster, and on this he based a new system of minor tactics. The infantry was to fire a platoon volley, advance four paces behind the smoke while reloading for the next volley and, when close enough to the bullet-racked enemy line, fall on with the bayonet.

In major tactics every one of his big battles of the war—Chotusitz, Hohenfriedberg, Sohr—was a deliberate repetition of the accident of Mollwitz. In each Friedrich pushed forward a heavily loaded right wing, took the enemy at the oblique, and rolled up his line. There were variations in the individual case, but this was the basic pattern, and it was noted beyond the borders of Prussia.

I V

This was the military background for the next act. Part of the political background was furnished by the fact that, having obtained what he wanted, Friedrich was opposed to war. "We must get rid of it as a doctor does of a fever." But there was now on the imperial side Wenzel Anton, Graf von Kaunitz, counselor to Maria Theresa. She had been rather reluctantly willing to accept Bavaria in compensation for the loss of Silesia, but the peace that ended the general war gave her neither, and though her husband secured election as emperor, there remained in her an inextinguishable fund of bitterness against the robber who had taken her province.

Wenzel Anton (who exercised by riding in a hall to avoid fresh air and kept dozens of kittens, which he gave away as soon as they became cats) exploited this bitterness, and he exploited it in the name of the balance of power. He argued that the presence of a new great power in north Germany—and with her army and accession of territory, no one could doubt that Prussia had become one—had deprived Austria of her proper place in Europe and freedom of action. If she was ever to recover either, if the French influence which had become so predominant in Europe through Friedrich was ever to be allayed, Prussia must be destroyed. Austria's traditional alliance was with the sea powers, England and Holland; but it was hopeless to expect these Protestant nations to support an enterprise against Protestant Prussia. The true line of Austrian policy was therefore in forming an alliance with France and Russia, the former of whom could be repaid in the Netherlands and Italy, and the latter in East Prussia, none of which lands were really part of the empire.

Thus Kaunitz to the empress. It was not hard to talk Russia into the combination, for Russia was perpetually ambitious and, for quite personal reasons, the Russian Empress Elizabeth had conceived a deep dislike for Friedrich. France and some of the lesser states—Sweden, Saxony—came harder, but Kaunitz was a diplomat of almost uncanny skill, who had a goodie for everybody. Also he was aided by the underlying feeling he used with the empress, more a sensation than a statable idea, that the balance of power had been overthrown by the expanding Prussian state, and there was no security for anyone unless this tendency was ruthlessly punished. France signed; and England promptly allied herself with Friedrich—the sea power to furnish money, the Prussians troops for the protection of King George's Hannover.

These were the roots of the Seven Years' War, the first of the true world wars, itself decisive in more than one way, but whose importance is often hidden beneath the overlays of later struggles.

The actual fighting began in August 1756, when Friedrich invaded Saxony without a declaration of war, occupied Dresden, and shut up the Saxon army in an entrenched camp at Pirna. His espionage service was exceptionally good; he had a man named Menzel in the Saxon chancellery who, incidentally, was discovered and spent the remaining eighteen years of his life in irons in prison growing a fine crop of hair. Friedrich published the documents Menzel furnished as a justification for his aggression against Saxony. Not that it did much good, since the adroit Kaunitz instantly summoned the Diet of the empire and persuaded all the smaller states to send contingents to an imperial army, which made part of the half million men who began to flow in for the demolition of Prussia.

Friedrich's aggression succeeded in its first object. Saxony was knocked out, and what was left of its enlisted troops was offered the choice of serving under Friedrich henceforth or going to prison. Friedrich invaded Bohemia for a second time, won a battle under the walls of Prague, threw a blockade around the town and pressed southward until he encountered an army twice the size of his own under Marshal Leopold Josef Daun at Kolin on June 18, 1757.

This officer was probably the best commander Friedrich ever faced. His plan was the same as that of the usual Austrian leader—draw up and await attack, since he lacked the mobility to compete with the Prussians in maneuver. But he chose his position very well, the left on a high wooded ridge, center running across little knolls and swampy pools, and right resting on another hill, with an oakwood on it and a marshy stream running past. Daun was in three lines instead of the usual two; all across the front, in reeds, woods, and tall grass, he scattered quantities of Croat irregular sharpshooters. Friedrich judged the Austrian left unassailable and angled to his own left to make an oblique attack on that wing, with each of what we would call his brigades to follow on in turn, swinging right-ward when they reached position to sweep out Daun's line. The leading formation, Hülsen's, did break through the ex-treme flank and drove back the first two Austrian lines; but those that followed had to cross Daun's front, with the fire from the Croats coming into their flank. One group halted and faced round to drive off these tormentors by firing a few volleys, and the brigade immediately behind, believing that the battle plan had been changed, also faced round and went into action.

That is, they had begun too soon, and in somewhat the wrong place. This should not have been fatal, for Friedrich had a strong column under Prince Moritz of Dessau coming up to form the link between Hülsen and the groups prema-turely engaged. But Friedrich chose this moment to lose his temper and order Moritz in at once, using a form of words that caused him also to make contact too soon. The conse-quence was that Hülsen was isolated. The Austrians counterattacked him, completely broke up his formation, turned in on the flank of the remainder of the Prussian line, and drove Friedrich from the field with 13,000 lost out of 33,000 men.

The allies now thought they had him and began to shoot columns at him from all directions. The Prince of Hildburghausen with the army of the empire, and Marshal Soubise with the French, together 63,000 strong, drove toward Saxony; 17,000 Swedes landed in Pomerania; 80,000 Russians moved in from their side, and Charles of Lorraine, with his own and Daun's troops, over 100,000, marched on Silesia from the south.

That summer there was fighting all around the circle, with Prussia slowly going down. The Swedes were incompetently led, accomplished nothing against the detachment that faced them, but they still forced Friedrich to make that detachment. The Russians beat a third of their number of Prussians in a battle, but their supply organization broke down, the machine ground to a halt just when it might have taken Berlin, and a large part of the army melted away in desertions. The Austrians, as might be expected, made a war of sieges, but it took 41,000 men to keep them from overrunning everything, and Friedrich could gather barely 22,000 men to meet the incursion of Soubise and Hildburghausen into Saxony.

There was some maneuvering west of the Saale before the two armies faced each other at Rossbach, Friedrich's at the western terminus of a sausage-shaped complex of low eminences, with the Janus and Polzen hills at his rear. The Austrians were moving in Friedrich's strategic rear, and however slowly they advanced, he was required to do something. He was proposing to attack the enemy camp, a rather desperate undertaking in a completely open plain dotted with villages, when on November 5 they saved him the trouble.

Soubise and Hildburghausen had been reading, and from their documents they learned that the King of Prussia won battles by throwing his full strength against the enemy's left flank. Now they decided to outdo him by hurling their whole army quite around his left and rear to take the hills there and cut his communications. They formed with their cavalry in the vanguard, the infantry in three columns behind, and began a wide sweep around the Prussian left through the village of Pettstädt, with their trumpets blowing.

There were only three defects in this plan. One was that the plain was completely open, and Friedrich had an officer on the roof of the highest building in Rossbach who could observe every move; the second was that the tracks were both sandy and muddy, and the march slow; and the third was that the moving column, in some witless idea of gaining surprise, threw out no scouts or cavalry screen. When word was brought to the king that the enemy had swung through Pettstädt, he calmly finished his dinner, then at the double-quick took up an entirely new disposition. Seydlitz, with all the cavalry, was posted out of sight behind the Polzen hill, with a couple of hussars as pickets atop; the artillery on the reverse slope of Janus, only the muzzles projecting; the infantry behind the guns, most of them rightward. The beginning of the movement and the apparent disappearance of the Prussian force were observed from the allied army; they assumed that Friedrich was retreating, and ordered hurry to catch him.

As they sped up, at three-thirty in the afternoon, Seydlitz came over Polzen Hill with 4,000 cavalry, "compact as a wall and with incredible speed." He hit the allied horse vanguard in flank and undeployed; rode right through them, overturned them utterly, and drove what was left from the field. Seydlitz followed till the rout was complete; then sounded a recall and formed in a dip of ground at Tagweben, behind the enemy right rear. The moment their field of fire was cleared the Prussian guns opened on the hapless allied columns, tearing down whole ranks, and as they strove to deploy, Friedrich's infantry came over Janus Hill, all in line and firing like clockwork. As the writhing columns tried to fall back, tried to get their rear battalions in formation, Seydlitz came out of his hollow and charged them from the rear. It was one of the briefest great battles of record; by four-thirty the allied army was a panic-stricken mob, having lost 3,000 killed and wounded,

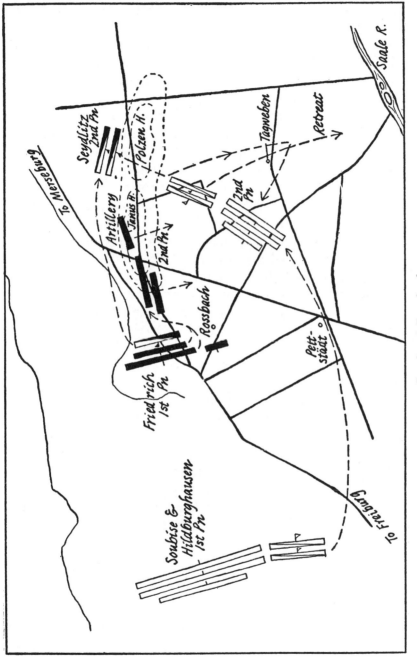

Battle of Rossbach

5,000 prisoners, and sixty-seven guns. The Prussian losses were 541.

Worst of all for the allies, what was left of their army was so broken that it could never be assembled again. Rossbach was decisive in the sense that it took France out of the war against Friedrich; he had no more fighting to do against the French except by deputy in Hannover. He had cracked the circle of enemies; and he had also achieved a focus for German nationalism and assured the support of England. After the battle Parliament increased his subsidy almost tenfold.

But there was still almost too much for any one man and any one army to do. While Friedrich was eliminating the imperial and French armies from the war, Austria had slowly rolled up all of southern Silesia, beaten the Prussian forces there in battle, and taken Breslau and Schweidnitz, with their huge, carefully assembled magazines. Friedrich turned over command of the beaten army to Ziethen, a thick-lipped ugly little man; picked up his forces at Parchwitz, and hurried forward to offer the Austrians battle.

He now had 36,000 men and 167 guns, of which one big battery was superheavy pieces brought from the fortress of Glogau. Prince Charles and Daun had nearly 80,000. The latter had expected winter quarters, but the news of Friedrich's approach drew him out of Breslau into a position in double line. The right was under General Lucchesi, resting on the village of Nippern, behind a wood and some bogs, the center at Leuthen village, the left on Sagschütz. The tips of both wings were somewhat drawn back, and General Nadasti, who commanded the left, covered his position with *abbates*. Forward in the village of Borne was a cavalry detachment under the Saxon General Nostitz, but most of the cavalry were in reserve behind the center.

It may have been that Friedrich had some doubts about the morale of the beaten army Ziethen now commanded; if so, they were dispelled on the freezing dark night of December 4, when he rode through the camp and all the soldiers hailed him with, "Good night, Fritz." He assembled his generals and told

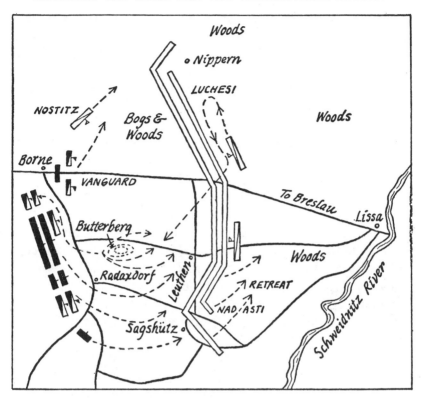

Battle of Leuthen

them that what he intended to do was against all the rules of war, but he was going to beat the enemy "or perish before his batteries," then gave orders for an advance at dawn.

It struck Nostitz and his detachment through a light mist. Ziethen charged the Saxons furiously, front and flank, made most of the men prisoners, and drove the rest in on Lucchesi's wing. There was a halt while the mist burned away and Friedrich surveyed the hostile line. He knew the area well, having maneuvered there frequently; rightward from Borne there was a fold of ground that would conceal movement, and he immediately planned to do what the allies had attempted on him at Rossbach—throw his entire army on the enemy left wing. As a preliminary, the cavalry of the vanguard were put in to follow up the Nostitz wreck in the opposite direction. This feint worked; Lucchesi, who like Soubise and Hildburghausen, knew of Friedrich's penchant for flank attacks, imagined he was about to receive a heavy one and appealed for reinforcement. Prince Charles sent him the reserve cavalry from the center and some of that from the left.

But the storm died down there, and to Charles and Daun, standing near the center, it seemed that this must have been a flurry to cover the retreat of inferior force, for Friedrich's army had passed out of sight. "The Prussians are packing off," remarked Daun. "Don't disturb them!" There is no record of his further conversation down to the moment a little after noon, when Friedrich's head of column poked its nose from behind the fold of ground and the whole array of horse, foot, and artillery did a left wheel and came rolling down on Nadasti's flank at an angle of maybe 75 degrees.

Nadasti, a reasonably good battle captain, charged in at once with what cavalry he had, and succeeded in throwing Ziethen back, but came up against infantry behind, and was badly broken. One can picture the hurry, confusion, and shouting as his whole wing, taken in enfilade by the Prussian volleys, went to pieces. But there were so many of these Austrians that they began to build up a defense around the mills and ditches of Leuthen, and especially its churchyard, which had stone walls. Prince Charles fed in battalions as fast as he could draw them from any point whatever; in places the Austrians were twenty ranks deep, and the fighting was very furious. The new line was almost at right angles to the old and badly bunched at the center, but still a line, heavily manned and pretty solid.

Friedrich had to put in his last infantry reserves, and even so was held. But he got his superheavy guns onto the rise that had concealed his first movement, they enfiladed the new Austrian right wing and it began to go. At this juncture Lucchesi reached the spot from his former station. He saw that the Prussian infantry left was bare and ordered a charge. But Friedrich had foreseen exactly this. The cavalry of his own left wing, under General Driesen, was concealed behind the heavy battery, and as Lucchesi came forward at the trot, he was charged front, flank, and rear, all at once. It was like Seydlitz's charge at Rossbach; Lucchesi himself was killed and his men scattered as though by some kind of human explosion, while Driesen wheeled in on the Austrian infantry flank and rear around Leuthen. Under the December twilight what was left of them were running.

V

Leuthen was the extremest example of Friedrich's oblique-order attack and also his most destructive victory. He lost 6,000 men, but the Austrians lost 10,000 in killed and wounded, besides 21,000 prisoners, and two weeks later Breslau surrendered, with 17,000 more. The effect was crushing, but it was not decisive, except locally and in a temporary manner, as to who should hold Silesia until the next campaign.

Austria was unable to get another army into the field until late in the following summer, but in the meanwhile the Russians, who had thus far been trying to assure themselves of the possession of East Prussia, pushed a column into the home counties as far as Frankfurt an der Oder, and Friedrich had to go fight it. He beat it at Zorndorf in a slaughtering battle in August, but by October the Austrians were on foot again, now under Daun, and at Hochkirch they beat the king.

They beat him in the way one would have least expected against so acute a commander, by leaving their watch fires burning while they made a night march and surprised him at dawn. That is, they caught him being careless. And in the following summer, 1759, a combined Austro-Russian army inflicted a paralyzing defeat on Friedrich at Kunersdorf, one in which he lost over 20,000 men—again through his own fault, for he sent his troops into action after two days without sleep, up a steep hill in broiling sun. "Will not some curst bullet strike me?" he cried afterward, and, "I believe everything is lost," he wrote.

But he had done better than he thought and everything was not lost; neither after Hochkirch nor Kunersdorf did his enemies make any follow-up. They could not; they were too disorganized in terms of lost officers, mingling of regiments, breakdown of supply. They had no such solid basis as the Prussian army; when any of them lost a battle, that particular campaign was over, when they won, it merely went on.

A realization that their sole real asset was numerical penetrated allied minds in 1761, and they adopted a plan of campaign to make numbers count. There were to be three columns, one operating through Saxony under Daun, one through Silesia under the Austrian General Loudon, and a Russian column through Poland. Each was to deplete Friedrich's resources by eating up the towns. He could maintain only one army large enough to deal with any of the three; whenever he turned against one, the others would keep moving stolidly toward Berlin.

This plan was modified by events. The Russians came slowly through northern Silesia. Daun also was slow, and when Friedrich turned against Loudon, the Austrian marshal thought he saw an opportunity to repeat the surprise of Hochkirch. He swung around toward the northwest of Friedrich's position at Liegnitz while Loudon marched by a circuit to close him in from the northeast, with the Russians under General Czernicheff pushing up from behind.

But Daun did some careful scouting from the heights above Liegnitz, which not only slowed his march, but attracted Friedrich's attention. On the night of August 14, 1761, the king turned the Austrians' trick right around on them, leaving a group of campfires burning and making a fast march along the road Loudon was to occupy. Loudon reached it cross country in the morning; was received by musketry fire, and being already too deeply committed to get out without battle, fought one that cost him 10,000 men and eighty-one guns. Daun reached Friedrich's former camp only just in time to see the column of smoke rising over the defeat to the north; his pursuit was not a success.

As for the Russians, Friedrich supplied a peasant with a message addressed to his brother, Prince Henri, who was facing them: "Austrians totally defeated today, now for the Russians. Do what we agreed upon." The peasant was to let himself be taken by Czernicheff and give up the paper to save his own life. There is something peculiarly pleasing about these devices of Friedrich the king; they are so firmly rooted in understanding of the men he was dealing with and so unexpected. This one worked precisely according to prescription. Czernicheff, beset by nameless terrors, marched right away from the area of action and the Russians were next heard of besieging Kolberg on the Baltic coast, which would be more use to them than another victory over Friedrich, anyway.

Two of the three attacking columns were thus eliminated, for Loudon had been so badly knocked about as to be out of it. Friedrich spent some weeks maneuvering in Silesia, but was recalled by the news that Berlin had been taken. He rushed north with his army; it turned out not to be a serious occupation, but a handful of Cossack raiders and a wing of Austrian light cavalry, who dispersed at once. But it was now evident that something would have to be done about the Daun column, which had taken nearly all Saxony and established itself at Torgau, 64,000 strong. By whittling down garrisons Friedrich managed to assemble 45,000 men, and approached the place at the end of October.

It was not Daun's intention to fight, except as he had done at Kolin, long ago, on terms that would force the king to attack under every disadvantage. He chose his position very well for the purpose, along a certain Siptitz Hill that runs roughly westward from Torgau. Its southern edge was covered by a deep, wide, muddy brook, the Röhrgraben, a good military obstacle; all around the height were sparse forests of pine, growing out of sand. The lines were so good that Prince Henri had previously held them against this same Daun with much inferior forces, and the Austrians now had no less than 400 guns.

Friedrich moved up toward the installation from the south.

It struck him at once that the place was unduly cramped for as many men as Austria had and offered poor opportunities for mounting a counterattack, and he determined to assault it from front and rear simultaneously. Ziethen, with nearly half the army, would take the southern side, across the brook; Friedrich himself would swing by a circuit through the woods in three columns, the outermost one of cavalry.

The king marched fairly early; it was nearly two in the afternoon when Friedrich, leading the innermost column, reached the edge of the woods, just in time to hear the boom-boom of guns from the southward. To him this meant that Ziethen was already engaged; there was no sign yet of his second column or his third, but he immediately hurled 6,000 grenadiers straight at the Austrian position.

The trouble with any converging-column arrangement is that it is impossible for the commander of one wing to know precisely what is happening to the other. Ziethen's engagement, in fact, was with some outposts of light troops, who had a few guns south of the Röhrgraben. These retired slowly eastward, in the Torgau direction, drawing the Prussians out of their true line of advance during hours, which caused Friedrich later to rate Ziethen roundly for his stupidity. But this was no help at the moment to the 6,000 grenadiers, who were met by the fire of nearly all the 400 Austrian cannon. Friedrich himself said he never saw anything like it; the Prussian artillery was smashed before it had a chance to load, the grenadiers were cut to pieces. Enough of them survived to reach the Austrian line for some deadly close work, but Daun brought up infantry, drove them out, and even tried a counterattack, which came to considerable grief in a heavy shower of rain. At the end of it not 600 of the 6,000 were left; it was three o'clock and the attack had failed.

Shortly later Friedrich's second column arrived; there was a pause for reorganization, and at about three-thirty it and the remnants of the first attack went forward again. This was the hardest fighting of the day, along the northwest portion of Daun's line; the Prussian infantry got in among the guns, and there was hot hand-to-hand work on Siptitz Hill, but Daun summoned his reserves from every quarter and after a long struggle drove the Prussians back again, the king himself wounded.

Not until four-thirty, with the sun down, was the coming of the cavalry, which had gone astray in the woods. Friedrich dauntlessly organized a third attack through gathering dark and smoke, cavalry and infantry together. This storm was at least a partial success: four whole regiments of Austrians were taken, with many of the guns; Daun's whole left wing was reduced to a jelly-like consistency, and there was confusion all through his lines, but the thing could not be carried forward. Friedrich gave orders to bivouac on the field and try again next day if possible; Daun, himself wounded, sent off a courier of victory that caused all the windows of Vienna to be illuminated.

But at six, under a night grown wet and very cold, there was a sudden glare of red in the sky southward. It was Ziethen, free at last of his preoccupation with the Austrian light forces, trying to close the sound of the king's guns, and he had taken the village of Siptitz, south of the Röhrgraben, and set the place afire. His men could not cross the stream through the blazing village, but an intelligent officer named Möllendorf found a bridge beyond it, and Ziethen poured through, up a saddle at the southwest angle of the ridge and down on the Austrians, his drums beating the Prussian march, muskets all in line blazing across the dark.

There is a famous picture of Friedrich, wrapped in his cloak, chin on chest and stick across his knees, waiting in deepest discouragement for the dawn at Torgau. The dawn came before the day, it is said, in the person of Ziethen himself, to tell the king he had won after all, the Austrians were driven through Torgau with a loss of 10,000 men and most of their guns. Daun's army was a wreck and the allied campaign with it.

VI

There was some bickering and some maneuvering the next year, with Friedrich on the defensive and neither Austrians nor Russians daring to besiege or attack; and early in 1762 the Tsarina Elizabeth died and Tsar Peter, her successor, made peace with Friedrich and sent a Russian corps to *his* help, while France could no longer pay subsidies to Austria, and Maria Theresa had to reduce her army to 20,000 men.

It may be put that Torgau ended it. It did not decide the war—probably the one battle that went furthest in that direction was Rossbach—but it decided that Austria could not carry the war to a successful conclusion. And in so doing it established in north Germany a new state and a new type of state, with a standing army, a centralized administration, officials who looked to the building of dams, canals, roads, bridges, internal communications, and who promoted agriculture and internal colonization. Before Friedrich the Great's death he had settled 200,000 people on previously unoccupied lands; and the efficiency of his administration was such that the other nations of Europe were forced to imitate him if they wished to remain level in the complex game of the balance of power. "It appears," he said once, "that God has created me, pack horses, Doric columns, and us kings generally to carry the burdens of the world in order that others may enjoy its fruits." His ideal of peace was to have the government help every citizen; his ideal of war was not to have the civil population know that a war was going on. His seizure of Silesia was doubtless anything but moral; but when he made it stick on the field of battle, he forced the rest of Europe into a new sense of the responsibility of government.

12. Quebec, Quiberon, America

I

The fog cleared in the afternoon to show the uneasy chop normal off Cape Race at this season, and British ships all around. M. de Hocquart, Captain of His Most Christian Majesty's ship *Alcide*, 64, knew enough about his English to suspect their intent, and made sail, but the necessity of tacking brought some of them always nearer, and at about eleven the next morning a two-decker was close aboard to windward and a heavier ship hauling up fast. A red flag snapped to the two-decker's gaff, the ammunition signal; Hocquart lifted his speaking trumpet and shouted across the swell, "Are we at peace or war?"

"*La paix, la paix,*" came the reply.

"Who is your admiral?" asked Hocquart.

"The Right Honorable Edward Boscawen."

"I know him well; he is a friend of mine."

"What is your name?"

Before Hocquart could reply there was a crash as every gun in the two-decker's broadside went off, and a moment later another from the big ship. *Alcide* made what defense she could, but the odds were too heavy and De Hocquart presently hauled down his flag, with eighty-seven dead aboard. Off to the west two other British were taking the transport *Lys*.

The date was June 8, 1755, and though the British captain

had been technically right when he called out the word of peace, De Hocquart was as well aware as he that matters must sooner or later come to the cannon. For the two French ships were stragglers from a fleet sent to reinforce Quebec, and in London there sat that strange, grumpy, gouty, and furiously able man, William Pitt, who had, as it were, an oath registered in heaven to put a period to the colonial ambitions of France. At the moment he was not actually in power, but it was his spirit that had driven England on, and no administration could draw back from the line he had taken.

The conflict was one of mutually incompatible ambitions, of opposed dynamisms seeking the same object. The strategic lines were extremely simple; France held the St. Lawrence and at least the mouth of the Mississippi, and was embarked on an effort to link them together in a cordon that should forever limit the British colonies to the eastern watershed of the Appalachians. The British were embarked on an effort to break that cordon, and the prize was a continent. (There is a curious parallel to the continuing French effort to pierce the Hapsburg cordon in Europe.) The taking of the *Alcide* was only accidentally the first tactical incident. At that very hour Edward Braddock was marching to his death on the Monongahela, Baron Dieskau was preparing to lead a motley column against the English establishment on the lakes that flow into the Richelieu, and the western frontier of the colonies was all one blaze of war.

It became formal in May 1756, and one of the leading protagonists stepped on the scene, Louis Joseph, Marquis de Montcalm, newly appointed commander of the French land forces in Canada. He was a small man, very vehement, ardent and uncompromising, who gestured rapidly as he talked; had fought with credit in Bohemia and Italy; was the complete antithesis of the man with whom he was supposed to work, the Sieur de Vaudreuil, Governor of Canada. The latter was a colonial, who regarded all officers from metropolitan France with dislike and suspicion, and most especially those belonging to the army, for Canada was under the naval establishment, and the troops

Vaudreuil commanded were technically marines. There were nearly 3,000 of these; Montcalm had about as many army regulars; and in addition there were available the Canadian militia, never called to the colors to the extent of more than 1,100 men, very good forest fighters and trackers, very poor in any stand-up battle.

On paper this was a singularly small defensive force for so important an area, and in fact it was, but the knowledge and attitudes of the time have to be taken into account. Nobody knew that the struggle for a continent was engaged; in fact, nobody knew there was a continent there. The general supposition was that the land ended somewhere not far beyond the Mississippi. To French policy makers Canada was another island like St. Domingue or Martinique; like them, a part of naval strategy and a matter for naval administration. Moreover, the current government of France was predominantly non-naval or even anti-naval. It was actually in the hands of the king's mistress, Mme. de Pompadour; she grudged every livre spent on a ship, and was interested chiefly in helping out her good friend, Maria Theresa of Austria, in putting down that evil man, Friedrich of Prussia, and in securing French predominance in western Germany. The number of French colonists in Canada was not above 80,000 as against the million in the British colonies.

However, there were countervailing factors which made the French military position much stronger than either population figures or home government indifference would indicate. One of these was that by their very organization the British colonies were unable to deliver in the field anything like the force their numbers appeared to indicate, but more important were the Indians. From the beginning British policy was to drive them out, dispossess them in favor of more British colonists; from the beginning French policy was to make friends with them, intermarry, and use them as bird dogs for the fur trade. It was no accident that the series of border conflicts was called the French *and Indian* Wars. Montcalm thought these allies were dirty villains, but recruited them all the way from

Lake Superior and the Des Moines River, and they were a ponderable force.

For the expanding frontier was by its nature open, and even the secondary line of defense could not always be made good against raids. Armaments that might easily have dominated Canada were pinned down to tasks of security, and military operations were directly affected. All the lines of communication between the French colonies and the British lay through woods, and while these woods were full of pro-French Indians, Montcalm could move easily and with a minimum of transport, his opponents only slowly and with difficulty, making heavy detachments for flank guards and outposts.

Although Montcalm got his training in the plains warfare of Europe, he turned out to be just the man to use the dirty villains, and one of those driving characters who overcome all obstacles besides. By August of 1756 he had an expedition landing at Oswego, one of the anchors of the English border, and when the colonial scouts arrived three days later, they found nothing but staved-in rum casks and burned buildings. Lake Ontario was wholly French, and middle New York open to Indian raids.

The following summer Montcalm launched an expedition against Fort William Henry, at the head of Lake George. There were promptly revealed some of the other factors balancing the over-all French deficiency in numbers. Everything went wrong on the English side. The commander in America was Lord Loudon, "whom a child might outwit or terrify with a popgun"; the colonial governors failed to call out the militia; the commandant at nearby Fort Edward had not men enough to attempt a relief, and in addition was a coward. Fort William Henry fell and a good many of the prisoners were massacred by the Indians among scenes that provided James Fenimore Cooper with his best novel.

The whole frontier quivered with terror.

This victory solidified the reputation of France and Montcalm among the Indians. But he could not control these unruly cattle, and when they all went home after the fall of Fort William Henry, he had to postpone the business of gradually eating up the British colonies for another year. And during that year there came to power in England not merely the spirit of William Pitt, but William Pitt in person, a man with a quite different set of ideas than his predecessors.

Their general theory may be described as one that the colonies could best be defended in Hannover; Pitt's that the essential struggle was naval and colonial, in which decision would be found on the banks of the St. Lawrence. A vast tide of energy and effort flowed from the man; he not only worked like a devil unchained himself, he demanded that everyone else do so. He recklessly promoted men without regard to their political connections and removed them with the same insouciance. The incompetent Loudon was replaced by General James Abercrombie; to help him Pitt jumped Colonel Jeffrey Amherst, who had done well in Germany, at one step to a major general, and for 1758 there were planned three expeditions to break the French cordon in North America.

One was against Fort Duquesne, in the Pennsylvania colony; Montcalm was too weak to hold it and the other places too, and it succeeded. One was against Louisbourg, the fortress France had built at immense expense on Cape Breton Island to hold the mouths of the St. Lawrence. It was under Amherst and the Admiral Boscawen who had begun the war, and after a long and incidented siege, it succeeded, too. The French lost not only their stronghold, but five battleships in the harbor. The third was led by Abercrombie against Ticonderoga; Abercrombie tried a frontal assault and failed, with the loss of 2,000 men.

I I

Two successes out of three was still a respectable result. The grip of the French cordon had been sensibly loosened, and some of the glitter rubbed off Montcalm. But Pitt had now advanced to a wider concept than merely breaking the cordon;

for 1759 he meant the destruction of France in America. Abercrombie was replaced by Amherst, who had demonstrated that he was a capable, if not very rapidly moving, soldier; he was to head the colonial forces against Ticonderoga and then down the Richelieu. But the main blow would be amphibious, delivered straight across the Atlantic against the heart of the enemy installations at Quebec. A fleet of twenty ships of the line was assigned, under Admiral Charles Saunders, some of them already on station out of Halifax under Rear Admiral Philip Durell, who was to blockade the St. Lawrence till the blow fell. The land forces were about 9,000 men under Brigadier James Wolfe.

He was a curious character, only thirty-two years old at the time, with a long, upturned nose, an amateur of the arts, as ardent as Montcalm himself. Wolfe had been the inspiration of the siege of Louisbourg and wrote angry letters home when it was not at once followed up by a push on Quebec. The Duke of Newcastle, technically head of the administration, was horrified at the disregard of precedent and seniorities shown by Wolfe's appointment, and told George II the man was mad —to which His Majesty, who did not want a certain wit on occasions, replied, "Mad, is he? Then I hope he will bite some others of my generals." All Wolfe's subordinate commanders were under thirty; "it was a campaign of boys." Wolfe and Saunders sailed from Spithead on February 17 to meet the rest at Louisbourg; the attack was to be a surprise.

But it was not a surprise. Durell had failed in his blockade, and before the British fleet reached Louisbourg, a French squadron was at Quebec with reinforcements and, what was much more important, a letter from Amherst, intercepted at sea, which gave the whole plan away. Montcalm was horribly hampered by the highhanded and incompetent Vaudreuil, and surrounded by such peculations that he could write, "Everybody appears to be in a hurry to make his fortune before the colony is lost." But the intercepted letter gave him a chance. He secured from Vaudreuil "provisional authority" to command all forces. Instead of concentrating toward Lake

Champlain and the Richelieu, as the British expected, he sent only a detachment there, while himself preparing to hold Quebec with his main body, now something over 10,000 men, including the militia.

The northern bank of the St. Lawrence is very high and precipitous; from the falls of the Montmorenci to above Cap Rouge he covered the whole range with a line of redoubts and intrenchments, most especially between the Montmorenci and St. Charles, which falls in at Quebec town. Floating batteries were established at the mouth of the St. Charles. The French ships were sent far upstream; their gunners came down to help man the batteries.

Landings below the Montmorenci, Montcalm did not fear; he could stop any advance at that stream. Landings above he feared still less; it would be impossible for ships in sufficient number to work up the river in support, and if they did and the men landed, they would be in just the kind of forest country most suitable for the French type of operation. There were some fireships and gunboats; Quebec held 106 guns, and was fairly immune to direct attack. By October fogs and gales would drive from the St. Lawrence any English ships that dared to enter it, and when they went, the troops must go too, for the essence of amphibious operation is that it must depend upon seaborne supply.

Considering that Montcalm had inferior numbers and many of his troops could not be trusted in offensive operations in the open, it was an excellent plan. The leading defect was that there were not enough men to held all the entrenchments solidly.

III

On June 9 the fleet entered the river, as bold a stroke as ever struck, for battleships had never before come that far through the fogs, rocks, and eddies that haunt the St. Lawrence. On the twenty-sixth Wolfe landed with his chief engineer on the Île d'Orléans to survey his problem, with a great many of the troops following. His plan had been to land on the north bank at Beauport, then push across the St. Charles into the rear of the fortress, but a glance told him this would never do; not only did guns on the heights rake the projected landing area, but it was composed of extensive mud flats with more batteries behind them. Two nights later the French tried their fireships, loaded not only with combustibles, but rockets, bombs, and grenades. The night was pitch-dark, but all the French got out of it was a rather spectacular show of fireworks; the ships were set alight too soon, and those that offered any real danger were grappled and towed ashore by imperturbable British sailors.

At Point Lévis, opposite the city, the river is less than a mile wide; Wolfe opened batteries here to bombard the town under cover of one of his brigades, Monckton's. With the other two he effected a landing east of the mouth of the Montmorenci, for an effort to bruise a passage across that stream. Quebec is terraced from the heights down to the water; the Point Lévis batteries soon tore to bits everything that did not burn, sending the inhabitants into huts in the fields, and under cover of the gunfire *Sutherland*, 50, and a frigate were shot through into the upper river. Montcalm was forced to detach 600 men to Cap Rouge in case the ships were there to cover a landing. The over-all French position could be regarded as unstable; food was short in their lines, except with Vaudreuil and the higher civil officers, who were living on pen-fattened chickens, while the rest had enough to do to get gruel. Many of the Canadian militia were deserting; they were perfectly willing to turn out for a raid, but not to take the discipline of a campaign.

It has been a matter of speculation why Montcalm did not sift his light forces through the woods on the upper Montmorenci for an attack on Wolfe's left flank, where "a Canadian in the woods is worth three disciplined soldiers." One answer is that a couple of nights after Monckton's brigade was established around the Point Lévis batteries some of the Canadians

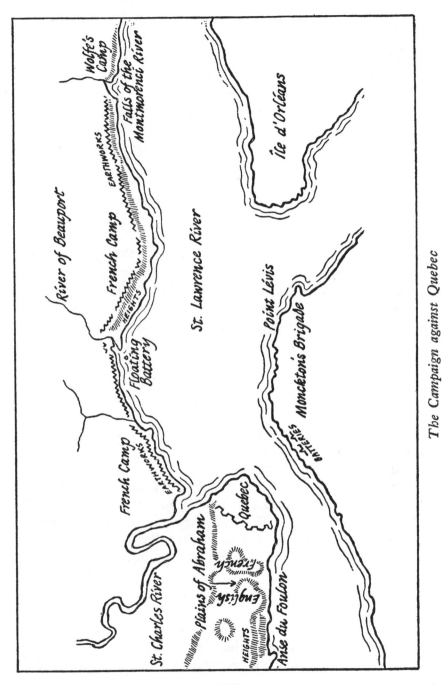

The Campaign against Quebec

tried this trick for themselves against him, landing west of the point for a night attack; they panicked and accomplished nothing. The other and more complete answer is that Montcalm was content to play a waiting game. Wolfe had declared that he would have Quebec if he had to stay till the end of November, but with every tick of the clock the date of storms and ice drew nearer, and no real progress, while the whole back country was filled with Indians, who picked off sentries and patrols.

The English were thus compelled by meteorology to break through somewhere, reach the high ground within the entrenched camp, and on July 31, Wolfe tried, just west of the mouth of the Montmorenci. At the base of the heights there the French had built a series of redoubts. Wolfe conceived that if he attacked them frontally, the French would come down from their summits and he would have the open battle he wanted. On the morning in question ships were moved in to give the place a long naval bombardment; when the tide went out to leave wide flats, the attack was launched from boats.

It was a dismal failure. The grenadier regiment in the lead made its rush without orders and without waiting for the rest; the French calmly abandoned their redoubts at the base of the cliff and shot the English down from the fortifications above, which were so high that they had not been at all damaged by the artillery preparation. Wolfe lost 450 men, most of them scalped by Montcalm's Indians, and he would have lost more but for a torrential storm of rain that wet all the powder. In the French lines "everybody thought the campaign as good as ended." It was true that Amherst had entered the strategic situation by forcing the French out of Ticonderoga, but he was still a long way from the St. Lawrence, and Montcalm sent his best officer, the Chevalier de Lévis, to Montreal for the defense.

There is a hiatus in the story at this point. Wolfe had a new plan for getting onto the high ground behind the city, but he told it to no one who recorded it, and in the meanwhile sent one of his brigadiers on a raid upstream to the Richelieu River and himself embarked on a perfectly deliberate campaign of burning out the countryside to force more desertions among the Canadians. He was despondent; in August he fell ill and lay incommunicado for a week.

In the meanwhile the British, always active on water, had been sending light ships and flat-bottomed boats through into the upper river, and Rear Admiral Charles Holmes, Saunders' second, had gone up to command them. This did not pass unnoticed in Montcalm's camp; he assigned Louis Antoine de Bougainville, later one of the most famous of navigators and a senator under Napoleon, to watch this force with 1,500 men. Holmes amused himself and drove Bougainville to distraction by keeping his motley squadron together and drifting with the tide, up and down, up and down, firing from time to time and occasionally embarking troops, compelling the French to march back and forth to keep pace with him. As soon as Wolfe was out of bed, the admiral and the brigadiers urged him to try a night landing between Cap Rouge and Quebec. He caught up the idea, and on August 31 ordered the abandonment of the lines on the Montmorenci, everything to be concentrated at Point Lévis. Wolfe himself reconnoitered the chosen spot, a cove named Anse du Foulon. The difficulty would be to hit it in the dark and with the tide running.

Montcalm had not missed the troop movement. He wrote to Bougainville, urging him not to let Holmes get out of sight, but on the afternoon of September 11, Saunders moved his big ships up toward Beauport and began firing and lowering boats. News of this apparent landing attempt affected Bougainville; when the tide began to ebb at two in the morning, he let his weary men rest instead of following Holmes down. Wolfe's expedition silently joined the drifters, twenty-four men in the leading boat, with Wolfe himself, who in a low tone recited Gray's *Elegy Written in a Country Churchyard* as far as, "The paths of glory lead but to the grave," and said, "Gentlemen, I would rather have written those lines than take Quebec tomorrow."

Twice they were hailed by French sentries, but each time a French-speaking Highlander gave the right word. The tide carried them a quarter of a mile beyond the destined landing spot, but this turned out to be good luck, for the only path where they could have mounted from the cove had a barricade and a post on it. The twenty-four pulled themselves up the steep by tree roots and bushes, and took the post in the rear with a few shots and a shout; the path was cleared and the English began to climb, while boats passed and repassed to bring those who had not been embarked at first. By daybreak slightly less than 5,000 English had formed line of battle across the bush-starred Plains of Abraham, west of the city.

Within it, and especially in the high command, there was a good deal of confusion. Montcalm, concentrated opposite Saunders at Beauport, began marching for the plain as soon as he heard of the landing, but Vaudreuil insisted that this was a feint, and would not release the men holding the lines from Beauport to the Montmorenci; nor would the Governor of Quebec give up the twenty-five field guns Montcalm wanted. Still, with what he had, about 5,000 men, approximately the same number as the English, he advanced to the attack, which was now his only resource—for if he so much as waited for Bougainville or Vaudreuil, the English would dig themselves in, and they were between him and his sources of supply.

Montcalm advanced, then, with five regular regiments, three guns, and his front covered by a cloud of Canadian militia, who lay among the bushes as sharpshooters. They did some damage, including wounding Wolfe in the wrist; but he made his own men lie down and not rise until the French came cheering within 130 yards, somewhat disordered by passing their skirmishers. Wolfe had trained those men himself, on lines learned from Prussian Friedrich, and he had them under close control. They stood there while the French came marching and firing forward until the enemy were within forty yards, then let go with a volley so co-ordinated that it sounded like a single cannon shot, advanced four paces and fired again, and then again. Within fifteen minutes it was all over, the French flying in disorganized groups, with many killed and Montcalm mortally wounded.

So was Wolfe; two bullets went through him and he lived just long enough to hear the French were running and remark, "Now God be praised, I die in peace." Quebec surrendered five days later, and though the decapitated snake writhed for a while, the French dominion of Canada was ended.

I V

But it was not exclusively ended on the Plains of Abraham. It was not because in December 1758 there had come to the head of affairs in Paris, Louis Étienne, Duc de Choiseul, who had the double advantage of being a great favorite of La Pompadour (he was so much of a gallant that even Casanova admired his amorous exploits), and a man of both drive and ideas, quite different from the lazy pedants who had preceded him. When he reached power, Rossbach had been fought, Canada was going, and India almost gone. Choiseul realized that it was eleven o'clock and only by the boldest throw could the game be won. He prepared the boldest of possible throws—the invasion of England by 50,000 men.

By at least one historian the plan has been called crackbrained; within terms of the means available it was nothing of the kind, and Napoleon Bonaparte, who was assuredly not crackbrained about military matters, adopted an inferior version of it in 1805. Troops were collected in the Austrian Netherlands, Normandy, and at Vannes in the Morbihan. Thurot, the gallant sea raider, was to take a squadron out of Dunkirk, sail north; this would draw off some British strength. Admiral de la Clue, with the Toulon battle fleet, was to pass Gibraltar and sail for the Morbihan. As soon as weather permitted, he would be joined by Admiral Conflans with the Brest fleet; they would sail together, covering a convoy for the south of England, then pick up the troops in the Netherlands and land them on the Clyde. Sentiment for the exiled house of Stuart was still a force in Scotland, and it was less than fifteen years since Bonnie Prince Charlie almost won. The over-all objective was not so much conquest as the attainment of a bargaining position for the peace table.

It was true that both De la Clue and Conflans were watched by superior British squadrons. But they were watched from a distance, the squadrons were not much superior, and the conditions under which sailing ships operated must be remembered. A heavy easterly gale, not unusual in the Mediterranean, would drive De la Clue's ships through without possibility of interruption. A strong westerly gale, common in the English Channel, would hold British blockaders to their usual base in Torbay, while the configuration of Brest was such that Conflans could work out against it, using the same wind to reach the Morbihan. Once there, once the transports were picked up, Conflans was to fight his way through, no matter what happened to his warships. In 1747, Commodore L'Étenduère lost six of his fleet of nine of the line to an English fleet of fourteen, but assured the safety of a convoy of 252.

The De la Clue part of the plan worked very ill. In August, when he tried to run Gibraltar, some of his ships missed orders and put into Cadiz, while the rest were caught off Lagos by that Boscawen who began the war and almost totally destroyed. This neither prevented nor discouraged the operation of Conflans, who had twenty-one line-of-battle ships against the twenty-five of Sir Edward Hawke, who was charged with watching him from Torbay.

This Hawke was a tall, strong, broad-faced man, who has left an impress on history by his actions, but almost none by his personality. He had indulged in the singularly dangerous pursuit of speaking against Pitt in Parliament, and the great minister did not like him, but George II did, and made the retention of the admiral in command a personal obstinacy. Since Hawke's war record was outstanding—it was he who had captured L'Étenduère's six ships in '47—Pitt was forced to give way.

The ships of 1759 were not copper-bottomed, and readily became so foul that they lost speed. It was thus the general custom of the age to fit out a squadron for a specific operation, then bring it home and clean house before starting again. Hawke was well informed on French intentions, and very early realized that this normal procedure would be playing the game exactly as the French wanted it. Even if he caught up with their fleet in the Channel, even if he beat them, it would not be hard for them to slip the convoy through—as the convoy of 1747 had got away. The only valid answer was to prevent the convoy from sailing under cover of Conflans' fleet, and the only sure method of accomplishing this was to keep fleet and convoy from assembling at the same place.

Hawke therefore kept the main body of his fleet in Torbay, where they could be quickly careened for bottom-scraping; off the exits to Brest he stationed four or five heavy ships, and off those to the Morbihan he placed Commodore Robert Duff, with four fifty-gun ships, two-deckers midway between a line-of-battle ship and a cruising frigate, both squadrons having instructions to whistle him up at once if the enemy began to move. It was an outrageously expensive procedure to keep so many ships at sea, and Hawke heard himself denounced in Parliament for wasting the king's guineas. A gale drove one battleship on the rocks off Brest; another became so leaky that she had to be retired from service; two of the fifties fouled up and had to go home; but all that summer and early fall the guard was maintained, and when he was criticized, Hawke replied only, "By the grace of God, we will give a good account of them."

There must, nevertheless, have been a considerable degree of strain and short temper in the Channel fleet that summer, while Wolfe toiled with the problem of reaching the heights behind Quebec. It would be sometime in October that news of the Canadian success came, and the windows were illuminated, but it had grown to November 15 and the season of autumnal gales when the light frigate *Gibraltar*, 24, came bursting into Torbay with the news that Conflans was out,

21 of the line, twenty-four leagues off Belle Isle, steering southeast.

The wear of service had cut Hawke's battle line to twenty-three, many of them smaller and less well found than those of the French, although he had four of the giant three-deckers that were like floating fortresses in a sea fight. He sailed at once for the Morbihan, sure that they were thither bound. The wind came in south by east and held Hawke westward for days; it was the nineteenth before the breeze turned fair and he could crack on sail.

Next morning early a frigate firing signal guns ran in on Commodore Duff, at anchor inside Belle-Île-sur-Quiberon with his fifties. It took him no time at all to realize that the French were on him in force; he ordered cables cut and made all sail for the south passage out, but the enemy came down so fast that his dullest sailer was almost under the guns of their leader, a little west and south of the island and the entrance to Quiberon Bay, when they suddenly abandoned the chase. Duff held his course and was out of it; the French bore before the wind for the bay, where there are numerous rocks, shoals, and intricate passages well known to them, but unknown to Hawke's ships, which they had seen in pursuit. All morning long the west wind freshened toward gale, with frequent heavy squalls.

This westerly stormwind pushed the heavy British ships along fast, rolling their lower-deck ports under and sending men staggering by life lines across the decks. They held on, Hawke flying signals from his flag that each ship should engage as it came up, not waiting to form. At two in the afternoon *Warspite*, 74, and *Devonshire*, 70, were in range of the rear ships of the rather confused French and opened fire; a little later seven other British ships were in action. Shot from one of them partly dismasted the French *Formidable*, 80, and each Briton fired into her as she passed; at four she struck, with 200 dead, including an admiral.

It was now falling dusk on a wild tossing sea among the shoals and rocks, British and French mixed in a mad combat against weather and each other. Hawke had no pilots but, reasoning that the enemy would serve him that purpose if he stayed close aboard them, held right on into night and storm. The French *Thesée*, 74, foundered when she opened her lower-deck ports against the English *Torbay*, 74, and 780 men went down with her; *Torbay* almost shared her fate. The French *Superbe*, 70, sank likewise; *Héros*, 74, struck just as she crashed on the rocks; *Soleil Royal*, 80, Conflans' flag, was so surrounded that she had to be beached and burned.

In the last of light, in the rising seas, Hawke made the signal to anchor. Morning showed that he had lost two of his battleships, wrecked on the inhospitable shores of Quiberon. But seven of the French twenty-one were gone and the remainder were driven up the little rivers, Charente and Vilaine in two groups, aground, unable to unite, all damaged, never to emerge.

V

Quiberon Bay was the crowning achievement of that *annus mirabilis*, 1759, when, as Macaulay says, "Men woke up to ask each other what new victory there was that morning." It was the justification of William Pitt, who made England an empire. The importance of the fall of Quebec and the ejection of the French from Canada needs no comment; the subsequent history of the American continent is its product. But it does need to be noticed that Quebec without Quiberon Bay decided nothing. In the previous war the New England colonists had valiantly taken Louisbourg, but it had to be given back at the peace table to recoup British losses elsewhere. Quiberon Bay made permanent the result of Quebec; decided that Choiseul would never attain his bargaining position. He would live to be an old man and somewhat recover France from her doldrums; but after Quiberon Bay the question was no longer which nation should dominate the seas and the empires, but how far England could be restrained.

Something else of the greatest importance had happened. Sir Edward Hawke had invented blockade; the idea not of meeting an enemy's overseas expedition with another expedition, but of closely watching his ports at whatever cost, whatever strain, and clobbering him as soon as he came out. The concept of blockade and such questions as enemy goods in neutral bottoms go back at least as far as Hugo Grotius, but no one ever before had thought of a blockade that prevented all ingress and egress of whatever nature; in technical terms, a close blockade. Boscawen watched De la Clue's Toulon fleet from the distance of Gibraltar, but Hawke watched Conflans from the distance of his doorstep. And this idea of close blockade was to dominate the story of war on the waters of the world for at least 200 years.

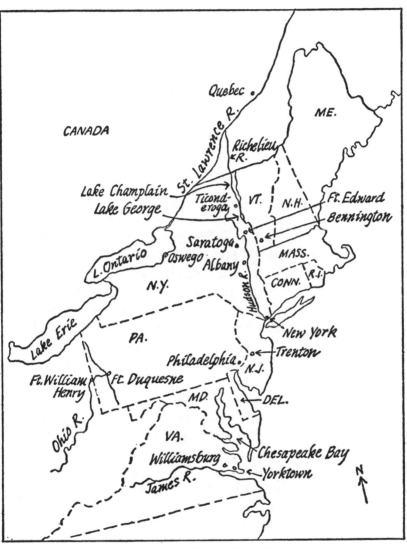

The Northern Colonies

245

13. Why the American Revolution Succeeded

I

When the troubles began in Boston in 1775, the Secretary of State for Colonies was Lord George Germain. He was a gay dog of an Anglo-Irishman, haughty and domineering, who had taken up the army as a career, and remained in it till the Battle of Minden in 1759, where he commanded the cavalry. When a charge of English foot broke the French line, Prince Ferdinand of Brunswick, who led the Anglo-Prussian forces, three times ordered Lord George to charge to turn the victory into a rout, and he three times refused to do anything of the kind. For this he was pronounced "unfit to serve His Majesty in any military capacity whatsoever." The order was entered in every regimental book, and a black cloak of cowardice was draped round him—somewhat unjustly, for there seems to have been nothing wrong with his personal courage, he had fought in battles before and been wounded. He was simply in a bad mood that day.

Still, he was cordially hated in the army, and in addition he knew nothing of its problems in the woods and vast reaches of America, nor cared to know. Whatever energies, whatever abilities he possessed flowed into politics, society, and the gaming table. It was vitally important to cry banco! And to maintain that balance among the forces represented by the king, the city, and the ruling gentry, on whom the administration rested. The conduct of affairs in the revolting colonies fell into his department, but he began by regarding it as a kind of police operation against mere rioters, and neglected everything he could possibly put aside.

There was thus no mobilization of energies into great thunderclouds that discharged destructive bolts of lightning, as with Pitt, no call to the national spirit. A good half of the soldiers for the police operation were rented from the minor princes of Germany. Lord George never learned that General Sir William Howe, his leading commander in America, had suffered a psychic block as the result of the Battle of Bunker Hill. That celebrated action was correctly counted a British victory, but Howe lost nearly half the storming party that participated, and he never again dared attack American sharpshooters in position. At Long Island, Harlem Heights, White Plains, he might easily have destroyed the Continental forces opposed to him by bold assault; instead he maneuvered, and George Washington's little army survived to slash back hard at Trenton.

To Germain, Trenton was merely an "unhappy affair." He had little concept of the kind of man Howe was up against, and in February 1777 there came to him Gentleman Johnny Burgoyne, dramatist and commander in Canada, with a plan of campaign for the year. It called for Burgoyne himself to move up the Richelieu and the lakes, Howe up the Hudson to meet him at Albany, splitting the colonies, and holding the split open by a chain of blockhouses. The conquest of New England would then be easy; it would be isolated from the sources of supply in the west. While this was being discussed, there arrived a letter from Howe with his own plan; he proposed a column from Rhode Island to reduce Boston, a second to ascend the Hudson to Albany and there meet a force under Burgoyne, and a third to deal with Washington. For this plan he needed a reinforcement of 15,000 men.

It was characteristic of Germain that he accepted both plans except for the single detail of the 15,000 additional men for Howe; that would throw his budget out of gear. He could spare only 2,900 reinforcements; and this would probably not be enough for Howe to carry out the full three-column plan. Therefore he dictated a letter to Howe saying that the Rhode Island-Boston project could be conveniently dropped, and of the other two, the Hudson River move was the more vital. If Sir William did not feel himself strong enough both to make it and to follow Washington, the Hudson should have precedence, a positive order. It was also characteristic of Germain that he was in a hurry to make a previous appointment for a country weekend, and went off without signing the letter. It was never sent.

Howe thus learned nothing but that he would not have all the men he needed for his three-pronged offensive. On the ground and in fighting contact with the Americans, he had quite other opinions than those entertained by Germain in London, and one of them was that General George Washington was the most dangerous man on the Continent. If Howe could not execute all his projects, that of dealing with Washington must have first place. Besides, he had an American prisoner, a general named Charles Lee, who assured him that the middle colonies of Maryland and Pennsylvania would return to their allegiance if the royal standard were raised there. Howe therefore cut the Hudson expedition to a raid, boarded his transports, and sailed for the Chesapeake.

The details of the campaigns that followed are often confused, but the main lines are simple. Howe beat Washington in battles at Brandywine and Germantown, and took the colonial capital of Philadelphia, a stroke that would have been decisive. Here it was decisive also, but in the contrary sense. For while Howe was beating Washington but failing to destroy his army, thanks to that psychic block, something perfectly dreadful happened to Burgoyne. A diversionary force that was to join him by way of Oswego failed to deliver, and was driven back with loss. Burgoyne took Ticonderoga and reached the head of the lakes without too much difficulty, but then found himself involved in a campaign in dense woods against woodsmen who every hour increased in number and in the intensity of their attacks. Their rifles were slow-loading, but very accurate and of a range far superior to the British muskets; and volley fire was no use against them.

Burgoyne's supply and transport problems became practically insoluble. It took him twenty days to cover less than that number of miles to the upper waters of the Hudson. When he sent a strong foraging party into the valley of Vermont in quest of povision, it was practically wiped out at Bennington in a battle that enormously raised American morale. By the date when the British reached the neighborhood of Saratoga, the Americans were much stronger than they. The Continental Congress, which had about as much military sense as Lord George Germain, placcd a "fussy old midwife" named Horatio Gates in command of its army, but they gave him the fiery Benedict Arnold as a second. When Burgoyne attempted to solve his difficulties by a battle on September 19, 1777, he was thrown back with the loss of a third of those engaged. Word drifted in that the Americans had taken the posts in the British rear and communications with Canada were cut. Burgoyne tried another battle on October 7, and was surrounded when Arnold led a charge that broke his flank. His whole army surrendered ten days later.

The fighting at Saratoga was decisive in one sense. It not only marked the failure of the Burgoyne plan and the loss of his army, it also decided the French court that the clandestine aid being given to the revolters should be converted into active alliance with a nation which had established its independence. Troops and fleets would help the colonists, and the theater of conflict was swung round the zones from the West Indies to the coasts of India. One must never forget India.

I I

The French navy that entered the war in 1778 was a far different organism from the one whose failures caused the loss of Canada. Choiseul started it; he wanted a fleet that could meet the British on equal terms, and he spared neither trouble nor expense in setting it up. A naval academy was organized, the calibers of guns were standardized, and a corps of seamen gunners established along the lines of the land artillery service; the civil housekeeping officers lost their former control of the movement of ships; new regulations prescribed that admirals, captains, lieutenants, and midshipmen should dine with each other; the best engineers of France were sought out to improve the breed of ships, and did so to an astonishing degree.

The French are peculiarly ready to take fire when a powder train of this sort is ignited, and something like a wave of national enthusiasm for the navy swept over the country on the heels of Choiseul's reforms. The estates of the various provinces donated ships, the city of Paris a huge three-decker, and the associated tax farmers a whole squadron—which, incidentally, they could very well afford. By 1770, Choiseul felt his new navy was strong enough in spirit and force for a war of revenge against perfidious Albion, and he wanted to try it; Louis XV disagreed, and the minister was dismissed.

But he had been given twelve years in which to build the new structure, and it stayed built. Moreover, when Louis XVI came to the throne in 1774, France had a head of state who was really interested in naval matters; and when she entered the war on the side of the colonies in 1778, there were not Continental commitments to distract her attention. It should, however, be noted that the French idea of naval strategy was by no means the same as the English. In French thinking the basic purpose of naval war was not to be an end in itself, to assure control of the sea for purposes of commerce and everything else that could be moved by water, but to support definite, specific operations ashore. This has been condemned by Mahan as false strategy, and he was doubtless right, but in the hands of such ships and seamen as those of the French naval revival, it could lead to results.

The first of these results followed close on the heels of the alliance. Comte d'Estaing sailed for the Chesapeake with twelve battleships, and forced Admiral Lord Howe, brother of the general, to take his smaller fleet out of there. That meant the army would have to go too, and Sir Henry Clinton, who had succeeded Howe in command of it, made his way back to New York, not without a battle at Monmouth, which ended in no decision, in spite of some heroic swearing by Washington at generals who were not executing his orders in the way he wished.

The British now held only New York and Newport, Rhode Island, and if they were to make any progress in putting down the rebellion, needed a new plan of campaign. Germain conceived one for transporting troops by sea and working up through the weak southern colonies to Virginia and Maryland. There were three basic assumptions behind this plan. One of them was correct: that the French were more interested in the rich West Indies islands than in supporting American operations on the Continent, and would send fleets thither only for brief campaigns, while the British could afford to maintain a permanent American squadron and move troops along the coast at will. The second assumption seemed to be correct: that there were no solid American forces in the South, and regular British troops could deal with anything there. The third assumption was never to be tested: that if Georgia, the Carolinas, and Virginia were overrun, "all America to the south of the Susquehanna would return to its allegiance" —a phrase which had an invincible attraction for Lord George Germain.

In accordance with the first two assumptions a force was dispatched to Savannah, which took that place with ease, practically subdued Georgia, defeated General Benjamin Lincoln without difficulty, and marched into South Carolina. Considerable maneuvering followed, but the essential feature of the campaign was that on May 12, 1780, Clinton himself took Charleston with Lincoln's whole army of over 5,000 men, the worst disaster suffered by the American arms, and a fair set-off for Saratoga.

During the previous fall D'Estaing and his fleet had briefly reappeared from the West Indies, and been roundly beaten in an attempt to recover Savannah. Atop this, General Lord Cornwallis, whom Clinton left at Charleston with 8,500 men while himself returning to New York, marched into the Carolina upcountry. At Camden on August 16, 1780, he virtually destroyed the American southern army, which had been placed in charge of Old Midwife Gates. Sumter, the partisan leader, was surprised in his camp at night and his force wiped out, too. British posts held down the whole countryside, and Germain's campaign was a thing of genius.

But the British now found themselves in the presence of a master spirit. To replace Gates, Washington sent to the South his quartermaster general, Nathanael Greene, a Rhode Island Quaker who had been ejected from that society over his interest in military affairs. At Charlotte, where he assumed command of the wreckage from Camden, he found 1,482 men, with equipment for 800; but he was a man who could perfectly analyze a situation and who knew exactly what he wanted to do. His advantage lay in the converse of Germain's third assumption: that wherever any small core of regular American fighting men appeared enough local assistance would rally round to make things impossible for lesser British detachments, while a major British force could continually be dogged.

The campaign that followed was the classic example of how small war should be waged. There was an incident at King's Mountain, where a group of backwoodsmen swarmed out of nowhere to annihilate a force of 1,100 British and Tory militia, and another at Cowpens, where Daniel Morgan of the famous Rifles nearly wiped out another British detachment. But the real weight of the campaign was in the marchings and maneuvers all through North Carolina, in which Cornwallis tried to pin the elusive Greene down for a fight, and in the work of the partisans in the background. It lasted all winter long. On March 15, 1781, Greene at last gave the British leader his battle at Guilford Court House. Cornwallis won it, but when it was over he found himself with no supplies, more wounded than he had wagons for, and a distance of 260 miles between him and his base. He left the wounded behind and, in order not to give an appearance of throwing up the campaign, made for the coast at Wilmington, which was still in North Carolina, under the wing of the Royal Navy.

Greene marched off to try his bag of tricks on the forces Cornwallis had left to hold South Carolina.

III

The importance of Greene's campaign lay in its effect on the mind of Lord George Germain. There was nobody to tell him that the remainder of the British army in the South was being subjected to a process of extraordinary and destructive erosion. In his view resistance in the Carolinas was practically over. Cornwallis had marched where he pleased through the states and won a battle over a force that could not now be much more than a disorderly rabble. Throughout the criss-cross of correspondence among the minister, Clinton at New York, and Cornwallis at Wilmington, with all sorts of sug-gestions and changes of detail, there runs the fixed idea that the South being now in strong hands, the British purpose should be the establishment of a solid naval station on the Chesapeake as a prelude to the reduction of Virginia. For that matter, Cornwallis himself did not regard the Carolina cam-paign as a failure, only thought that "until Virginia is in a manner subdued, our hold of the Carolines must be difficult."

He marched to Virginia then, in the spring of 1781, picked up a detachment that had been operating in the area and, with reinforcements from Clinton bringing him up to over 7,000 men, began to look for his naval base. Opposing him was Wash-ington's friend, the young French volunteer, the Marquis de Lafayette, with strength so limited he dared not risk battle. Cornwallis tried to bring him to book and failed, as with Greene; and was engaged in an intricate correspondence which contained continual changes of plan, with the letters taking from six weeks to three months to reach destination. The essential feature that emerges is that, after investigating the

Hampton Roads-Portsmouth area, Cornwallis decided that the facing positions of York and Gloucester on the river of the former name would be the best station for ships of the line, and in the closing days of July established himself there and fortified.

It was about the same date that there arrived in Washington's camp outside New York a reinforcement of four strong regiments of French infantry with artillery and engineers under the Comte de Rochambeau. He came overland from Narragansett Bay, having been convoyed in by Admiral de Barras, with eight of the line; and Barras bore word that the main French battle fleet, twenty-five to twenty-nine ships, would operate on the American coast sometime that summer, the fleet of De Grasse. There was a British fleet in the West Indies, with which De Grasse had engaged in an indecisive action. But now he not only had the more ships, the British must see their huge summer sugar convoy to England; he was confident that he could slip their vigilance.

Since the beginning of the war Washington had not ceased to insist on how British control of the sea permitted them to strike where they pleased. "The amazing advantage the Enemy derive from their ships and the command of the Water keeps us in a state of constant perplexity," he wrote as early as 1777. Nor since the forging of the French alliance had he relaxed his efforts to obtain the help of a fleet. "A constant naval superiority on these coasts is the object most interesting," he set down in 1780; but Versailles was interested in the sugar islands. Now, however, De Grasse was coming; the point was where should he come?

Washington's own taste had been for an attack on New York, and he submitted the idea to De Grasse as one of three possible plans; but the more he considered it, the less good it looked. The British had eight ships of the line under Admiral Thomas Graves on the New York station. It would be very difficult for even a largely superior squadron to beat into New York Harbor against these and the forts. On the land side Clinton now commanded 16,000 men; even with the three additional regiments De Grasse was bringing, Washington would have less, and would be faced with the problem of crossing a river against fortified lines.

There is one thing to be remembered about George Washington. He has received so much admiration for constancy and character that he is in danger of becoming a plaster saint. General Howe was perfectly right in regarding Washington as one of the deadliest military opponents in history. His instrument was often weak or flawed; but there runs a consistent strain through every campaign in which he was involved, every battle he ever fought. He made no effort to maneuver the enemy out of position, but sought to destroy, to annihilate; and under the conditions of the American Revolution this only had to be achieved once or twice. After Saratoga the British hold on the northern colonies was gone; and since calculation showed there was no very good chance of wiping out Clinton in New York, the decision was for annihilation on the shore of the Chesapeake. De Grasse replied that he would leave the Indies for that area on August 13 with ships and troops; would remain until October 15, when he must return. He would be perfectly at Washington's disposition until the latter date.

The commander of the British fleet in the West Indies was Sir George Brydges Rodney, and he was one of the greatest seamen in English history, but that summer he made a serious miscalculation. Only July 5 one of his frigates reported that De Grasse had been seen coming out of Port Royal Bay of Martinique with twenty-seven sail of the line and 200 merchantmen, the latter being the French summer sugar convoy. There had been some intelligence that they intended summer operations off the North American coast, and to Rodney it was perfectly clear what this movement meant. De Grasse was going to send a detachment to co-operate with the Barras squadron at Newport against New York, while with his main body he covered the passage of the sugar convoy. To provide against this Rodney detached fourteen sail of the line under Sir Samuel Hood, his best fighting junior, to join Graves at

New York; this would give the latter twenty-two battleships, superior to anything the French could assemble. Rodney himself sailed for home with his own sugar ships. He did not know that the French merchantmen had gone back to Port Royal to wait until November, or that De Grasse with his whole fleet had slipped up the Old Bahama Channel, north of Cuba, south of the Bahamas; nobody used that route. He did know that Hood detested Graves, but as he hated the man himself and you cannot always choose your bedfellows in the service, this did not seem important.

On August 21, Washington and Rochambeau crossed the Hudson at King's Ferry and began one of the great marches of history, leaving only General Heath with 2,500 men opposite Clinton's 16,000. Twenty-eight days later, through a country of unmetaled roads or no roads at all, with utterly inadequate transport, Washington had covered 400 miles and was on the Chesapeake, joining Lafayette and the troops just brought by De Grasse, and closing his jaws around Cornwallis.

When Hood reached New York and anchored outside Sandy Hook, Clinton was still uncertain that Washington and Rochambeau were after Cornwallis, but he had reliable intelligence that Barras had sailed from Newport with eight battleships, eighteen transports, and a siege train. This situation might be dangerous to Cornwallis. Graves came out with the only five ships he had in sailing condition and the combined squadron of nineteen made for the Chesapeake. Toward noon on September 5, Graves raised the entrance of Cape Henry and found De Grasse coming out to meet him, with twenty-four battleships in line.

I V

Admiral Thomas Graves was certainly not the type of man who would invent gunpowder, and he had nineteen ships against the French twenty-four, but he was a British sea dog and he knew precisely what to do in the presence of an enemy who was threatening something vital—fight a battle. He had the weather gauge, the wind on his side, as the French formed a rather straggling line east from Cape Henry, and he bore down on them from the northward. The signals he hung out from his flagship *London*, 98, midway along the line were for "Close action" and "Line ahead at half a cable."

The fatal words were "Line ahead." There existed in the British navy of that date something called the Fighting Instructions; in the most decided terms they prescribed that when a line of battle had been formed every ship must follow directly in the wake of her next ahead, and in 1756 an admiral had been court-martialed and shot on his own quarterdeck (*"pour encourager les autres,"* according to Voltaire) for having violated this absolute rule. When the British leader, *Shrewsbury*, 74, bore down to engage *Pluton*, 74, at the head of the French line, the rest of the British ships followed her, head to tail, instead of making directly for their French opposite numbers. The consequence was that the British line came in on the French at an acute angle; the leading ships were hotly engaged, those at the centers of the lines very little, and those at the rear not at all.

The commander of the British rear division was that fighting admiral, Sir Sam Hood, and it is possible that he could have fallen on the French rear, which was in some disorder. But he was not going to break that signaled line ahead in violation of the Fighting Instructions and expose himself to a court-martial in order to get that fool of a Graves out of his difficulties; and he did not. When dark closed over a mild swell, the French seamen gunners at the head of the line had done so well that the British had three to two of their losses and several ships badly battered, one of them so much that she had to be burned a couple of days later.

Next morning Graves tried to close again, but the French kept away across the entrance to the bay and the English battle cripples fell behind. If Graves had had an anchorage where he could make repairs, it might have been different, but it was De Grasse who held the anchorage. Three days more they maneuvered, the French now in possession of the weather gauge, thereby permitted to fight only under conditions most favorable to themselves. On September 10, Graves discovered that Barras had joined De Grasse, who now had thirty-two battleships to his eighteen. These odds were too heavy even for a British sea dog; Graves called a council of war to make sure that nobody was going to criticize him seriously, then went back to New York to repair damages.

On September 27, Washington's army was assembled at Williamsburg, 16,645 strong, nearly half French. Cornwallis has been criticized by some military men for not trying to move past him, but this ignores the question of where he was to go in a completely hostile countryside, opposed by the fast-marching Washington and French regular troops quite equal to his own in numbers and training, plus some excellent French cavalry. Formal siege operations were opened on September 29; the parallels were vigorously pushed forward. Alexander Hamilton led a brilliant night assault which took two redoubts, and the 24- and 18-pounder guns brought by Barras pounded everything in sight. On the morning of October 17, four years to the day after Burgoyne's surrender, a red-clad drummer mounted the Yorktown ramparts to beat the chamade, and two days later Cornwallis and all his men marched out and gave up their arms.

V

The effects of the success of the American Revolution have received sufficient comment to need no more here. It was not only the establishment of the new nation, but also the cradle of the French Revolution. Yorktown decided a revolution ideological as well as physical. But although Lord North threw up his hands and cried, "Oh, my God, it is all over!" when he heard the news from the Chesapeake, there were still points at which the decision could be proved in reversible error, and if Frederick the Great's was the first of the world wars, that of the American Revolution was the second.

An England victorious elsewhere in the circuit of the zones could easily have built up Clinton's forces in New York to attack point, or enabled those in Charleston to undertake something else than the quiet defense to which Greene's operations presently reduced them—even an England under the administration of Lord North and George Germain.

The reasons why England did not make or even attempt an American rally have been hidden behind the hurricane of events that blew along the corridors of that second world war. Spain and Holland joined France in August 1781, and while Washington was debating the question of New York or Yorktown, there was a bloody dingdong battle between British and Dutch off Dogger Bank which resulted in a draw. The West Indies fighting reached a climax six months after Yorktown in a battle off the Saintes. There Rodney took five French ships of the line, including the three-decker flagship *Ville de Paris*, 110, with De Grasse in person aboard, and so prevented an attack on Jamaica, but by no means drove the French from the islands. A year after Yorktown the Spaniards attacked Gibraltar with ten huge floating batteries and the help of French troops, but were foiled amid immense thunders, with the loss of all the battering ships and 1,500 men.

The sum may be stated as defensive success and negative decision. Some of the sugar islands changed hands and changed back again, but the allies lacked the power and skill to drive home a real offensive against the widespread British possessions, while the British lacked resources to take the offensive themselves. Thus the situation remained fairly static down to the late months of 1782, by which date the most serious of the allied attacks had been beaten off, and it became possible for Britain to consider a counterstroke in America or elsewhere. At this point there arrived a piece of news that made it imperative to abandon the American venture.

VI

One of the results of the Seven Years' War had been the ejection of the French from India, except for a few "factories," with which communication was maintained through Mauritius, then called the Île de France. A smallish French squadron operated from there to India under M. le Comte d'Orves; it was opposed by a British force of approximately equal weight under another of the sea dogs, Sir Edward Hughes. The British were having infinite trouble with Hyder Ali, Sultan of Mysore, the only prince of India who ever beat them in battle, but D'Orves refused to amalgamate the wars, or in any way to help the sultan; was himself beaten in the manner of the Seven Years' War, and retreated to the Île de France, while the British snapped up French outposts.

Early in 1781, with things going pretty well for them (Cornwallis had "conquered" the Carolinas and was getting ready to move into Virginia), the British decided to improve their own communications with India by seizing the Dutch colony at the Cape of Good Hope. A squadron was fitted out under Commodore George Johnstone, one seventy-four-gun battleship, a sixty-four, and three of the fifty-gun intermediates so useful in colonial service, with numerous transports, supply ships, and frigates. After operations at Good Hope were completed, Johnstone was to move on and join Hughes, giving him a sharp superiority over D'Orves.

The existence and purpose of this force were not hidden from the French cabinet; on the same day that De Grasse sailed from the West Indies on the voyage that was to take him to Yorktown, there left Brest a squadron of two seventy-fours and three sixty-fours, with a convoy of troops to reinforce Good Hope. Its commander was a newly made rear admiral, Pierre André de Suffren, who had done some service with the Knights of Malta and there acquired the title of bailiff, *bailli*. In the Seven Years' War he had been twice a prisoner of the English and learned to dislike their arrogance; an enormously fat man, ardent to the point of violence, filled with a desire that was almost an obsession to restore the honor of the French marine.

On the voyage down the latitudes one of his ships ran short of water. He determined to put in at Porto Praya in the Cape Verdes to fill up, and on the morning of April 16, Suffren arrived off the harbor and found it full of English ships, Johnstone's ships. These were neutral waters, but it was in neutral waters that he had been taken prisoner by the British in '57; he hung out the red flag for battle from his flagship, *Héros*, 74, and drove right in, neglecting the British transports, anchoring in the middle of their warships, and opening both broadsides. Unfortunately his own captains were as much surprised as the British. *Annibal*, 74, was not completely cleared for action; she came in boldly enough, but fired ineffectively. The captain of *Artésien*, 64, was killed by a musket ball at the first fire; she did not do much in the confusion but carry a big Indiaman out. The other French ships only marched through the roadstead, firing as they went, and after an hour or so of it Suffren pulled out. At the mouth of the bay *Annibal's* masts went over the side.

Yet it was anything but a setback, anything but a failure. Suffren had sent his convoy on ahead; now he got *Annibal* in tow, formed line of battle in the offing, and waited for Johnstone to come out. In the afternoon Johnstone did; the masts of one of his own ships promptly crashed down from the damage they had received, most of the others had been more or less hurt, the French were down to leeward on a rising sea. If he followed them he might not be able to get back to his convoy at all and would be involved in a night battle against superior forces. He turned back, therefore, and wrote a report speaking of the anguish of his cruel situation.

As might be expected, the French were in full possession when he reached the Cape; Johnstone sent three of his battleships on to reinforce Hughes off India and turned back with the rest and the convoy, expedition aborted. Suffren had to stay at the Cape for two months while arrangements were made and his damaged *Annibal* repaired; he reached Île de France in October, just after Yorktown surrendered. It was now the hurricane season, and the year had rounded before he and D'Orves sailed for the Coromandel, or east coast of India, to take some French troops to the help of Mysore. This was probably Suffren's urging, for D'Orves would hardly have thought of it for himself. On the way two things happened: Suffren's *Héros* fell in with and took one of the British fifties, and D'Orves died.

The Bailli de Suffren was now commander of the fleet. His objective was to land the troops at Mysore, then, if possible, take Trincomalee, which controlled Ceylon. Trincomalee had an excellent harbor, though, like all others except those in English hands, devoid of supplies that would support a fleet. On the morning of February 17, 1782, French and British sighted each other off Sadras, the French covering their convoy northeast of the British; twelve French, nine British battleships, but the latter heavier ones. The wind was mildly off the land from the French side. Hughes began to form his line heading eastward downwind, so that when the usual afternoon sea breeze rose he would be in a good position to attack from windward, in the best tradition of British sea dogs. Before he got things completely in order he was startled by a sight no

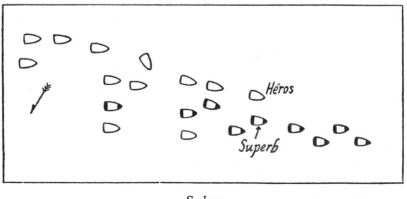

Sadras

one had seen for a hundred years, the French coming down like a herd of charging elephants to attack him.

Suffren himself led the line; he ran along the port side of the British formation as far as number 4 from the head, Hughes' own flagship, *Superb*, 74, hove back and began to fire at pistol shot. The three British ships ahead were now downwind and would have an exceedingly difficult time tacking back to get into action, which was precisely what Suffren intended. He also intended that the rear ships of his fleet should run up the leeward side of the British rear and so double on them; but in the French service, as in the British, there were Fighting Instructions that prohibited breaking the line of battle. Most of Suffren's captains either did not believe he meant what he said when he gave the doubling order, or were so bound by custom that they could not bring themselves to obey. Only one ship really doubled, and she was a fifty, though toward the end another made it; but even so the British had enough to do. When the sea breeze did rise after two hours of fighting, the British had two ships badly damaged.

Suffren saw he could accomplish nothing more that day, landed his troops, and ran south to cruise off Trincomalee, writing furious letters to the Ministry of Marine about the conduct of his captains. "I should have destroyed the English squadron," and, "My heart is wrung by the most general defection." Hughes had to go to Madras to refit; there he was joined by two fresh battleships and sailed for Ceylon, reasonably worried about Trincomalee and anxious to throw supplies into the place. On April 11, about fifty miles northeast of the port and off Provédien, the French ships were in sight again to the windward. In spite of the fact that the two new ships gave him slightly more than the French strength, Hughes was not especially anxious to fight a battle; he had another mission. But the experience of Sadras had taught him that if this fat Frenchman wanted a fight he was going to have it, and when dawn of April 12 showed the leading French overtaking his rear ships, he formed line and waited.

This time Suffren forbore anything fancy; he simply ordered

all ships to form on a line of bearing, which is at an angle to the line of approach, and bore down for a ship-to-ship attack, with his one extra, *Brillant*, 64, to double on the British rear ship. But the sailing qualities of the ships were very unequal and a line of bearing is very hard to maintain. Moreover, as the ships at the head of the French line came under fire, they luffed up and replied, and so, ultimately, did those at the tail of the line. Led by Suffren himself, the French at the center pressed in, and seeing a gap, so did *Brillant*. The consequence was a French line in a curve, concave toward the British, with ship after ship crowding toward the center until there were no less than five French ships engaged in the closest kind of action with three British, and there ensued one of the bloodiest naval combats in history, at a range where it was almost impossible to miss.

The British *Monmouth*, 64, was beaten out of line with a third of her crew casualties, her mizzen- and mainmasts down; Hughes' flagship lost nearly as many, and so did *Monarca*, 68. *Héros* was much disabled in rigging, but stayed in tight action till three-forty in the afternoon, when Hughes wore away out of the fight and there was too much damage and laxity among Suffren's ships for him to follow. Even a direct order by signal for *Artésien* to take possession of the completely disabled *Monmouth* was not obeyed.

For two days the fleets lay at anchor making repairs, and temporarily it looked like a draw. But in reality Hughes had been so hard hit his fleet operations were paralyzed. He had to put into Trincomalee and stay for six weeks, while Suffren ramped all around Ceylon, mopping up British convoys of supplies and transports and seeing his own through. The sultan took the British stronghold of Cuddalore; there was no fleet to cover it.

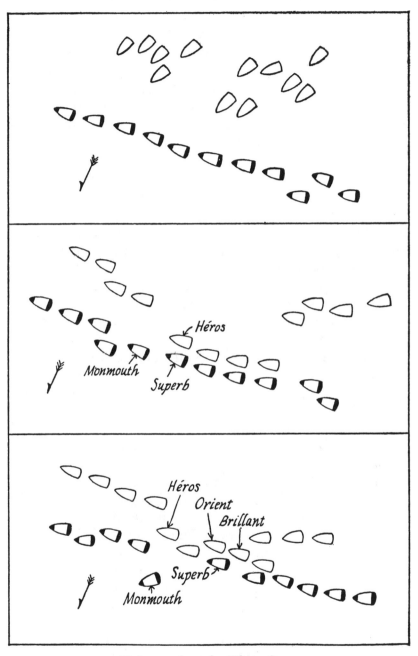

Trincomalee; the Three Stages

VII

This was the news that, reaching Europe late in the summer —when the British got their hands free enough from other entanglements to afford an expedition somewhere—determined that the expedition should be to India, not America. It was the news that the French had a new kind of sea captain, one who always attacked, who fought terribly, who beat British sea dogs at their own game, and who had a high sense of strategy. They did not know of Suffren's difficulties with his captains; or that he was so short of spare spars that he had to take the masts out of his frigates; or that he was so short of men he had to embark land artillerists.

They did not know his troubles, but they knew their own. The fact that there were three more of those desperate combats later, with the bailiff always victorious in spite of increasing British reinforcements, has made historians and readers alike regard the fighting off the Coromandel Coast as a flowing, continuous campaign—which, indeed, it was. But the continuous campaign has drawn attention away from the vital factor, which was the time factor, the date the news reached Europe that the British fleet off India was faced by an antagonist who thought in terms of destroying it, and who possessed the will, the skill, and probably the means.

For on that fleet the British empire in India depended. The American colonies were about as good as gone, and under the conditions of the time, they were as much of a liability as an asset anyway, but the empire of India was the great cash crop of Britain. It not only furnished the widows and orphans and retired colonels with their pensions, it provided much of the means by which the British government itself existed. Let America go, then, but for heaven's sake, save India—this was the unspoken principle, the line on which Whitehall was forced to act. It is not too much to say that if De Grasse made it possible for the British to be ejected from the thirteen colonies the Bailiff of Malta, halfway around the world, was the man who kept them from recovering.

When word of the peace came, Suffren's return to France was like a triumphal progress down an avenue of cheering; even the British captains came aboard at Table Bay to honor the man who had fought them so hard. In 1788 a dispute arose between England and France, and Suffren was appointed to command a great fleet fitting out at Brest. He died on his way thither and the dispute was settled. One can only wonder.

14. Trafalgar, Austerlitz, and the Fall and Rise of Empire

I

It is important to view events in their contemporary context.

In October 1797, General Bonaparte, officially "captain of artillery in temporary command of the Army of Italy," signed a peace with the Austrians and returned to Paris to face an unstable government of five Directors, who were practically without popular support and intensely jealous of their all too popular army commanders. The war on the Continent was over; the only remaining hostility to the Revolution was the absolutely implacable hatred of England. General Bonaparte was appointed to command an army for the invasion of the seagirt isle—with an implied threat that non-acceptance of the commission would result in his being returned to his captaincy.

In February 1798 he accordingly inspected the coast of Normandy and the flotilla of small craft gathered there, and reported in a sense unfavorable to the enterprise. Of his own capacity and that of the French soldiers he entertained no doubt; the difficulty was to bring them into contact with the British. To do that would require the extremely dangerous enterprise of stealing a crossing during one of the long winter nights in the face of heavy English ships that could easily scatter the whole flotilla. He advised, however, that the preparations be kept up to fix British attention at the Channel and confirm them in that withdrawal of fleets from the Mediterranean to which an otherwise profitless French naval expedition to Ireland in 1796 had so effectively contributed. Bonaparte himself would be glad to undertake an expedition through that now friendly Mediterranean against Egypt, a practically independent suzerainty of Turkey, a storehouse of immense resources, and the gateway to the East, "where there are a hundred million men." The East, even more importantly, from where the English drew those resources which enabled them to dominate the financial exchanges and markets of Europe.

The English war against the French Revolution was primarily a war about those markets, though it had been prettied up with a good many phrases about lawlessness let loose in the world, insatiable ambition, and the murder of divinely anointed kings. In the address which was the younger Mr. Pitt's proclamation of that war, the only physical act charged against the French government was the opening of the Scheldt to make Antwerp a port of entry, a place closed to commerce by treaty ever since the southern Netherlands became Austrian. The Anglo-French section of the wars of the Revolution was thus a separate struggle, a continuation under new terms of the sempiternal English effort to exclude all others from the business of delivering both home and colonial products to the Continent—in fine, to establish and maintain a commercial monopoly, a monopoly of gold. Down to the date when General Bonaparte was sent to the Channel, this war had followed the normal course, with English fleets beating the French on the seas, English expeditions snapping up colonial possessions, English money supporting the armies that attacked France on land, and English bankers profiting hugely on the whole transaction through an involved structure of international debt.

This was the system that Bonaparte proposed to break in on by giving France a new colonial area, peculiarly her own. If this new colonial empire did not emancipate her from the need for overseas products, it at least would provide a medium of exchange for them other than the gold that was being indirectly drained out of the country, even in wartime. Something of the kind was more or less necessary if France was to make the Revolution permanent. Up to this time the government had been largely financed by seizures from the Church and nobility, but the end of that resource was in sight. As for the strategy of the operation, Bonaparte thought in the essentially military terms of deception and speed—and calculated that by the time the British could react they would be faced with the *fait accompli* of a French Egypt, with Malta as a guard post on the line of communications.

The government of the five Directors decided that an expedition to Egypt would relieve them of the awkward problem of providing for some thousands of soldiers who had been defending the country for so long they had become professionalized, and the movement was approved. But Bonaparte failed—understandably since it had not been that way before—to calculate on the aggressive strategy of the new group of British admirals, and his deception deceived too well. The destination of the armament fitting out at Toulon was put forward as Ireland, and the British believed it. But instead of falling back from his blockade of Cadiz and the Gibraltar Straits to cover the Channel approaches, Admiral Lord St. Vincent of the Gibraltar command jutted forward into the Mediterranean a squadron of thirteen battleships and a fifty under orders to find the Toulon fleet, wherever it was, and to destroy it.

The commander was a little one-armed, one-eyed sailorman named Sir Horatio Nelson, recently made rear admiral for gallantry in an action with the Spaniards. The evidence is that the appointment was due to the personal intervention of dim-witted old George III, who liked the man without being at all aware that he had some very unusual qualities indeed. For one, this Nelson was perfectly prepared to give literal obedience to the order to destroy the enemy, instead of merely defeating him and confounding his projects, like all previous naval commanders with the sole exception of Suffren. He wanted everything; once he wrote, "Now had we taken ten sail and allowed the eleventh to escape, when it had been possible to have got at her, I could never have called it well done." In the second place he called his captains "a band of brothers," and treated them as such. It is hard to realize today exactly what that meant in 1798. For over a century every naval battle in which the British were victors, as they usually were, had been followed by a court-martial in which the captain who did least well was condemned and dismissed from the service as a kind of booby prize. It was part of the tradition, like flogging and the Fighting Instructions. Nelson laid it down that, "No captain can go far wrong who lays his ship alongside the enemy," and left his band of brothers to their own devices, apart from the most general orders.

He concentrated his fleet off Sardinia on June 7 and shortly afterward learned that the Toulon armament had left port on May 19. It had certainly not gone through the straits for Ireland or he would have met it. His instructions mentioned the possibility that the revolutionary army was sailing for the twin kingdoms of Naples and Sicily, then under the misrule of a monarch called "Ferdinand the Burglar," a perfectly fit object of attack to a government that had proclaimed its intention of abolishing monarchy everywhere. Off Sicily, Nelson learned that the French had taken Malta and gone east; he had no orders but those for the destruction of their fleet, but he followed, and the succeeding weeks were filled with looking for them at Alexandria (where he arrived too early), Crete, Turkey, Greece.

On the late afternoon of August 1, Nelson found them at last, fourteen ships of the line, anchored in Aboukir Bay, heads to the wind, which was light from the north. Sir Horatio, who had taken practically no food at all for a week, ordered an ample dinner, remarking, "Before this time tomorrow I shall have gained a peerage or Westminster Abbey." Without orders beyond the preliminary general instructions, the British battleships formed and rushed down on the French line, the four leading British ships doubling around its head on the inshore side while the others took station outside. Thus each French ship at the head of their line had two opponents, usually with one of them in position to rake her lengthwise along the decks;

nor could the French ships at the rear beat up against the wind to join the battle. As the head of the line was crushed into striking their colors, the British moved down. All night the cannon roared across the bay, the French flagship caught fire and blew up, and in the morning there were only two of them left to escape.

Sir Horatio had carried out to the letter his orders to destroy

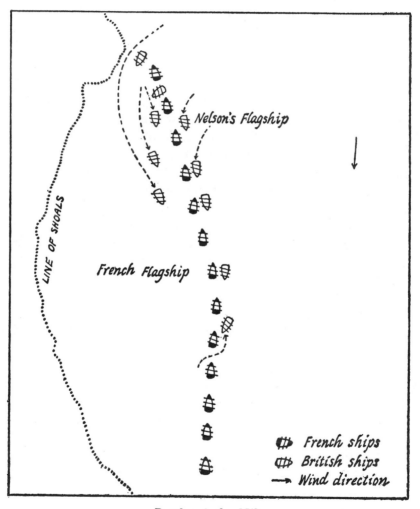

Battle of the Nile

the French fleet (for the two refugees did not last long) and gained his peerage; the Abbey would come later.

II

The Battle of the Nile, as it came to be called, was decisive in more than one sense. It said no to Bonaparte's Eastern dream and placed him in a dangerous position. The wars for the colonies during the eighteenth century had been fought out on land; English sea power gave tremendous advantages in the transmission and support of expeditions and the English usually won, but French fleets remained in existence even when beaten, and it was possible for them to provide at least intermittent help to the overseas areas, as it had been given to Montcalm. The night in Aboukir Bay wiped out the only part of the French navy that mattered in that area. Not even precarious communication with metropolitan France was any longer possible. The load of maintaining Egypt had become one that not even military genius could carry; there were too many shortages at the colonial end of the severed line of supply.

Bonaparte was perfectly conscious of the fact that this demonstrated no French overseas dominion could be established in the face of such naval power except on a self-supporting basis. When he became First Consul of France, already emperor in all but name, one of his first projects was to set up such a dominion—in Louisiana, with San Domingo as a way station. The project is generally held to have foundered on yellow fever and the resistance of the San Domingo blacks, but First Consul Bonaparte was a persistent and intelligent man, and it is not at all impossible that he would have succeeded in setting up his system—given time. Probably few wars were ever begun for reasons having less to do with the realities than the one which ended the brief Anglo-French peace in 1803. On the British side the pretext was Bonaparte's interference in Switzerland and Holland; while the French claimed that Britain had not evacuated Malta and Cape Town, according to treaty.

Actually, both sides were fully aware that the real issue was the French laws excluding British ships and products from ports under Bonaparte's control and the British failure to get a commercial treaty that brought this state of affairs to an end.

Bonaparte was rebuilding the French navy, but it was still well short of the almost parity point he needed. A war with England on the basis of overseas possessions maintained by occasional expeditions that evaded British fleets was the classical formula. The new strategy, the new tactics of the Nile demonstrated that his means were inadequate for such a project. He knew that only a radical solution would do, and the only radical solution that would be permanent was to strike England down on the home grounds; that is, get an army into the island and smash up those dockyards that were the nexus of her fleet and overseas trade.

Bonaparte estimated that 100,000 men and six hours' undisputed possession of the Channel would be about right. The army, called "of the Coasts of the Ocean," assembled from the Texel to Brest, was one of the finest ever brought together anywhere, far more effective than that army he had refused to lead in 1797. For the crossing there were to be provided 2,000 vessels of the type called praams, designed by the distinguished naval architect Pierre Alexandre Forfait, tubs just barely able to sail, but with oar power in addition, and armed with guns heavy enough to keep light British craft, such as frigates and sloops, at a distance. They were built at every place where ships could be built from the Dutch harbors down to the upper waters of the Loire.

It is hard to tell precisely what the master plan for their employment was because of Bonaparte's habitual policy of concealment and still more habitual method of leaving himself alternatives, but in the beginning it seems to have been for the invasion fleet to concentrate at Boulogne and make a crossing under night, storm, or fog. This was dropped out early in the game. Tests showed that Forfait's design was imperfect. The praams could not work along the coast to concentrate in the face of opposition. It would take a full forty-eight hours to get them loaded and across the bar at Boulogne, and when the wind blew strongly enough to move the clumsy vessels, they could not work their guns.

Bonaparte was thus driven to revise his plan in the direction of obtaining genuine naval command of the Channel for the necessary crossing period and using big ships. He counted on deception again, as when he went to Egypt. A new fleet had been built up at Toulon under Admiral Louis-René de La-touche-Tréville, eleven battleships strong. It was being watched by Sir Horatio, now Lord Nelson, who had twelve of the line, but the shape of the coast was such that no intimate blockade could be maintained. Bonaparte, always so prescient in following the mental qualities of his opponents, believed that Nelson had a fixation toward Egypt. If Latouche-Tréville were sighted steering south out of Toulon, Nelson's scouts would inform him, and he would almost inevitably be off to Alexandria. But Latouche-Tréville would go in the opposite direction, out into the Atlantic, making for Rochefort, where five French ships were blockaded by an equal number of British. These he would release, and having picked up one ship from Cadiz in friendly Spain, he would have seventeen, a force superior to the fifteen British ships under Admiral Cornwallis who were blockading the other major French fleet of fourteen in Brest. If Cornwallis stayed close to Brest, Latouche-Tréville would hurry to the Channel and cover the invasion; if Cornwallis instead chose to fight, it did not matter whether Latouche-Tréville won or lost, the British would be in no shape to prevent the Brest fleet convoying the army across.

This was quite a good plan, which encountered only one obstacle: before it could be executed, while Latouche-Tréville was still training his crews to an efficiency such as no French fleet had possessed since the Revolution, the admiral died.

And he was the last of the admirals. All the others senior enough to command a fleet bore what Bonaparte himself called "the souvenir of the Nile." They had been in that horrible disaster, and it had been borne in on them in a way hardly to be expressed in words that no French officer could conquer the English at sea. The first consul, always peculiarly sensitive to matters of morale, was fully conscious of this. When he appointed Pierre Charles Jean Sylvestre Villeneuve to replace Latouche-Tréville at Toulon, he altered the plan to one which involved no fighting except in possession of enormously superior numbers.

Villeneuve was to dismiss Nelson to Egypt as before, but instead of making for Rochefort and the Channel, would run for the sugar islands of the West Indies. News of this would reach London, and as the sugar islands were almost as important to England as India, it would cause a squadron to be sent there. Villeneuve was to stay among the islands only long enough to pick up six battleships that would escape from Rochefort to meet him there, then return to Europe, wipe out the five British blockaders who were holding a French group of equal strength at Ferrol in northwest Spain; then, avoiding Cornwallis off Brest (if he had not already been sent to the West Indies), make for the Channel and the invasion. He was not to fight except with the blockaders of Ferrol, twenty-three ships against five.

In execution of this plan Villeneuve duly put out of Toulon. Nelson was deceived according to prescription and went off to Egypt. But the French fleet met a storm and had to put back, and Nelson closed in again. A new factor was introduced when friendly Spain decided that going to war with England would be cheaper than paying the treaty subsidies that enabled France to continue her war "for the mutual benefit." Everybody told Bonaparte that the Spanish navy was not in good shape; but his motto was always, "There are no bad regiments, only bad colonels," and the attraction of a number of Spanish battleships that would give him a clear superiority on the water was irresistible. He again altered the plan to include Spanish squadrons.

It now became an enormously complicated device for moving British fleets around as though they were under Bonaparte's orders. Villeneuve was to escape from Toulon again, sending Nelson to Egypt, pick up Spanish ships at Cartagena and

Cadiz, and sail for the West Indies. There he would meet the Rochefort squadron, whose blockaders would of course imagine that it was making for Ireland and go there. The big Brest fleet would escape blockade and meet him there. Admiral Cornwallis, with the Western Squadron (as it was called) would obviously pursue the French to the West Indies, in accordance with the principle of making the main enemy force the objective. The Brest fleet would elude him, join Villeneuve, return to Ferrol and, on releasing the squadron there, attain the Channel for the vital six hours. This was the plan actually put into operation, and it all depended upon the idea that the British must concentrate to follow any French fleet that put to sea.

The working out was as complex as the plan itself, and it had features Bonaparte had failed to count on. One was that Nelson could not be hoodwinked a second time; instead of going to Egypt he followed Villeneuve to the West Indies, and news that he was among the islands brought the French admiral back to Europe prematurely, in order to avoid fighting the battle he had been forbidden to fight. The Cadiz and Rochefort Franco-Spanish squadrons got out, but instead of following them their blockaders simply joined with the Western Squadron at the gates of the Channel. As soon as a French fleet reappeared anywhere, one adequate to deal with it was detached from the Western Squadron. That is, the British did not concentrate against the moving French fleets, but at the point where these fleets must take decisive action. Even Nelson joined this concentration when he returned from the Indies. Villeneuve simply dared not try to run around this concentration. He made for Ferrol instead and, after an indecisive action with the British blockaders there, pushed in.

There were twelve Franco-Spanish ships inside, which brought Villeneuve's strength to the paper-potent figure of twenty-eight. Bonaparte expected him to come to the Channel at once, and even addressed a letter to him at Brest; but as the head of the French state failed to grasp the basic British strategic plan of reinforcing the Western Squadron every time a

French fleet disappeared, so also he failed to understand that there was no fundamental identity between a military base and a secure harbor. At the former all things needed by an army are almost automatically provided by the surrounding country; but a fleet requires such specialized items as masts, tar, timber, and cordage. There were none of these in Ferrol, and Villeneuve's ships had returned from their double transit of the Atlantic so worn down in precisely these items that most of them would need refit before attempting battle or even another cruise. Ferrol was for the time being not under blockade; Villeneuve accordingly sailed for Cadiz, where he could get his supplies.

This was the decisive event; all the rest was appendant.

III

It was evident to the man who had now become the Emperor Napoleon I that this ended any chance of his gaining control of the English Channel for the necessary time. Villeneuve had succeeded in effecting a concentration of thirty-three battleships at Cadiz, but this was a long way from the western approaches, where there was already a far greater British concentration. The admiral was accordingly ordered to get out of Cadiz and report to Toulon for a different campaign, whose precise nature has never been determined, but which would be a part of the new policy Napoleon instantly adopted on the arrival of the news from Cadiz. "You have much to do to regain His Majesty's confidence," read part of the order; Villeneuve decided that the only way to that accomplishment was to accept battle and win when he put out of Cadiz.

And he would have to accept battle. British cruisers had of course spotted the retreat from Ferrol to Cadiz, and Lord Nelson was at once ordered to the latter point. He had thirty-three ships of the line, the same number available to the allies, but six of them had gone to Gibraltar for food and water, so there were only twenty-seven when on October 21, 1805, the

Franco-Spanish fleet was sighted off Cape Trafalgar, running down for the straits under light airs from north and northwest.

Nelson had already formed a battle plan—an outgrowth of the one at the Nile—to advance against the allied line in two columns, break through it in both places, and double against their center and rear while their van would have to work back against the wind to help, and could hardly arrive until the other ships had been crushed. (Sailing battleships maneuvered very slowly against the wind.) This would apparently involve each British ship being subjected to end-on raking fire as she approached the allied line, but the danger was less than it looked, because once the first ships had broken through and counterraked the allies at the point of penetration the latter would no longer be able to fire effectively, and as successive British doubled down the allied line the gaps would grow. Nelson led one column of twelve ships himself in the three-decker *Victory*, 100; Admiral Cuthbert Collingwood headed the other in *Royal Sovereign*, 100.

A rather odd and often unnoticed thing about the plan was that it was exactly what Villeneuve anticipated, though he had not foreseen the detail of Nelson's two-column arrangement. In the earlier action off Ferrol the British had tried something like it; a fog which partially concealed movements and a quick-witted turn by the Spanish Admiral Gravina foiled them. This time Villeneuve placed the same Gravina in charge of a whole division of ships at the head of the line, with instructions to operate independently, at his own discretion, to prevent any British line-breaking, doubling attack. But just as Nelson's two columns began their slow-motion rush across the gently heaving sea, Villeneuve was visited with an inspiration. He turned his fleet simultaneously till it pointed nearly northwest, close-hauled, almost head to wind; and this had the effect that instead of being at the head of the line Gravina was very near the tail of it, in no position to make a counterattack or signal anyone else to do so.

In the British fleet Nelson hung out his famous signal, "England expects that every man will do his duty," and there was a burst of cheering from the line of battleships, as *Victory* headed for the huge four-decker *Santissima Trinidad*, 130, largest warship in the world, Nelson being certain that the French flagship would not be far from her. It was just falling on noon when the allies opened fire against Collingwood's column, slightly in advance of Nelson's. *Royal Sovereign's* sails were rags and she had a good many dead before she reached contact point, but when she did, her first tremendous raking broadside brought down 400 men aboard a Spanish three-decker. Now as ship after ship piled through the gap Collingwood opened and the allied vessels on their line of sailing began to bunch toward the area, the battle at the rear of the line turned into a disorderly, smoke-shrouded tangle; but it is to be noted that there were always two or three British ships to one of the allies, usually in raking position.

The cloud of smoke and thunder had been collecting over this area for quite half an hour when *Victory* plunged through the line, just where Nelson wanted to be, under the stern of the French flagship, *Bucentaure*, 80. *Victory* had lost a tenth of her people during the advance; now she repaid it all in one terrible broadside that dismounted twenty of *Bucentaure's* guns and wrecked the ship, then locked side to side with *Redoubtable*, 74. The French ship should have been, and was in fact, no match for the three-decker, but her Captain Lucas had trained his men carefully with small arms, and from her tops there poured down a devastating fire of musketry onto *Victory's* upper deck. Captain Hardy saw the admiral beside him spin around and sink to his knees, saying slowly, "They have done for me at last."

"I hope not, sir."

"Yes, my backbone is shot through."

It was true. All afternoon, as the admiral of England lay dying, the whole ocean area around Trafalgar was covered with rocking, blazing warships, broken masts, and accumulating debris. At four-thirty Captain Hardy went to the cockpit to report a victory and Nelson closed his eyes for the last time. He had taken eighteen of the allied ships, another went to

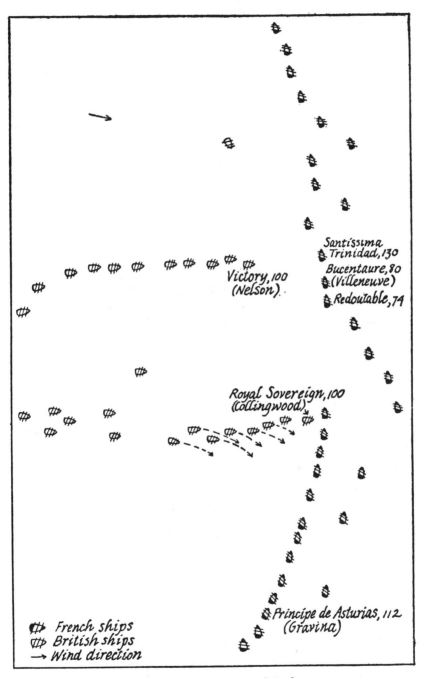

Santíssima
Trinidad, 130
Bucentaure, 80
(Villeneuve)
Redoutable, 74

Victory, 100
(Nelson)

Royal Sovereign, 100
(Collingwood)

Principe de Asturias, 112
(Gravina)

French ships
British ships
Wind direction

Trafalgar—Nelson's Attack

281

wreck that night, and four more were captured as they tried to escape, while nearly all the rest were so damaged as to be useless.

Except for the always immobilized Brest squadron, Napoleon now had no navy. There would be none of the "ships, colonies, commerce," that he regarded as the foundation of a sound polity; no emancipation from the commercial toils; and Britain was free to deliver her goods, her resources, her troops to any point touched by salt water.

IV

The night he received word that Villeneuve had gone to Cadiz was spent by Napoleon in dictating orders which flung the Army of the Coasts of the Ocean, now become Grande Armée, halfway across Europe to the banks of the Danube. For if he could not "end all coalitions at London," as he had hoped, he must at least deal with the land arm of the one confronting him, the most dangerous of all the coalitions faced by France in the post-Revolutionary period. In inception it owed a good deal to that morose, flighty, ambitious, and personally charming character, Alexander I of Russia, who took his own name seriously and wanted to be great. In form this coalition was a general European congress of peace and mediation, whose basic purpose was to put an end to the quarrel between England and France, a kind of precursor to the United Nations. In fact, it was a general alliance against France and the Revolution, for although Alexander referred to himself as a liberal, his liberalism did not extend to people who decapitated hereditary kings.

Of course, the thing was not altogether that simple. The trigger event in determining Alexander to launch the war of the Third Coalition, and Austria somewhat hesitantly to join, was Napoleon's assumption of the crown of (north) Italy. In the eyes of diplomats with memories this made the new France into an expanding state of the Louis XIV type. But the basic Continental idea was that espoused with considerable skill and passion by Friedrich Gentz, the publicist—the idea of eliminating from the world a system utterly subversive of all society and good order. The fact that its head now called himself an emperor did not conceal from either Gentz or Alexander that this "empire" rested on usurpation, the confiscation of Church and landed properties, and the execution of those who had held them by "the canaille."

Austria and Russia agreed to go to war against this system even though they could not persuade the Prussians to join their pan-European peace union at once. A plan of campaign was drawn up by General Karl Mack of the Austrian service. Along the frontier in Italy he established a "cordon sanitaire" of troops, technically to prevent the spread of a yellow fever epidemic from Tuscany, actually to hide Austrian mobilization and strength. The main theater of war would be there, in Italy, where Austria could hope the greatest gain, and it was assigned to the ablest of the Hapsburg princely soldiers, Archduke Karl, with 94,000 men. North of the Alps, the Austrian army of 84,000, under Mack's personal command, would first coerce Bavaria into joining the alliance, then push forward to Ulm, where the Iller falls into the Danube, ready to strike at the heads of any French columns coming through the Black Forest. The first Russian army of 40,000, under General Kutuzov, would arrive in Mack's rear on October 16, 1805, closely followed by 30,000 more under General Bennigsen; they would operate north of the Danube, sustaining Mack as he pushed forward from the Iller. Fifty thousand more Russians under General Buxhöwden would follow through Silesia and Bohemia, operating down the Frankfurt gap against the middle Rhine. Mack was pretty well informed about the force of the French army. It would have to leave troops at the Channel to provide against English invasion, and on the basis of this and logistic problems, Napoleon could hardly reach the upper waters of the Danube through the Black Forest before November 10, and then with not over 70,000 men.

Ample allowance was thus made for accident and error, but

there were two errors Mack failed to take into consideration. One was introduced by his personal intelligence officer, the man who collected the information about the French army, theoretically a young Hungarian nobleman named Schulmeister, who had been in France for some time; actually a French spy, who was feeding the Austrians whatever information Napoleon thought they ought to have and sending to Paris everything he could find out. The second error was that in the staff conversations with the Russians nobody but Schulmeister had noticed that they were talking according to the Orthodox calendar, while the Austrians were referring to the Gregorian, which had a twelve-day difference. Schulmeister sent this information to Paris instead of referring it to Vienna.

The Russians would thus be nearly two weeks late, and the French would arrive many weeks too soon, not with the 70,000 Mack had been led to expect, but with nearly 177,000 men, propelled from the Channel at Napoleonic marching speed. Moreover, this was a new kind of army. The normal arrangement attached a force of cavalry to each division, and artillery to each infantry battalion. In the Grande Armée the guns were taken away from battalion to be concentrated in divisional parks, and the cavalry assembled in one huge corps, 22,000 strong, with its own artillery. Its mission was to screen the movement, which flowed in parallel rivers of steel, not through the Black Forest, as expected, but across the whole northwest of Germany to a series of points on the Danube between Mack's position and Vienna.

In the later days of September, Mack's outposts at the debouches of the Black Forest began to encounter French horsemen; from the fact that they had guns with them he deduced that infantry could not be far behind, and ordered a concentration in the Ulm area. The first solid news came on October 7, and it was appalling: the French were already south of the Danube, across his line of communications, in great force.

The Austrian general did his best to cut his way out, first along one bank of the river, then the other, but he was outnumbered at every point of contact, bewildered, surrounded. A week later he was bursting into tears as he delivered his sword to Napoleon, with, "Behold the unfortunate Mack!"

V

Nearly 70,000 of Mack's men were dead or prisoners, but Napoleon's problems were only beginning. His line of communications stretched back a hundred miles to the Rhine, and many troops were required to maintain it; considerable forces had to be detached to cover the south flank against Austrians in the Tyrol and Italy; and in late October, before the advance down the Danube could begin, Kutuzov reached Vienna with the first Russian contingent. The next six weeks were occupied by a campaign of maneuver down the funnel of the Danube valley toward where Vienna stands at the eastern gate of Europe. After the disaster at Ulm and the arrival of the Buxhöwden contingent with their emperor, the Russians had much the larger proportion of the allied forces and were able to call the strategic tune. They greatly shocked the Austrians by their doctrine of giving up space and even Vienna city for time, but it was done, and in a fighting retreat the French were drawn through the mountains into Bohemia just east of Brünn at the end of November.

A not unimportant element in the situation was stiff Austro-Russian diplomatic pressure on Prussia to join the league of mediation with her 180,000 soldiers, drilled in the manner of Frederick the Great. This pressure had reached its peak; as French and allied patrols bickered along the road between Brünn and Olmütz, the Prussian foreign minister was at Napoleon's headquarters to deliver an ultimatum and the allies knew it. They were also fully conscious that successive retirements toward reserves had given them a field numerical superiority (the cold figures were 85,000 to 70,000), that the French cavalry had for several days been showing a want of enterprise, the French infantry advances had stopped. Napoleon seemed to regret having been pulled so far from his base and to be preparing a withdrawal. To strike him at such a moment of doubt would not only take advantage of the moral and numerical factors, but would undoubtedly draw Prussia in. Colonel Weyrother, the Austrian Kaiser's chief of staff, was appointed to draw a battle plan.

Patrols had located the French in a roughly northeast-southwest line across the Brünn-Olmütz highway, on some hills with steep slopes but flat tops, just behind a brook called the Goldbach, which flows south into some pools, now frozen. East of this brook is a high hill, the Pratzen, just in front of the village of Austerlitz, which the French had held but abandoned, one of the reasons for thinking they meant retreat. At the village of Sokolnitz, on the French side of the Goldbach, the hills occupied by them break sharply southwestward toward the road running south to Vienna. This road was Napoleon's line of communications, and Weyrother, who was a great student of Frederick the Great, perceived that the position offered an admirable opportunity for an oblique attack in Frederick's own manner, the weight to be directed against the French right wing, their sensitive flank.

The detail of the plan was that Austrian General Kienmayer, with the Austrian cavalry and some light infantry, would work close along the ponds around the French right toward Raigern Abbey, on the Brünn-Vienna road. Russian General Dokhtorov, 8,500 men, would strike the extreme French right; General Langeron, a French émigré in the Russian service, with 12,000 men was to attack Sokolnitz, next in line; General Przebyschevski, 14,000 strong, to assault Sokolnitz Castle, just upstream from the village. While this triple attack was breaking the French right, their left center would be contained by General Bagration, striking along the Brünn-Olmütz highway toward a little round hill called the Santon, supported by 6,000 Austrian cavalry and the Russian imperial cavalry guard under Grand Duke Constantine, 8,500 men. Concealed behind the Pratzen were 25,000 more men, a heavy column under Russian Miloradovitch and Austrian Kollowrath; they would follow

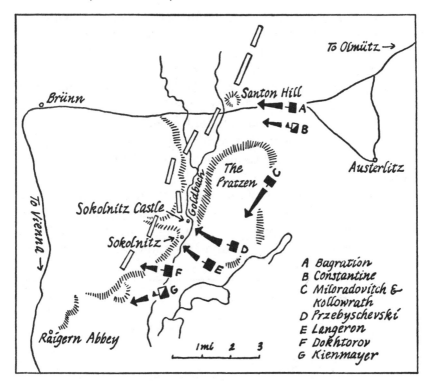

Austerlitz; the Austro-Russian View of the Situation and Their Plan

the Dokhtorov-Przebyschevski-Langeron columns, rolling up the French line after their right was broken.

The plan was explained at a council of war on the night of December 2, 1805, and the attack was set for dawn. It was indeed the sort of battle plan the great Frederick might have conceived, and there was only one thing wrong with it—that it was exactly what Napoleon was inviting the allies to do. In view of the menace of Prussia it was even more necessary for him to win a battle than for them, and he had planned not merely to win, but to destroy. His left did not extend beyond the Santon hill; but there he placed Marshal Lannes with three heavy and very good divisions, ordered to hold hard. On his right, along the hills from Sokolnitz to Raigern Abbey, he stationed his very best fighting commander, Marshal Davout, with orders to hold like hell; all the rest of the army, over 40,000 men, were arranged in depth between the Santon and Sokolnitz, a coiled spring under heavy pressure waiting to be released, a torpedo waiting to be launched. That evening the Emperor of the French rode along the lines, and as the soldiers made torches of straw and shouted at him, said, "Before tomorrow night I'll have that army," gesturing toward where the allies had taken up position precisely as he had hoped they would.

The morning broke thick, with a growl of cannon out to the allied left, the French right. Kienmayer found he did not have room to work up his horse for a swing on the extreme flank, and as Dokhtorov's column crossed the Goldbach, it met sharp-

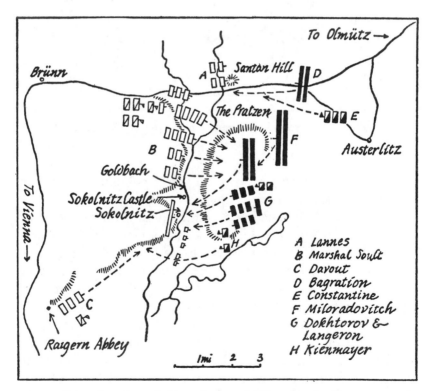

Austerlitz; the Actual Situation and Napoleon's Counterattack

shooters on vineyard-covered slopes, slowed up and pinched in by the fact that the neighboring columns occupied so much room that nobody could deploy properly. The Russians came on with their usual Slavic resolution, and Langeron even took Sokolnitz village in fighting so fierce that both sides were shooting across parapets of corpses; but the assaulters could not make their numbers count, and at the very moment when they began to close on Sokolnitz Castle, Davout violently counterattacked them with a storm of heavy cavalry. The advance against the French right was halted dead by eight in the morning.

At the same hour the sun—the sun of Austerlitz, as it came to be called—burst through the clouds and Napoleon, looking across the clear valley at the Pratzen, said to his Marshal Soult, "How long do you require to reach those heights?"

"Less than twenty minutes."

"In that case, let us wait a quarter of an hour more."

He waited, while smoke and thunder erupted from the valley where Davout was struggling against the three allied columns, and then launched his torpedo just as Miloradovitch began to slant across the eastern edge of the Pratzen to the support of the allied left. His men were in column, totally undeployed, and their guns were in limber at the tail of the mass. The hasty line they tried to form as thousands of French came across the Pratzen was swept right away; the men of the column surrendered by hundreds and thousands and the whole high plateau was French by ten o'clock in the morning. The allied center had disappeared; its right and left were now separate forces.

On the allied right, the French left, Bagration hit hard at the French infantry, but Lannes' men formed square, and Bagration was himself struck in the flank by cuirassiers dispatched from the Pratzen by Napoleon. By eleven the allied right was broken; Napoleon turned his attention to their left, where the columns of attack had come to a stand, laced them with artillery and musketry fire, and ordered the guns to break the ice on the frozen pools across which some were attempting to escape. When the shouting twilight closed in, Austrians and Russians had lost 30,000 men, all their baggage, guns, food, ammunition, and transport, and this particular war was over.

VI

Austerlitz was decisive in two dimensions, one military and one political. It changed the whole art of war, the method of obtaining decisions in battle, by introducing grand tactics. In the system of Gustavus, in that of Frederick the Great, and even in the earlier Napoleonic battles, it was possible for a commander to change his mind while the fighting was going on, to reinforce one wing from another or alter the direction of an attack. Not so at Austerlitz; the major units were irrevocably committed to a course of action the moment the fighting began.

Napoleon was the first to perceive that the masses had grown too large for anything else; that with 70,000 men on a front seven miles long, no one eye or brain could exercise continuing control. Oriental armies had often been larger than those that fought at Austerlitz, but in them there was no effort at any co-ordinated tactical plan; it was simply a case of achieving contact and awaiting the result of a melee. That is, Austerlitz introduced the system that made it possible to handle in the field and with precision the new large national armies that were the product of the universal conscription introduced by the French Revolution.

But this was attained at a price. The Napoleonic grand tactics involved committing a unit up to a 15,000-man corps to an assigned course of action and being unable to change its operations thereafter until it had accomplished its mission. (The columns of attack on the Pratzen did swing in other directions, but not until they had demolished Miloradovitch.) This involved not only pre-planning the battle; it also required that subordinate commanders should be deprived of all but local initiative. At least it did in Napoleon's day, before anyone but himself understood what the new tactics meant.

In the failure to give initiative to subordinates, in the failure to develop juniors who seized it for themselves, may be found one of the causes for the ultimate military downfall of the Napoleonic empire. The general criticism of Napoleon's marshals is that they could lead but not direct. Davout and Masséna were exceptions, to be sure; but in Napoleon's effort to extend grand tactics into strategy and personally to control armies operating across the whole face of Europe, even these two never got an opportunity to make the most of what they had. The French Empire may be said to have perished because it had only one man who could command an army of over 50,000, and his method of grand tactics did not allow him to bring up successors. When the allies overwhelmed Napoleon, they did it by beating all the armies but the one he personally commanded. They had no generals of his ability; but they had many equal to his subordinates.

Yet the defect in the Napoleonic method was not in the method itself, but in the physical techniques that supported it; specifically, those of communication. During the campaigns in Spain officers accustomed to receiving very precise orders that launched them in a certain course kept getting directives that no longer related to the changed conditions. Napoleon had invented something he lacked the tools to apply to any larger field than Austerlitz, yet tried to apply everywhere. The French Empire perished through this fault; but it was the French Empire, not the French Revolution and the changes it stood for.

If the idea of the universal state died at Lützen and that of the Empire of all Germany at Torgau, at Austerlitz there fell the final claim to imperial dominion over those lands that had once been Charlemagne's. Before the campaign of 1805 there remained such a claim, however shadowy; George III of England was still *Elector* of Hannover, Maximilian Joseph was still *Elector* of Bavaria, each with at least a theoretical share in the government of the empire. After that campaign the Holy Roman Empire became one frankly of the Austrian crown lands alone, a kind of zombie which would stagger around for another 113 years before falling down, but whose fate was really decided on that one field.

There had ceased to exist any real point of focus for the forces represented by Friedrich Gentz, or any power that stood a chance of successfully challenging the ideas and policies of the Revolution as consolidated by Napoleon. The war would last as long as he lasted, but beneath it the work of consolidation went on, and after the allies got rid of the man they called "the Monster," they found they could not do more than throw a veneer over the solid work that remained. The new society was established; the most the rest of Europe could do was to get rid of the man who had given it permanence.

15. The Things Decided at Vicksburg

I

In the beginning no one realized how important Vicksburg was. It was not even a major item in the system of fortifications by which the Confederacy hoped to secure its natural frontiers in the West and to exert pressure on the northern states of the Mississippi valley by blockading the outlets for their products. That was the original concept; a land blockade of water traffic. In the terms of 1861 thinking this was a logical project. Ever since the Old Northwest began to fill up after the Revolution, the natural outlet for its wheat, beef, pork, lumber, and even the manufactured products of Pittsburgh had been by way of the Mississippi. The lakes carried some items to Buffalo for transshipment down the Erie Canal and the railroads were beginning to extend steel fingers to the plains, but the great river remained the main artery.

To dominate the upper river General Leonidas Polk of Confederate Department 2 lunged forward into "neutral" Kentucky and built a great fortress on high bluffs at Columbus, armed mainly with the guns taken in the huge windfall at Norfolk Navy Yard. Forts Henry and Donelson on the Tennessee and Cumberland covered his rear areas, and it is interesting to note that they should be regarded as adequate for that cover; the movement of the armies, like that of commercial traffic, was regarded as ultimately dependent on water transport because of the supply problem. No one believed that any serious military advance could be made through the tangled western Kentucky country between Columbus and Fort Henry without exposing its flanks and rear. Below Columbus, at the Tennessee-Kentucky line, low-lying Island No. 10 was heavily fortified, and the high ground on the Tennessee side opposite. At spaced stages between the island and Memphis, wherever geography offered a field of fire that would make downcoming ships slow up and take difficult turns, there were other forts— Pillow, Randolph, Harris. Even Pillow received forty guns; Vicksburg, so far downstream that its function was considered that of a guard post, got only a few.

The Confederate strategic concept of 1861 was thus that commercial necessity would force the Union to make a campaign down the Mississippi; and that this campaign could be slowed up, brought to futility against a chain of fortresses, like those that held the Belgian frontier against France in the old wars. The plan had this advantage: that, while in the flat plains of Europe any one of several lines of operation was available to an invading army, the Union forces were practically compelled to work down the Mississippi, supporting their drive on river traffic.

That was how it looked to Richmond, specifically to Jefferson Davis, graduate of West Point and book-learned soldier. The strategic concept seemed to be confirmed in November 1861, when a Union force dropped downstream with a couple of gunboats and temporarily occupied Belmont, opposite Columbus, but was easily driven off. Not until word came through that the Yankees were building warships at Cairo and St. Louis was any thought given to defending the river on the river itself; then there were laid down at Memphis two powerful ironclad rams of the general type of *Virginia* (ex-*Merrimack*). Down at New Orleans there was a naval command, but it was solely concerned with the area between that city and the sea. When General Mansfield Lovell arrived to take military command of the New Orleans district late in 1861, he became so exercised over naval defense on the stream that he

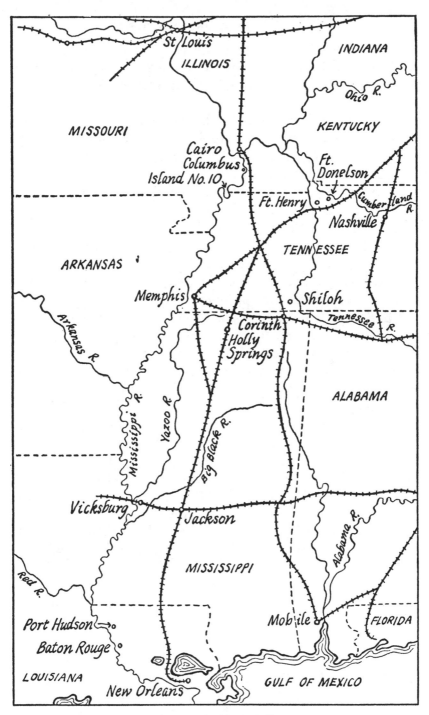

The Mississippi Valley

seized twelve river ships and converted them to rams, bulwarked with timber and pressed cotton bales. Most of them were sent to Memphis as the "River Defense Fleet" under army command.

The reason for this was that by the time they were ready Union strategy in the Mississippi valley had unfolded along lines utterly different from the original Confederate conception. The major method of operation was less thought out than felt out, but began to develop fairly early in the fall of 1861, when Brigadier General U. S. Grant, in military command of an area of vague definition out of Cairo, Illinois, made contact with Commodore A. H. Foote, who had been sent west to lead the Mississippi naval squadron.

This squadron had been in process since summer, and its principal units were the product of the mind and drive of James B. Eads, a remarkable man who started as an apple boy, taught himself diving and engineering, and became a millionaire. The ships were nine gunboats, intended specifically to deal with fortifications ashore. They were aptly likened to turtles, with iron plating around their prows, carrying three heavy guns ahead and four 32-pounders on each beam. Foote hit it off at once with Grant, and loaned him two earlier-built wooden gunboats for that operation to Belmont. It was really a raid, intended to attract attention from operations elsewhere, and when the Confederates who crossed to the Missouri shore tried to mop up the little force Grant had brought, they were stopped cold by the heavy guns of the ships.

The difference in conception as to what had happened at Belmont had important effects. It confirmed Confederate strategists in their view that the river could be closed by forts, and it convinced Grant that guns carried by ships could be moved so fast and in such numbers that it would be almost impossible for field troops to stand up against them when also assailed by infantry. In other words, he had this early attained at least a rudimentary concept of combined operations, and it was to this type that he addressed himself as soon as ice-free rivers permitted, at the beginning of February 1862.

But he did not project this operation down the Mississippi, as the Confederates expected. A reconnaissance up the Tennessee in January convinced him that Fort Henry was weakly held. With some difficulty, he persuaded his departmental commander, General H. W. Halleck, to let him attack the place, and moved upstream against it, with seven of Foote's gunboats leading. On February 6, while the troops were struggling through drowned land and forest toward the rear of the fortress, the ships shot it all to pieces, and Grant arrived only in time to find that it had surrendered to the navy.

It was characteristic of Grant that instead of asking Halleck for any more permissions, he should telegraph that he was going to take Donelson, too, and start marching his men for the place while the gunboats went around by the rivers. Donelson was a far different proposition than Henry; instead of being almost water level, it was mounted up the sides of a steep bluff, its cannon commanding a bend. The consequence was that when the gunboats moved in on February 14 they took a plunging fire into their upper decks, where there was no armor, and were driven off, with several of them disabled and no particular damage to the fort.

But while this was going on Grant closed on the fort from the rear. An attempt at a sortie failed, Grant counterattacked and took enough of the works to make the position untenable. On February 16, Donelson surrendered with 15,000 men.

It was a turning point in the Civil War in the West. The Confederacy was all along to suffer from manpower shortages, and the loss of the Donelson garrison was a serious blow. Still more serious was the facet that the Confederate defense system was invalidated, and most of the essentials of war along the western rivers worked out. The gunboats cruised up the Tennessee clear into Alabama, and on the Cumberland took Nashville without help from the land forces. It was also demonstrated that they would have a decidedly rough time against artillery mounted high for plunging fire, but could cover and support the operations of troops to take that artillery from behind.

II

The Henry-Donelson debacle made nonsense of the great fortress at Columbus, which could be outflanked and cut off along fairly good lines of communication from Grant's position on the Tennessee. It was abandoned, the guns being moved to places farther downstream, while the troops were called in to Corinth, Mississippi, by General Albert Sidney Johnston, over-all Confederate commander in the West. He also summoned troops from every other area under his authority for a great smash to demolish Grant, who had moved up the Tennessee to Pittsburg Landing, a position very dangerous to the Confederacy. It was the normal transshipment point where goods left the river to reach at Corinth both the rail line running deep into Mississippi and the long lateral road Memphis–Corinth–Chattanooga, one of the only two such lines crossing the Confederacy. Halleck ordered General Buell with the Army of the Ohio to join Grant; he was going to undertake a campaign against Corinth.

On the morning of Sunday, April 6, 1862, Johnston delivered his attack, achieved surprise, and almost did demolish Grant's army. Thousands of them fled to the cover of the bluffs along the river; but the rest, sustained mainly by Grant's personal leadership and the hard fighting around Shiloh Church by a hard-faced, red-bearded brigadier named William T. Sherman, made it into the most savage battle yet fought on the American continent. The Union right was driven far back. But early in the afternoon Albert Sidney Johnston was killed and there was some confusion in the Confederate command. The decisive attack on the other wing, intended to pry Grant away from his river landing and communications, did not come till very late. By this time the Union line had impacted around the landing with its artillery in position. The Union gunboats in the river shelled the rebel lines all night, while Buell's steady battalions crossed and filed into line. In the morning the Union forces counterattacked, drove the Confederates from the field, and it was Grant's victory.

It is natural that the early battles in any war should lead to a good deal of deducing, as it becomes evident that the current conflict contains elements that have not been present in any other. Shiloh told both sides that the apparent ease with which the South had won at Bull Run and the North at Fort Donelson was illusory; that a hard and probably long struggle was in prospect—and this was true. It also founded in the North the reputation of Grant as a smash 'em, hard-bitten fighter who did not do much thinking, and though this was not true at all, it clung to him to the end, and was reinforced by his taciturnity, his immobile countenance, and a certain deliberation of physical movement.

Probably more important to the progress of the war were the deductions drawn by the commanders. One of the reasons Grant got himself surprised was that he failed to entrench. Halleck, who now assumed command of the combined armies of Grant and Buell for the drive on Corinth, did not intend to let that happen again, and conducted his drive by digging, which achieved the lightning speed of a mile a day. He got Corinth, all right, but not until May 30, 1862, and then found he did not know what to do with it. His army numbered above 100,000 men; the Confederates had torn up the north-south railroad down from Columbus so that all supplies had to come by the Tennessee, but that river was now so low it would hardly any longer carry the necessities for so many troops. Moreover, the Confederates, relieved of immediate pressure, had set up an area of operations around Chattanooga, and it was important to prevent the army there from jabbing northward. Just before he was called East to take general direction of the armies of the republic, Halleck accordingly divided, sending Buell to counter the force around Chattanooga and leaving Grant to conduct operations from Corinth.

But the most significant of the lessons from Shiloh was in the work of the river navy, which supported the army at the end of a long line of secure communications and furnished that invaluable artillery cover for the endangered Union left wing. The point was underscored by an event that took place farther west at almost the same time. This was the fall of the great Confederate river barrier at Island No. 10. General John Pope approached the place along the Missouri shore with an army of some 20,000, but was prohibited from crossing to pinch it out from the Tennessee side by field guns along the narrow strip of dry ground there. But on the night of April 4, Commander Henry Walke of the ironclad *Carondelet* ran his ship downstream right through the batteries in a storm of thunder and lightning. After a day's rest the gunboat knocked out the field guns on the east bank, escorted Pope's troops across, and Island No. 10, its communications completely gone, had to surrender with 7,000 men.

Another term had been added to the complex of combined operations on the rivers. Ships could run past batteries, no matter how formidable and, once past, could support troops to cut in behind them.

This was presently reinforced in resounding terms from the other end of the Mississippi, where old Flag Officer David Glasgow Farragut brought up a strong fleet of ocean vessels and some bombardment mortars to try conclusions with the two powerful forts covering New Orleans. Three days of bombardment failed to tame the forts; Farragut impatiently ran his ocean-going ships past them, destroying the Confederate fleet on the lower river in a terrific battle, and on April 25 anchored off New Orleans. Two days later the forts surrendered, and the largest city in the Confederacy was gone.

This was the event that suddenly made the importance of Vicksburg vital, for after Halleck took Corinth on May 30, the forts on the upper river became useless; he was behind them. Pillow and the lesser works were evacuated peacefully on June 4, and two days later the Union gunboats wiped out the River Defense Fleet off Memphis. The city surrendered to the navy and became Grant's downstream base. Vicksburg was now the only barrier to Union domination of the whole stream, the only cover for communication between the east and west Confederacy. The rebels began fortifying it heavily in April, just after Island No. 10 fell, and neither effort nor expense was spared.

III

There was a certain amount of misapprehension on both sides, and at this point the Confederates had already paid for most of theirs. The thing that bothered Richmond from the beginning was those Union ironclads on the upper river. The attack on New Orleans from the sea fell as a stunning surprise, and the defenses were neither co-ordinated nor fully prepared. At a date when Farragut's ships were already moving up to begin the bombardment, the Confederate Navy Department sent a stern order that a strong ironclad building at New Orleans should be sent up to Memphis at once. That is, they recognized—too late—the defects of the fortress system in the face of amphibious operations, and tried to make good the deficit by supporting the forts with floating defense. But the floating defenders were now all gone except the ram *Arkansas*, which had been towed down from Memphis and then up the Yazoo River for completion. There was nothing left to do but try to make the fortress system work through better control of the inland areas behind. The process was sensibly aided by the fact that all available forces could be concentrated in support of the only major fortress remaining, and by the lack of a good water route leading to the rear of that fortress.

On the Union side there was still comparatively little understanding of the fact that success had really been due to combined operations. Halleck's army at Corinth had had quite as much to do with the movement of the gunboats down past forts Pillow, Randolph, and Harris as the gunboats had with the fall of Island No. 10. It was too easily assumed, on the basis of both river operations and successes along the coast, that no sort of fort could stand up against ships with heavy guns. Farragut at New Orleans received very positive orders to go upstream and help the gunboat fleet take Vicksburg. The only military support allotted consisted of 3,000 men from the New Orleans occupation command.

It was somewhat unrealistic to expect this force to climb the 200-foot bluffs of Vicksburg in the face of the defenders, who now amounted to an army, and the unreality was compounded by the fact that the deep-draft, long, unarmored ocean vessels were about as unsuited for work in a winding river filled with uncharted snags and sand bars as any ships could well be. Farragut went up, nevertheless, and after numerous groundings and accidents, was just south of Vicksburg on June 25 and in communication across the isthmus opposite the place with Flag Officer C. H. Davis, now commanding the gunboat squadron. The mortars that had bombarded the New Orleans forts were brought up to shell the batteries, and on the night of the twenty-eighth Farragut's fleet ran fighting through to join the gunboats at the mouth of the Yazoo, just above the town.

Now the operation rapidly turned to failure in spite of the ships' not being much hurt. Against the midnight hills the ships had to fire at flash and they obviously did no damage to speak of. As for the river gunboats, they were once again facing plunging fire, as at Donelson, Columbus, and Pillow, and could do no more than assure the communications and cover the flanks of an army that was not there. For two weeks the naval commanders discussed the situation, then sparked apart, Farragut back through the batteries to New Orleans, Davis to base at Helena, Arkansas.

It was merely one of those ventures into the domain of the fantastic in which the Civil War is so rich that the event which touched off the splitting of the fleets was the wholly unexpected appearance of the ram *Arkansas* from the Yazoo, running through the combined squadrons to anchor under the guns of Vicksburg. Her career lasted just twenty-three days. When she tried to go down and supply naval support for a Confederate army attack on Baton Rouge, her engines gave out in the presence of Union gunboats and the crew had to burn her up. But the Vicksburg fortress had fulfilled its mission so well that the Confederates now built another farther down at Port Hudson to keep the ocean ships from coming back, and to hold open communications with the West via the Red River.

The leading military event of the late summer and early fall in the West was Confederate Bragg's invasion of Kentucky. Troops were drawn off from Grant to help against this move until he had barely 30,000 in his mobile force, and this with the railroad supply line from Columbus to Corinth to cover. In October, Grant decided to take the offensive, Bragg's invasion having been turned back at Perryville, a Confederate force having been defeated at Corinth, and word having arrived that new troops were coming downstream to Memphis, as well as some reinforcements from the trans-Mississippi. His line was down the Mississippi Central Railroad, which projects from Corinth to reach the rear of Vicksburg at the junction of Jackson. The plan was this: Grant was to move down the railroad line, rebuilding destructions as he went, while Sherman picked up the new troops at Memphis, came downstream in transports and, with the help of the gunboats, attacked the Chickasaw Bluffs just north of the mouth of the Yazoo. The Confederates did not have force enough to be strong both against Grant's advance and the bluffs; one of these attacks should break through, communication with the river from the high ground would be established, and a campaign against Vicksburg from the rear begun.

This plan ignored two factors, one of which was not immediately apparent. The Confederates had become very alarmed about the safety of their fortress, and had appointed General Joe Johnston to command the whole area west of the Alleghenies; he built up the forces under General John C. Pemberton in the Vicksburg area to a strength that permitted freedom of movement. As Grant pushed down his railroad line, reaching a point over 200 miles from his major base at Columbus, he established an advanced depot of stores at Holly Springs, east of Memphis, and unconnected with that town except by inefficient wagon tracks, the railroad connection having long since gone. On December 20, the day Sherman's expedition left

Memphis for downstream, the Confederate cavalry of Van Dorn fell on the Holly Springs depot, burned it out and, with the help of other cavalry raiders, tore up many miles of track toward Columbus. Grant had to go back to Memphis at once, the troops marching on three-quarter rations, and there was no way to tell Sherman what had happened, since the wires were down and a letter would have to reach Memphis before proceeding downriver.

The consequence was that Pemberton was quite free to concentrate against Sherman and did so, bloodily beating off his attack when the gunboats proved no more capable of dealing with artillery on high bluffs than they had ever been. The essential fact was that this was the mirror image of the naval attempt on Vicksburg in June, not really a combined operation. Sherman's men were carried by ships and supported by them, but this was an amphibious attack, quite a different thing. At no time was Grant's own striking force in touch with or aided by the fleet. In a country so wide and generally flat as the Mississippi valley, communications that did not travel a great deal of the distance by water could be protected only at ruinous cost in detachments.

IV

When Grant reached Memphis after a hard march, he made the appalling discovery of the second factor of ignorance. Back in September one of his corps commanders, John A. McClernand, had gone to Washington on leave. This was a politician who had been commissioned out of civil life; a Democrat from Illinois of outstanding loyalty to the Union and somewhat more outstanding loyalty to his own advancement. In the capital he told Lincoln that it would be easy for a man of his popularity to recruit an entirely new army in Indiana, Illinois, and Iowa for a campaign down the river against Vicksburg. The recruiting problem was becoming serious, the word "draft" was being mentioned and it was rather a dirty word; Lincoln was persuaded to give McClernand a secret order empowering him to raise and command an "Army of the Mississippi." McClernand performed the recruiting part of his mission very well; many of the levies that came to Memphis were of his provision. But many also were not, and neither were the troops from the trans-Mississippi or the other formations Grant had left with Sherman. All the same, McClernand turned up at the bluffs of the Yazoo just after the repulse, brandished his secret order and, in virtue of it, not only assumed command of half Grant's army, but went off with it up the Arkansas on a private expedition against a fort there.

Of course the command arrangement was straightened out after a somewhat acrid exchange of telegrams with Washington, and McClerland returned to his position as a corps commander under Grant. But the operative fact was that Grant now had to go down to the lower river base at Young's Point and take command in person, with enough troops from the inland expedition to make it clear that this was not McClernand's army but his own. At this point the politics of strategy entered the picture. The news of the dreadful defeat of Fredericksburg had just shaken the North, and it came on the heels of the failure of the Lincoln party in the fall elections. If Grant now brought all his troops back to Memphis and replanned an overland campaign, it would be an admission of defeat and the effect might well be disastrous. Grant was perfectly conscious of this and of the fact that although the setback had really taken place, it was vitally important not to let people know about it. McClernand's action had thus politically committed him to a campaign against Vicksburg from the low west bank.

In itself there was nothing wrong with this. It ensured another combined operation, and Grant had become rather partial to working with the gunboats, now under command of the vain, irascible, dynamic, and able David Porter. But it imposed a virtually insoluble problem of means and communications. Below Vicksburg, all the way to Port Hudson and beyond, the highlands follow the east bank of the stream. It would be possible to march an army down the west bank and win a crossing by one of the methods established in the military art since the days of Gustavus Adolphus, but once across, how would that army maintain itself? On the basis of previous experience, the armored warships could be expected to run through the batteries with an acceptable amount of loss, but there were needed vessels that could provide a steady flow of supplies for over 30,000 men, ships making round trips. It was idle to suppose that such thin-shelled craft could work back and forth past those heights which daily grew more formidable.

Thus Grant's problem was to secure logistic support for a move across the river to some spot south of Vicksburg. The first attempt (on a suggestion from Washington) was by digging a canal across the neck of the land opposite the city. Grant never had much faith in it, and it never produced more than enough water to float a rowboat, while the Confederates set up new batteries opposite the exit, but it did keep the people busy during an uncomfortable winter in the Louisiana lowlands.

The next attempt was double. South of Memphis the high ground slants wide to the eastward before turning back to touch the Mississippi again at Vicksburg, forming the great diamond-shaped area of marshy flatland, cut by slow-paced watercourses, known as the Yazoo delta—nearly 200 miles long, nearly fifty miles broad, across which troops cannot march. The rivers of the eastern high ground flow west before they break through to attach themselves to the Yazoo in this delta. With the coming of January and freshet water it should be possible to shoot gunboats into the maze of streams in the delta, win a way into one of the westward-flowing streams where it breaks the highlands, and there establish a beachhead fed by naval support.

Far up the line a levee closed an old gap called Yazoo Pass, where the Mississippi had earlier annually flowed through into the Coldwater River and thence the Yazoo. This levee was blown on February 3, 1863, and four days later, the flood having reached sufficient height, eight light gunboats passed in, with transports carrying 800 troops. Overhanging branches and underwater obstructions tore at them and slowed progress; the Confederates got word of the movement and had time to erect a brand-new fort at the mouth of the Tallahatchie, surrounded by waters so that it would not be taken from the land side. The stream was so narrow that only two gunboats could approach at a time; they proved nowhere near enough to deal with the new fort, the commander of the Union expedition went insane, and it miserably pulled out.

While this was still undecided, Admiral Porter in person, with a squadron of ironclads, was trying to work through the maze of bayous and rivers from near the mouth of the Yazoo to reach high ground north of the bluffs that had stopped Sherman. He had better luck than the Yazoo Pass expedition in encountering no forts; and worse, in that at a critical point in his progress he encountered a stream-barring bed of underwater willows which his ships could not break through. Confederate snipers attacked him from the banks; he had to unship rudders and drift downstream to safety, with everything on the upper decks carried away by branches, and the only gain of the expedition was a pair of fine turkeys for General Sherman's table.

There was, then, no way of reaching the Vicksburg high ground via the Yazoo delta, and while these projects were under way, another canal effort failed. West of the main stream was an old course named Lake Providence, which it seemed might be deepened to lead into the Red River below Vicksburg. The channel was cut; Lake Providence flooded indeed, but then ran out into marshes and there was no passage for ships. By mid-April people in Washington were condemning Grant in unmeasured terms, and there was still no visible means of furnishing an army with logistic support for an advance along the high ground on which Vicksburg stood. The general asked Porter whether he could run enough gunboats through the batteries to cover a crossing and, being told yes, gave orders for the army to march down the right bank.

There was a great moment during that march, the moment when William Tecumseh Sherman sat beside Grant on a log and asked what he meant to do.

"Cross here and reach the high ground," said Grant.

Sherman said, "That would be putting yourself voluntarily in a position which the enemy would be glad to maneuver a year to get you in." He urged that Grant should go back to Memphis, fortify, build a road. Grant heard him out and said shortly, "The country is tired of retreats. I shall cross here."

Sherman said, "But your communications? You cannot get supplies down the west bank."

"No communications. We will live off the country."

At the time Sherman said nothing at all, only stared, he was too amazed to do more, but later he was to remark, "I am a better general than he is, but I lack his iron nerve."

V

There was no precedent for any such thing since Napoleon's first campaign in Italy, and even this was not a solid precedent, since the Corsican cut loose from one line of supply only long enough to uncover a new one. It would be utter disaster for Grant and the country if he failed, and the elements of failure were present. He had not over 41,000 men in the three corps of McClernand, McPherson, and Sherman, while Pemberton had at least 40,000 in the Vicksburg area, and Joe Johnston was eastward in range with unknown but formidable numbers. When the gunboats ran through the batteries with seven transports to test matters, only one of the latter was sunk, but several were reduced to barges that had to be towed, and the first attempt to shoot out a foothold at Grand Gulf ended in a beating for the ships. There could be no turning back; and if the army failed, the ships were faced with the prospect of being caught in a steadily narrowing area of fire from high places.

But Grant gave himself every chance for success. The initial crossing was made by the corps of McClernand and McPherson at Bruinsburg, well south of any fortified point and three miles from the foot of the bluffs, a place where surprise could be achieved. Sherman stayed behind temporarily at the mouth of

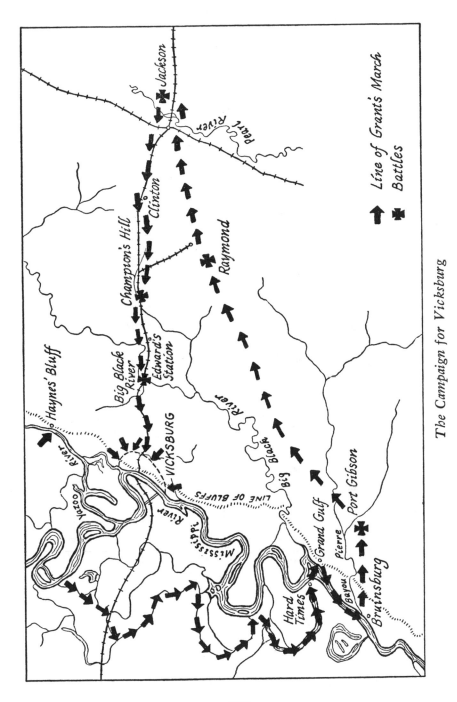

The Campaign for Vicksburg

the Yazoo with several gunboats to make a noisy demonstration toward the bluffs where he had been hurled back before. This worked; Pemberton shifted some of his strength in that direction and did not even begin to change arrangements until he heard of what was happening farther south.

The news was the landing of McClernand's whole corps, 16,000 men, at four on the afternoon of April 30, with three days' rations in their haversacks. Grant, at last on high ground, but with all the perils yet to come, nevertheless "felt a degree of relief scarcely ever equalled since" as he watched Illinois, Indiana, Wisconsin, Iowa swing past, no parade soldiers, but dusty and competent. The bands did not play; there was only the inexorable tramp, tramp, tramp of marching men, and after them, the guns. By twilight the corps was on the cliffs at Port Gibson; at dawn contact was made with the enemy.

There was a division of some 7,000 men under General Bowen, who had been in command of the Grand Gulf garrison, and who had, of course, been advised of the landing as soon as it took place. Pemberton had spent most of the night getting off telegrams to assemble his various commands, and off to the east Joe Johnston was assembling men at Jackson, the obvious point of impact if the Federal line of advance were prolonged.

The country around Port Gibson is composed of high ridges slashed by ravines filled with brush and canebrake, admirable for defense, but McClernand had too many men, and by noon two brigades of McPherson's joined him; in a sharp little battle the Confederates were thrown off northwestward, with 600 prisoners lost. Near Grand Gulf they were joined by another division Pemberton sent in support and various scattered groups that brought Bowen up to 17,000 men. He did not consider Grand Gulf safe, and got behind the Big Black River, his men much worn with marching. A division of McPherson's slashed out to keep him going, the rest of the Union army pushed on toward Jackson, officers and men working together in waist-deep water to build bridges. Sherman came crowding up behind the advance.

They marched. There was no bread, the country was rough

and the roads were bad, but there were local bacon, beef, and molasses, and by God, they marched; not in the direction of Vicksburg, as Pemberton was expecting, but toward Jackson. On May 12 at Raymond more Confederates were encountered, a brigade being called in on Pemberton from farther south. They were beaten by McPherson and lost 400 prisoners.

"Its effects were trifling," wired Johnston, but he considered McPherson's force a detachment with which the nearly 12,000 men he had assembled at Jackson could deal, and urged Pemberton to fall on the rear of Grant's main body. Pemberton's main ideas at this point were that he must not get too far from his base at Vicksburg, but that if Grant were as far east as Raymond the Union line of communications back to the river was becoming excessively long. He therefore stayed generally *in situ*, shifting his weight slightly to the right for a blow at that line of communications when he had a good chance.

Thus both Confederate commanders had an incomplete and inaccurate picture of what was going on. Actually, as soon as the Battle of Raymond was won, McPherson shot off leftward to strike the Jackson–Vicksburg railroad at Clinton, while Sherman moved straight on Jackson. On the thirteenth McPherson took Clinton and was between Johnston and Pemberton. It rained in torrents, the water was often a foot deep as the men marched, but they were in high spirits, with a taint of victory in the air; they cheered their general wildly as he rode past. On the fourteenth both McPherson and Sherman were before Jackson; they assaulted, Sherman got a division around a flank, Johnston was driven from the town, with 800 prisoners and seventeen guns lost. He turned north with what he had left, sending a message to Pemberton to urge that general to join him in that direction for an attack on Grant's rear.

But Grant's flowing mass of force had no real rear, and Pemberton was already moving south toward the attack on the nonexistent line of communications. In addition, Grant got a copy of the Johnston message, which the Union cryptographers promptly deciphered. He turned everything toward Pemberton, McPherson from Jackson with Sherman shoving along behind, McClernand from Raymond. Fighting contact was made on May 16 at Champion's Hill—a high hill slanting southwest to the considerable stream of Baker's Creek. Mc-Clernand, who was to break through on the left, was inexcusably tardy in going in, but after four hours of fighting two of McPherson's divisions got around and stormed the peak on the Union right. Ruin spread along the Confederate line and they were driven from the field in rout. They lost 3,000 in killed and wounded, 3,000 prisoners, and twenty-four guns. Grant personally drove McClernand's men in on their collapsing right so fast that what was left of a whole Confederate division, unable to find a ford across Baker's Creek that was not already in possession of the Yankees, wandered off far southward to turn up at Mobile.

Grant followed hard. Next morning he found the refugees from the battle ensconced in a bridgehead at the Big Black. Sherman was already pressing forward on the right to gain a passage farther up the stream. The other two corps moved up to the bridgehead, and just at this moment there arrived before Grant a colonel who had ridden hard with a telegram from Halleck in Washington, transmitted through New Orleans. It ordered the disorderly general to return to his base at Grand Gulf. Grant remarked that it was rather late in the game for that; the colonel started to argue, but just then there was a burst of cheering on the right, and General Lawler of McClernand's command went past in his shirt sleeves, leading a charge for the bridgehead. It broke right in; the Confederates lost 1,751 more prisoners and eighteen more guns, and by the next night the coils were closing around Vicksburg and Pemberton was telling his chief engineer that his career was ended in disaster and disgrace.

Down on the river the crews of the gunboats looked aloft to see men in blue capering on those bluffs so long inexpugnable. Among them was Sherman; he turned to Grant and said, "Until this moment I never believed in your success. But this *is* a campaign; this is a success, if we never take the town."

VI

The measure of the success is statistical; in seventeen days Grant had marched 130 miles, won five battles, put out of action, killed, or captured 14,000 of Pemberton's men, taken over sixty pieces of artillery; his own loss was 2,000. Of course he took the town; there were six weeks of assaults repulsed, hard bombardment, exploding mines, and endurance to follow after that meeting of the generals, but it had become a fully combined operation once more. Down the river, covered by the navy, there poured an inexhaustible flood of ammunition, supplies, reinforcements until Grant had 75,000 men in the lines and there was no chance of relief. A few days after Vicksburg surrendered on July 4, 1863, Port Hudson gave up to a force operating out of New Orleans and the Mississippi became fully Union territory.

The obvious economic result was that communication between the Northwest and the Gulf was restored, though it never again regained the proportional importance it had before the war. The obvious tactical result was that Pemberton surrendered 30,000 men, which was more than the Confederacy could afford. The obvious strategic result was that the Confederacy was cut in two, and not only were all the forces west of the river almost as effectively out of the war as though they had been prisoners too, but also the Confederate east at once began to go hungry for lack of goods from the producing lands of western Louisiana and Texas. General Dick Taylor, in command there, remarked that when the Union river blockade clamped down he had twelve loaded steamers on the Red, on one of which alone there were 300,000 pounds of bacon for the eastern armies. None of this, or any other supplies, ever was to get through.

Vicksburg thus condemned the operative parts of the Confederacy to slow starvation by completing the iron ring the Union navy had thrown around the coast. It was a combined operation, but its effect was to extend the blockade to inland waters. The only real chance remaining to the seceded states was that of crushing one of the great northern armies in a battle, and the event which took place at Gettysburg on the day Pemberton signed the surrender papers indicated how improbable that was. Of course, there was some chance also in the political area—that war weariness would drive the Lincoln government from office in the 1864 election, as Lincoln himself at one time thought it might. But Vicksburg was also directly operative in this field, a political as well as a military victory, a visible evidence of progress; and indirectly it helped provide the means for the military success which made the political position secure. Many of the troops who went hammering into Atlanta behind Sherman at the crisis of the political campagn were those released from other preoccupations by the fall of Vicksburg.

In a sense, Atlanta, the Chattanooga battles, the Wilderness fighting, Cedar Creek may be called decisive. They ruined the morale and much of the physical equipment of the staggering Confederacy. But they all rested firmly on the foundation of Vicksburg, and it is necessary only to ask what would have happened had Grant been defeated there.

He never received qualitative credit for the accomplishment. The correspondents could not get their dispatches out during those terrific seventeen days of marching and fighting, and when it was all over the victory so stood in the shadow of Gettysburg that hardly anyone realized that the man usually set down as a dull plodder was actually a general who hurled troops along the roads at Napoleonic speed, deceived and bewildered the opposition. The campaign against Lee in Virginia looks at first sight like mere hard pounding, but when the details are examined, it contains an astonishing amount of maneuver. Grant is always pulling a corps from the right of his line and performing the extremely delicate operation of bringing it around to the left through the rear areas of forces already fighting; and it was Grant who conceived the strategy that brought an end to the war.

There is also something that, if more tenuous, goes rather deeper. The Revolution left the American army a heritage of confidence in the aimed fire of the individual infantryman. In the same way the Vicksburg campaign, as the culmination of a series of combined operations, left an inbred tradition in favor of this method of making war. And this was not to be without value some eighty years later, across the vast reaches of the Pacific and on the beachheads of Europe.

16. More than Midway

In considering the point at which decision was reached in World War II, one's attention is almost irresistibly drawn to the events of November 1942, when within a few weeks the Germans were driven from the frontiers of Egypt, the Allies made good their combined operation against western North Africa, Hitler's drive into Russia was crushed at Stalingrad, and Japanese battleships went down in flames off Guadalcanal. It is possible that the European war was indeed decided at Stalingrad, but we do not now know for certain, and perhaps we shall never know. The deliberate falsification of history by both sides was so elaborate and so complete that there is now not recoverable any account of the operation that makes military sense. For instance: the German story has been that Von Paulus was ordered to retreat from the trap and failed to do so; the Russian story is that he wanted to retreat and was not allowed. There is equally contradictory testimony on such matters as the behavior of the Rumanian troops and the efficiency of the Soviet artillery.

And Stalingrad may also be viewed as a dependent event—the product of the failure of the tank columns before Moscow in the bitter winter of 1941. The other battles of the November 1942 series were more obviously the activation of decisions already reached. None, of course, was strictly inevitable; any one might have been an Allied defeat. But it was not necessary to the outcome of the general war that all should have been Allied victories. The forces mobilized against the Axis were already so tremendous that if Stalingrad, Alamein, Casablanca, and Guadalcanal had never taken place substitute decisions must have brought the same result.

A somewhat better case as decisive actions can be made out for the air battle over Britain in 1940, the failure of the German tank columns to take Moscow in the winter of 1941, and the Allied success in overcoming the submarines in '42 and '43. But these were negative decisions, preventive victories; they determined that the Axis was not going to win in a particular way, but failed to decide that it could not win at all. That decision was reached when the industrial power of the United States was released to give full support to Britain and Russia in Europe and to take the counteroffensive against Japan. "You want a hundred airplanes for this mission?" an acute French observer reports an imaginary American officer saying to his ally. "Wouldn't a thousand be better?"

The decision that liberated such forces, that turned the Allies from a parsimonious defensive to a richly supported attack, was a battle decision.

II

No comment on the complex Japanese naval command arrangements and staff planning is necessary beyond remarking that they were outrageously intricate, and a Japanese plan of campaign was the result of a kind of badminton game played at Imperial headquarters with ideas for birds. Documents now available show that after the success of the "first phase operations" was assured as early as January 1942 the question of whether to hold an established line or to continue the offensive against the United States came up; and the decision worked out in conferences at which admirals argued with tears running down their cheeks was in favor of the occupation of Midway

Island early in June, when a full moon would make night landing operations possible.

It would take the entire strength of the "Combined Fleet," which was in effect the Japanese navy; but it had certain advantages. The consent of the dominant army people was easy to obtain since it involved the commitment of only a single regimental combat team of the forces they were so carefully hoarding; and the United States fleet would almost certainly be involved, so that what remained of it could be brought to action and destroyed. That fleet was the chief preoccupation of Admiral Isoroku Yamamoto, head of Combined Fleet, though not of the Naval General Staff, of which he was theoretically the servant. His intelligence network in Hawaii had ceased to operate, but he was fully aware that the American battle line had been smashed at Pearl Harbor. His worry was about the heavy cruisers and the carrier task forces they supported; and when Doolittle bombed Tokyo on April 18, all objections to the Midway plan ceased. Quite apart from strategic considerations, it was an absolutely intolerable loss of face that any such thing should happen. Land- or lagoon-based patrol planes must be established to prevent a repetition.

The plan for the occupation of Midway, with an appendix of the western Aleutians as a diversionary measure, was therefore definitely laid on for the full moon in early June. The proponents of the idea of first severing American communications with Australia were nevertheless strong enough in the badminton game to get their plan adopted too; a task force built around two heavy carriers and one light was accordingly dispatched to secure Port Moresby in southern New Guinea and Tulagi in the Solomons in preparation for a more serious movement against New Caledonia, the Fijis, Samoa in July. In May, while war games were being played at Japanese headquarters to determine the probable outcome of the Midway operation, this task force encountered American naval vessels in the Battle of the Coral Sea. In spite of the fact that the light carrier was lost, one of the heavies so damaged that she was barely towed back, and the other deprived of her air groups to an extent that made her inoperative, the thinking of the Japanese high command about Midway was not in the least disturbed.

They had positive evidence that two of the big American carriers had gone down at the Coral Sea. That this evidence turned out to be spurious did not affect their thinking at the time. The estimate was that the U. S. fleet had only the carriers *Enterprise* and *Hornet,* and there was a strong possibility that these were still in the Solomons late in May. To be absolutely certain, the Japanese made allowance for the possibility that they had come back north or that *Wasp* had arrived from the Atlantic and threw out a double scouting line of submarines off Hawaii to report any carrier sorties from Pearl Harbor.

Even if the American carriers did come north, even if they were joined by *Wasp,* there was little they could accomplish beyond giving the Japanese the general fleet action Yamamoto desired after Midway had been taken. Admiral Chuichi Nagumo, in charge of the carrier striking force, had *Kaga, Akagi, Hiryu,* and *Soryu,* the largest in the Japanese navy; they would launch a surprise air attack on Midway from 250 miles out, destroying shore installations and any planes based on the island. Behind them would come the Midway invasion force, covered by the "Main Force" under Yamamoto in person, to fight the Americans on the surface as soon as they reacted to the occupation of Midway. By this time the carriers would have the help of land-based air-, or at least seaplanes, from the captured islands. These were counted on merely to soften up the enemy in preparation for the battleships to step in and deliver the decisive punch.

The fleet was organized in separate units in a somewhat complicated fashion. They would operate in mutual support, according to the tactical system that had yielded such happy results at Tsushima and had since become classic in the Japanese service. The essential feature was that Yamamoto could bring into action no less than eleven battleships and ten heavy cruisers against an enemy whose gunnery forces were estimated as consisting of five heavy cruisers at most.

In the north two light carriers would knock out the small American base at Dutch Harbor, the only one in the area, as a preparation for occupying Attu, Kiska, and Adak. This would take place three days before the Midway attack. As the American fleet might be drawn in that direction, north of Midway, one wing of Yamamoto's fleet would slant in that direction during the approach; once contact was made, the others could close in quickly. Nagumo would swing out to approach Midway sharply from the northwest, with Yamamoto behind him. The invasion force would stage from Saipan and approach Midway from the west-southwest. After the occupation and the battle Nagumo's group would go to Truk to prepare for the occupation of New Caledonia and the Fijis, this in itself a preparation for bombing raids against eastern Australia, then turn back to capture Hawaii sometime in August.

The fleet sailed on 27 May, "everybody singing war songs at the top of their lungs."

III

That same day the carrier *Yorktown* arrived at Pearl Harbor from Coral Sea, badly damaged internally and leaking. The estimate of the time necessary to repair her was ninety days; it was done in two by 1,400 yard workmen who toiled right around the clock. The reason for this frantic haste was that ever since 10 May, Naval Intelligence had been feeding Admiral Chester Nimitz of the Pacific Fleet most precise information as to the composition and purposes of the Combined Fleet, information secured chiefly as the result of having broken the Japanese radio code. At the time Nimitz had the carriers *Enterprise* and *Hornet* and seven heavy cruisers in addition to *Yorktown*, and that was all he had. There were six American battleships ready for service, but they were in San Francisco, whence they could hardly reach the scene of action in time, and were a good deal slower than the Japanese ships of similar class.

Nimitz did not count on them; in diametrical opposition to Yamamoto, he was counting on no gunnery battle at all.

The ships put out on the last day of May to an area northeast of Midway under a somewhat peculiar command arrangement. Rear Admiral Frank Jack Fletcher had his flag in *Yorktown* and, as senior officer present, was technically in charge, but he had no air staff, and most of the real direction of affairs was in the hands of Rear Admiral Raymond A. Spruance, who had moved up to carriers from the cruisers. This was "the human machine," visibly cold as the mountains of the moon, who drank a pint of the strongest black coffee ever seen every morning and was supplied with a brain that was a metronome and never ceased its accurate tick. Ashore on Midway, Captain C. T. Simard was in charge; as soon as Nimitz got the word of the coming attack, he began reinforcing the land elements there. The place held a total of 121 planes, including some army B-17s and a good many navy patrol planes, besides light bombers and a torpedo unit. The patrol planes were flying day and night searches up to 700 miles out on all directions on the arcs west of Midway, but bad weather hampered them much. The shore defenses had a heavily reinforced marine defense battalion, the two islands that comprise Midway were ringed with guns and obstacles, and there were ten motor torpedo boats in the lagoon. Bombproof shelters were supplied for all hands. A cable connecting Midway with Hawaii insured that there would be no abnormally heavy radio traffic to attract Japanese attention.

The sortie of the American ships on May 31 introduced a first and violent element of error into the Japanese plan. The submarine scouting line sent to watch for them was not yet in position, so they saw nothing. As Yamamoto approached Midway through rain and fog that gave him admirable concealment but made navigation and communications difficult, he had no positive information whatever as to the number or whereabouts of the American ships.

There was an arrangement that might have rectified this lack. The Japanese planned to have Pearl Harbor and its approaches watched by four-engine flying boats working out of Wotje beyond their normal range and refueled by submarines at French Frigate Shoal, between Midway and Hawaii. But they had already tried that one in March, and when the flying boats then showed up at Pearl, Nimitz deduced precisely what was going on. The Japanese submarines that were to refuel planes for the Midway operation found the approaches to French Frigate Shoal mined and the place crawling with American patrol craft, so the air scouting program had to be dropped. Thus Yamamoto had to depend for intelligence on the Naval General Staff in Tokyo, which continued to advise as to the possibility that the two American carriers were in the Solomons, which would deprive him of the chance for a showdown battle with the United States fleet. He "seemed in unusually low spirits." The opinion of his staff was that the Imperial fleet would have plenty of time to deal with the Americans after the occupation of Midway. They would have 1,100 miles to run from Pearl after they heard the news of the attack.

I V

The background was now complete; the rest was up to the operators. Those in the Aleutians achieved next to nothing on either side. The two light Japanese carriers ran their bombing raid against Dutch Harbor on June 3 without damaging anything important or suffering any important damage in return; but when they tried a second attack, the planes were sent on out of the fog by army fighters, P-40s. This meant that the Americans had in the area an air base of whose existence there had been no previous report and of whose location the Japanese had no idea; and the photos taken during the Dutch Harbor raid showed a far more solid installation than had been expected. Hosogaya, the admiral in charge, turned back and settled for Attu and Kiska; Adak would be altogether too near that new American air base. His effort at drawing American strength northward had failed because of Nimitz's prior information as to the real objective.

The curtain raiser for the big show came at 0900 on the morning of June 3, when a patrol plane sighted the Japanese invasion force 600 miles southwest of Midway and dogged it for several hours. The B-17s, which had the range, were sent out to make a high-level bombing attack in the afternoon. Actually, they hit nothing but, in a manner that was to be highly characteristic of Army Air during the entire operation, reported damage to two battleships and a transport and persuaded Navy to send out a submarine to look for cripples. During the night four of the big patrol planes took off with torpedoes under their wings, the first time they had been used in this way. They ran in on the convoy, loosed torpedoes down a path of moonlight, and one of them got a hit on a tanker that caused twenty-three casualties, but the ship was able to maintain station.

At 0430 on June 4 the Japanese striking force for Midway, 108 planes, took off from Nagumo's carriers, with the deck crews shouting the *Banzai* as each machine cleared; half an hour later came another 108. The ships were 240 miles from Midway, still under cloud cover and low visibility. At the same hour a search for American ships was flown, and Japanese accounts make it clear that this operation was formal, perfunctory; hardly anyone in the Japanese fleet expected the Americans to be at sea, far less that they would be looking for the invaders with violence in their hearts.

The American ships got the word of enemy carriers present at 0534 from a patrol plane; then successive messages that spoke of many enemy planes heading for Midway and two Japanese carriers with battleship cover. As it happened, the reported position of the Japanese was wrong. A little later Admiral Fletcher, whose ship had flown the American dawn patrol and who wanted his planes back, signaled Spruance to proceed southwest with the other two carriers and strike, promising to follow with *Yorktown* as soon as possible.

This was at 0607; and at almost the same moment radar

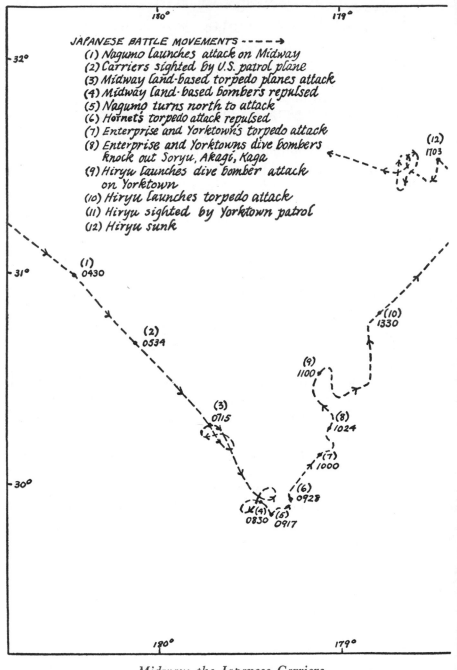

JAPANESE BATTLE MOVEMENTS - - - - →
  (1) Nagumo launches attack on Midway
  (2) Carriers sighted by U.S. patrol plane
  (3) Midway land-based torpedo planes attack
  (4) Midway land-based bombers repulsed
  (5) Nagumo turns north to attack
  (6) Hornets torpedo attack repulsed
  (7) Enterprise and Yorktowns torpedo attack
  (8) Enterprise and Yorktowns dive bombers
      knock out Soryu, Akagi, Kaga
  (9) Hiryu launches dive bomber attack
      on Yorktown
  (10) Hiryu launches torpedo attack
  (11) Hiryu sighted by Yorktown patrol
  (12) Hiryu sunk

(1) 0430
(2) 0534
(3) 0715
(4) 0850
(5) 0917
(6) 0928
(7) 1000
(8) 1024
(9) 1100
(10) 1330
(12) 1703

Midway; the Japanese Carriers

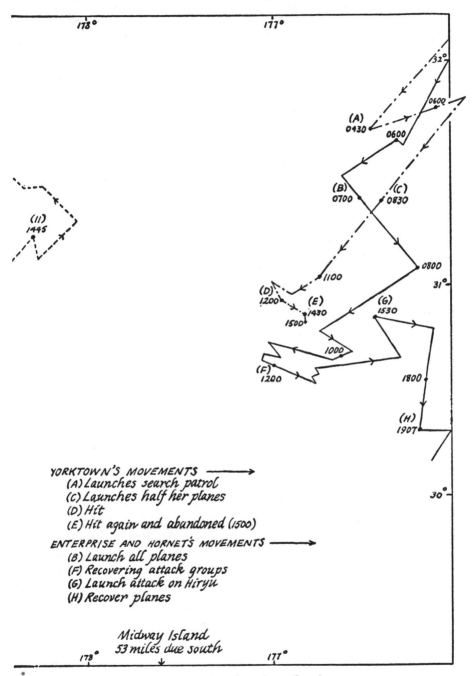

178°   177°   32°

0600

(A)
0430   0600

(B)   (C)
0700   0830

0800   31°

(11)
1445

1100

(D)   (E)   (G)
1200   1430   1530

1500

1000

(F)   1800
1200

(H)
190T

YORKTOWN'S MOVEMENTS ⟶
  (A) Launches search patrol
  (C) Launches half her planes
  (D) Hit
  (E) Hit again and abandoned (1500)

ENTERPRISE AND HORNET'S MOVEMENTS ⟶
  (B) Launch all planes
  (F) Recovering attack groups
  (G) Launch attack on Hiryu
  (H) Recover planes

30°

Midway Island
53 miles due south

178°   177°

Midway; the American Carriers

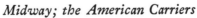

warning sent every plane off Midway—patrol planes to the rear, out of trouble, a marine fighter group to attack the incoming Japanese, a formation of six navy torpedo planes, another of marine dive bombers, four army B-26s carrying torpedoes, and sixteen of the B-17 Flying Fortresses, all for the counterattack.

At the island the Japanese came in through what they described as fierce anti-aircraft fire, burned out a hangar and a fuel tank, blew up a storehouse which scattered packages of cigarettes all over the island, and did assorted damage to other aboveground installations. In the air their tactically superior, too numerous Zero fighters made mincemeat of the marine squadron, fifteen of whose twenty-seven did not return. But the attackers did little damage to the airstrips, caused only twenty casualties, and they were sadly surprised at not obtaining surprise and catching American planes on the ground. As the attackers soared back to their carriers with the black plume of the burning fuel tank beneath, the air group leader radioed, "There is need for another attack. Time: 0700."

He was perfectly right; not even an invasion force supported by battleships and heavy cruisers could readily have struck home against the shore installations remaining. But a decisive factor in what happened next was the failure of the land-based Midway planes. The torpedo carriers came first; they got not a single hit and only three out of ten came back, two of which crash-landed. Then came twenty-seven dive bombers, half of them shot down, again without damage to the ships; and the B-17s, whose efforts produced nothing but boasts from the army air force. At 0715 the land-based air attacks from Midway were over and not a Japanese ship had been damaged. This carried conviction to Admiral Nagumo; the Americans were not going to hurt him, and their Midway base needed another strike. He had on the decks of his carriers ninety-three planes armed with torpedoes and armor-piercers on the off chance that enemy surface forces might be encountered. Now these were taken down to the hangars to be rearmed with fragmentation bombs for the second strike on Midway.

While this was going on, there came a report from a Japanese cruiser search plane which had taken off belatedly; it had found five American cruisers and five destroyers, and twenty-five minutes later it brought the surprising news that there was an American carrier present. By this time the re-armed planes were on the flight decks again, and Nagumo had a baby in his lap without an adequate supply of diapers. The ninety-three were all torpedo-type planes, which had to fly level for an attack, and the fate of the unescorted American torpedo planes showed they stood little chance without fighter cover. But the first wave of Japanese fighters was just begin-ning to arrive overhead with the planes of the Midway strike, low on gas and needing to be taken aboard. The second wave of fighters was flying combat patrol, and certainly could not accompany a preventive strike.

Under the circumstances, Nagumo decided to play it safe. He turned north to get deeper under cloud cover and avoid attack while the planes of the Midway strike were taken in. The combat patrol remained up; the planes on the decks were struck below for a second time, to be rearmed for work against ships. This would give Nagumo plenty of strength for an attack, but the second reloading was done so hurriedly that there was not time to send the fragmentation bombs back to the magazines, so they were arranged in racks on the hangar decks. It still took time to recover and rearm the planes of the Midway strike, and the action against the American force of "five cruisers, five destroyers, and one carrier" was scheduled for 1030.

Spruance originally intended to run southwest until 0900 and launch his strike 100 miles from the Japanese force, now accurately located. The news of the attack on Midway changed his mind; if he launched early, though the distance was so great that he was likely to lose many planes through running out of gas, he just might catch the Japs refueling. He launched then, a little after 0700, a full strike of every operational plane he had, itself a daring decision. *Yorktown,* coming along behind, did not launch for more than another hour, and then only half her planes.

The air squadrons made their getaway in standard formation, torpedo planes low down, dive bombers higher, and fighters above all. But Nagumo's turn north and floating layers of cloud introduced an element of uncertainty. The Japanese ships were not where they were expected to be; *Hornet's* dive bombers and fighters swung southeast toward Midway to search for them in that direction, missed them entirely, and had to put in at the island, out of the battle for that day. But underneath, Lieutenant Commander John J. Waldron, with the fifteen planes of *Hornet's* Torpedo 8, saw smoke northwestward; he turned in that direction and about 0917 made out the four Japanese carriers in a diamond formation. Nagumo had just finished recovering his planes and was again turning toward the Americans to launch his attack.

Waldron had no fighter cover and had flown so far that he knew his chances of return were poor, but he bored in. He was promptly jumped by no less than fifty Zero fighters and ran into a terrific curtain of flak. Very few of his planes survived to launch torpedoes, and of those that did, every one was shot down. There was a single survivor, Ensign George H. Gay, who came up to find a bag floating free from the wreck of his plane, with a rubber life raft in it. He hid under a seat cushion to keep out of sight of low-flying Japanese fighters and from that ringside position saw the next wave of attack come in.

This was Torpedo 6 from *Enterprise*, under Lieutenant Commander Eugene E. Lindsey, which had lost its fighters in the clouds. Doctrine called for him to wait and attack simultaneously with the dive bombers, but he was short on fuel. He went in, therefore, and the tragedy of Torpedo 8 was repeated. Zeros and flak got all but four of his planes, and again there were no hits on the Japs. The attack was hardly over when *Yorktown's* Torpedo 3 arrived; they had fighter escort, but nowhere near enough to meet the swarming Japanese patrols. Only five planes got torpedoes away and three of these were shot down; again no Japanese ship was hit.

Thus at a little after 1000 the American torpedo attack had been utterly suppressed without doing the slightest damage, and only four of its planes got home to mother. On the Japanese carriers they were feeling high; deck crews cheered the pilots of fighters returning for ammunition and patted them on the shoulder. The radical maneuvering to avoid torpedo attack had prevented getting planes away, but now it was over; at 1020, Admiral Nagumo gave the word to launch, and the four carriers turned into the wind, their decks covered with planes, engines revved up and ready.

V

There were still, however, the thirty-seven dive bombers from *Enterprise* under Lieutenant Commander Clarence McClusky, the seventeen from *Yorktown* under Lieutenant Commander Maxwell Leslie. The latter had been instructed that if the Japanese were not in the anticipated position he was to search for them on a reverse course. McClusky, flying longer, got off on an errant west-northwest course, but saw a Japanese destroyer beneath and projected its line of motion. The consequence was that both forces arrived simultaneously over the Japanese carriers at 1024, while all their fighters were at the low level, where they had been demolishing the torpedo planes, in time to treat Ensign Gay on his rubber raft to such a spectacle as no man had ever seen or would again.

Back on the American carriers they heard McClusky's ardent swearing as the first three bombs missed. Then *Kaga* was hit forward of the island, killing everyone on the bridge, hit three times amidships, with all the planes on deck set afire, and one bomb penetrating the hangar to the gasoline tanks; she drifted, a mass of flame. *Akagi* took two, one a 1,000-pounder just behind the midship elevator, that sent it drooping into the hangar as though it were rubber, and all those bombs and torpedoes began to burn and go off; the other on the port side aft, which left the armed planes on deck belching flame, smoke, and explosions. Everything began burning, even the fireproof doors burned down and the fire mains melted. *Soryu* took three hits from the *Yorktown* planes, one that folded the forward elevator back against the bridge, two amidships; the whole deck became a sheet of flame in a matter of seconds and the fires were joined by those from the hangar so rapidly that "Abandon ship" was ordered in twenty minutes.

In five minutes of attack the entire complexion of the battle had changed, and the Japanese no longer had their margin of superiority.

There remained *Hiryu*, bearing the flag of Rear Admiral Tamon Yamaguchi, one of the most highly regarded officers of the Imperial Navy; at the point of the diamond formation the ship had been farther north and more under cloud cover than the others and thus escaped attention during that devastating attack. Nearly a day's steaming farther north still were the two light carriers that had bombed Dutch Harbor. They were already on their way south; Yamamoto ordered them to speed up to join *Hiryu* on the morning of June 5 for a renewal of the battle, which had not gone well this day, while the battleships and cruisers covering the occupation force joined his own to press east for a night surface action and *Hiryu* launched an attack on what was still believed to be the only American carrier present.

This happened to be *Yorktown*. After launching their attacks the American carriers turned southeast and away into the wind to recover planes, but Fletcher's flagship was still some distance behind the others and was being dogged by a search plane from a cruiser shortly after the three Japanese carriers began to burn. Yamaguchi launched eighteen dive bombers, with six fighters for cover, at 1100; two hours later (it takes time to ready these strikes) ten torpedo planes took off with another six fighters. It would be just after noon when the first wave reached *Yorktown*, which was just preparing to take in her own dive bombers. They were waved off to land on *Enterprise;* fighters and escort took on the attackers and knocked down all but five, but the ship was hit three times by 500-pounders.

The fires they set were quickly brought under control, but the third bomb disabled two boilers and snuffed out the fires in others, so that the big carrier gradually ground to a stop. The damage control parties worked hard; by 1340 they had the ship up to eighteen knots again, but at 1430, when the torpedo attack came in, she still did not have her full speed and maneuverability, and though five of the torpedo planes and three of the fighters were shot down, *Yorktown* took two torpedo hits that cut off all power and gave her a deadly list. "Abandon ship" was ordered, and only salvage parties were aboard when she was finished off by a Jap submarine on the morning of June 7.

But while *Yorktown* was taking it, two important things happened. One was the return to *Hiryu* of a new type search plane, sent out earlier, whose radio had failed. The pilot verbally brought the news that instead of a single American carrier there were three, *Enterprise*, *Yorktown*, and *Hornet*, two of which were not supposed to be there and one of which was supposed to be at the bottom of the Coral Sea. The second event was that before *Yorktown* was knocked out Admiral Fletcher ordered a wide ten-plane search. At 1445, after three hours of hunting, it found *Hiryu*, and at 1530, Spruance (now in command, since Fletcher was aboard a cruiser) launched a strike of twenty-four dive bombers, a mixed group from all the carriers, with McClusky leading.

It had no fighter cover, but aboard *Hiryu* there were only six fighters left; their pilots had been working since before dawn and were at the utmost limit of exhaustion. When McClusky's planes roared in at 1703, there was practically nothing but anti-aircraft fire to oppose them and they landed four hits in the bridge area. The whole foredeck was peeled back, all forms of control were lost, and gigantic fires began to run through the ship. Like the others, she was doomed; but it was not until dawn that she went down; all three of them were under water by 1925.

During the night Admiral Yamamoto underwent a change of heart. He had been steaming east, still hoping for that night surface engagment, but as the constellations streamed past and intelligence slowly ironed out the details of the shimmering picture, it became more and more likely that instead he would have a dawn attack from those dive bombers that had wrecked his four beautiful carriers; there were no contact reports and the Americans appeared to be retiring eastward. (This was perfectly correct; Spruance had not the slightest intention of fighting Japanese surface forces at night, when his carriers could not operate, but still desirous of being in position to break up a dawn landing, turned west again at midnight.) The Americans clearly still had two big carriers operative; Yamamoto's own light carriers would not reach the scene until too late and, with the attrition their air groups had taken in the Aleutians, would be no match for *Enterprise* and *Hornet* even if *Yorktown* were badly used up, as his flyers claimed. At two in the morning he signaled the powerful squadron of four new heavy cruisers that were to have bombarded Midway during the night to give up the idea; at 0253 he turned westward himself and the conquest was abandoned. Next morning he sat on the forebridge of the largest battleship in the world, sipping rice gruel with a pale face and staring eyes. Few men have come down farther in twenty-four hours.

But Yamamoto was not yet through with Spruance. When the heavy cruiser squadron began its retreat during the night, it both saw and was spotted by an American submarine. The admiral in charge ordered a sharp simultaneous turn away, but the last ship in line, *Mogami*, did not get the signal soon enough. She came so violently in contact with the stern of *Mikuma*, next ahead, that *Mogami's* bow was all staved in. She could not make more than sixteen knots, and dawn of June 5 found her pushing westward with the slightly damaged *Mikuma* and two destroyers in company, a good deal to the south of Yamamoto's main body, which now comprised practically all the other ships present. A patrol plane sighted the two cruisers; the B-17s went out from Midway but, as usual, accomplished nothing, this time because they could not find the ships. There were six of the marine planes left at Midway; they were sent out also, picked up an oil slick and charged in, a glide-bombing attack, the only kind they could make. The flak was so heavy that it bounced them around and spoiled their aim, but when Captain Richard E. Fleming's plane was hopelessly hit, he crash-landed on *Mikuma's* No. 4 turret, and a damaging hit that was. It spread fire over the air intake to the starboard engine room, brought about a fume explosion that killed everyone in the compartment and disabled the engine itself, so that both cruisers were now cripples.

Spruance was not involved in this attack. At dawn on June 5 he was still without assurance that *Hiryu* had gone down, and late reports from patrol planes seemed to indicate that she was still afloat. The weather was thick; it was afternoon before a strike of fifty planes could be flown, and all they found was a single destroyer, dispatched by Nagumo to pick up *Hiryu* survivors. They attacked her, with the worst luck of any strike flown during the battle; she shot down one plane and was not hurt.

The Japanese main body was now out of range, but the damaged cruisers were not and Spruance held on after them all night, launching the first of three strikes before dawn. The cruisers had no cover but their potent anti-aircraft fire, and the planes hit them hard. *Mogami* got a bomb that penetrated a turret and killed everyone within, and another that sealed a burning engine room and killed ninety men. *Mikuma* took six hits from heavy bombs, fires raged through the ship, her own torpedoes exploded, and finally a magazine went. She sank about noon; most of the survivors were killed by another bomb as they stood on the deck of a destroyer. *Mogami* escaped, but in such shape that she could not put to sea again for two years.

That was the Battle of Midway. Spruance was getting so close to range of land-based planes from Wake that he turned back.

V I

The battle has been subjected to more detailed analysis than any other sea fight except Jutland, and deservedly, for it was one of the two naval battles in American history in which the distinctly inferior force won crushingly. (Lake Champlain was the other.) It is easy to make a catalogue of Yamamoto's mistakes. He was the great apostle of aviation in the Japanese navy, the man who organized the Pearl Harbor attack as a purely naval air operation, yet here he assigned the carriers to a secondary role and tried to do everything with his battle line. The heavy ships were not even near enough to furnish gunnery cover for the carriers—and it is to be remembered that later in the war no carrier that had a battleship in company was sunk.

The fact that the Americans had cracked the Japanese code was not properly Yamamoto's fault, of course, but the fact that he failed to allow for so many of their carriers' being in the area is; and this was doubly compounded by the failure to take any precautions against the chance of their being there. A submarine scouting line is very useful but, in the nature of things, not infallible; they cannot see very far and are apt to be driven underwater just when it is most important that they should be seeing. When the air reconnaissance via French Frigate Shoal failed, Yamamoto should have realized that there was a large area of ocean in which he knew absolutely nothing about American movements, and that area included the space it was most vital for him to know about.

Nagumo shares the fault here. His dawn search of June 4 employed far too few planes and they did not go far enough. Japanese sources place the fundamental blame on a doctrine that called for all possible planes to be used for attack instead of for search; and behind that on an arrogance that made a fatally easy assumption of victory, because everything had previously gone well in their campaigns. Even Coral Sea did not disturb this complacency; at Combined Fleet headquarters it was counted a victory on the basis of the two American carriers sunk, and Admiral Inouye, who ordered the withdrawal, received a severe wigging for not pressing on.

So the Japanese allowed themselves to be surprised because they felt too strong to be surprised. But there is no negative without a positive, and on the positive side of the American victory there is not only the work of the cryptographers, who laid the foundation for the whole business, but also the speed and thoroughness with which the information was exploited. There may have been complacency in American councils before Pearl Harbor; there certainly was none at the date when *Yorktown's* repairs were rushed through in forty-eight hours of round-the-clock work or Nimitz's provision for moving every available form of force up to Midway; or in the continual painstaking searches flown by American planes. The afternoon search that located *Hiryu* after the other Jap carriers were already fatally hurt, after the American planes had been flying and fighting since before daybreak, actually contained more planes and covered a wider area than Nagumo's search at dawn, before he had any information at all.

That is, the Americans took pains and the Japanese were too confident to take them. At first sight there seems also an element of luck involved in the opportune arrival of the dive bombers over the Japanese fleet at the precise moment when their attack would prove fatal. But luck will not explain the fact that Spruance cleared his decks in expectation that he would catch the Midway strike returning. It was, rather, bad luck that the American torpedo planes, through one accident or another, had to go in piecemeal, without fighter cover and unco-ordinated with the bombers. The basic planning and tactics were sufficiently good too for such an onset of unfavorable circumstance. Later in the war the American forces had some luck, for example the single torpedo that sank the giant carrier *Taiho* at the Philippine Sea; but there was none of that elusive component at Midway.

And the battle ruined Japan, as the title of a Japanese book about it says. Nobody on the American side realized it, even though Admiral Nimitz delivered himself of a pun about being "Mid-way to victory" in his communiqué. But the Japanese realized it, at least at the topmost level. Even their official documents glozed over the matter, even within the Japanese navy it was almost treason to discuss what really happened. Nagumo's air officer, who escaped wounded, was taken from the rescue ship by night in a covered litter and held incommunicado in a hospital for weeks until it was certain he would not talk; and he was not the only one subjected to isolation for fear the dreadful secret might leak. But it was not a secret from Yamamoto; he now knew that he could not gain his decisive victory before the industrial power of the United States was cast into the scale.

Not only were the four carriers so nearly irreplaceable that their loss caused a revision of the entire Japanese ship-building program, to the detriment even of the escorts that were so bitterly needed when the American submarines got to work. This was serious enough, deadly enough; but the control of the sea air was more. At the hour when the battle was fought, there were already nine new United States carriers on the way against two for Japan, and the latter could never catch up after the Midway subtractions. Not only was there a crippling and unforeseen loss of planes. The sinking of the carriers cost the Japanese 250 of them, and the naval air squadrons that were supposed to have a one-third reserve suddenly had no reserve at all.

But the most serious loss was among the pilots who were shot down or killed when the bombs fell among the planes ready for flight on the carrier decks. It can be said that the Japanese would have come out of the battle better if they had never tried to make the attack on *Yorktown* at all, even though they eventually sank her. They spent too many pilots.

Before the war there was opinion and even a certain number of flat statements that "the Japanese do not make good aviators." At Pearl Harbor, Coral Sea, and Midway this seemed to be disproved. The Japanese flyers there yielded nothing to the Americans in any aspect of their art. But in the long run the prewar statement turned out to be true. The Japanese made good flyers only after careful selection and prolonged training under experienced men, much longer training than that required by American aviators, and at Midway the seed corn was eaten up. The indispensable teachers and squadron leaders with combat experience were shot down or went down with their ships, and in spite of the desperate combats that some of the new men later waged in the Solomons, the service never recovered. New men were trained to fly after a fashion, but it was not a good fashion, and two years after Midway, 404 of them were shot down in a morning at the Philippine Sea, when Spruance collected his dividend on the investment he made on June 4, 1942.

Bibliography for Further Reading

It would be impudent (and imprudent) to attempt a thorough bibliography for a book which covers most of the course of recorded history, but some indication of sources used and places where further information can be found by anyone interested may not be out of place.

For Alexander the Great the sources are very good, considering the lapse of time and the disappearance of the works of so many ancient authors. Arrian is the chief one, and though he wrote some time after the events he chronicles, he had the great advantage of having before him the memoirs of two of Alexander's generals, Ptolemy and Aristobulus. Plutarch, Diodorus Siculus, Curtius, and Justin have also given connected accounts of Alexander, and though they often used inferior source material, they just as often check on each other, so that it is fairly easy to get at what went on.

As to Pyrrhus, the sources are just as bad as they are good for Alexander. The books of Livy that cover the period are among the lost; Diodorus does not supply much, and Polybius hardly anything. Dionysius of Halicarnassus and Hieronymus give accounts, but only in flashes; the main reliance among the ancients is Plutarch. Colonel T. A. Dodge (*Hannibal*) went over the battlefields and worked out the course of events with a keen military eye.

G. P. Baker's *Justinian* is a tower of light for anyone dealing with the period. Of course, he based on some secondary sources, such as Gibbon and J. H. Bury's *History of the Later Roman Empire,* which have also been used here. The basic oiriginal sources are Marcellinus and Procopius. Delbrück (*Geschichte der Kriegskunst*) is too much of a debunker by half, but useful on details of arms and equipment.

Most of the ultimate sources for Kadisiyah are Moslem chronicles and, besides being romantic and highly mendacious, they have little regard for either figures or dates. The best is that of Al Tabari, written in the ninth century, and translated in the *Journal of the American Oriental Society.* Modern writers have done a good deal of emendation and deduction; those in the *Cambridge Medieval History* are worth reading, and also Huart's *Ancient Persia and Iranian Civilization* and Sir Percy Sykes' *History of Persia.*

The excellent papers in the *Cambridge Medieval History* are most of the background for Las Navas de Tolosa. The Spanish chronicles are windy and picturesque, without throwing a great deal of light, but they have been winnowed by several English authors, notably George Power (*History of the Enpire of the Mussulmans in Spain and Portugal*), H. E. Watts (*The Christian Recovery of Spain*), and Stanley Lane-Poole (*The Moors in Spain*).

An excellent book, *The Sieges of Vienna,* was translated from the German of Karl Schwimmer "and other sources" by the Earl of Ellesmere. R. B. Merriman's *Suleiman the Magnificent* is worth a look, as is Eversley's *Turkish Empire.* An article on Salm by Johann Newald appeared in the *Verein für Geschichte der Stadt Wien, Berichte.*

As for Leyden, J. L. Motley's *Rise of the Dutch Republic* still stands up after nearly a century, and he went so thoroughly into the original sources that no one need do so again. Also see Frederick Harisson's *William the Silent* and Avermaete's *Les Gueux de Mer.*

Gustavus Adolphus, by Colonel T. A. Dodge, is a first-class military work. Behind it stand a number of other sources, one of the better being C. V. Wedgwood's *Thirty Years' War,* a book of the same title by Anton Gindely, and Bryce, *The Holy Roman Empire*. The quotations are from *George Fleetwood's Letter to His Father*, which was not dug up and published in the *Camden Miscellany* until 1847.

For Frederick the Great nobody is quite up to Carlyle, even at this date. His research was enormous and painstaking, and he is surprisingly good on military detail. Dorn's *Competition for Empire* is also good. Most readers will not want to bother with the numerous German sources.

Parkman's *Montcalm and Wolfe* is, of course, the classic for Quebec. The general background is nicely covered by Dorn's *Competition for Empire*, naval and strategic matters by Mahan's *Influence of Seapower upon History*, and *Types of Naval Officers*, while there is excellent detail on both Quebec and Quiberon Bay in the monumental *History of the Royal Navy*, edited by W. Laird Clowes.

On the American Revolution the best authorities are F. V. Greene's *American Revolution* and Douglas Southall Freeman's huge *George Washington*. Naval matters are covered by Mahan and Clowes, mentioned above, and the *Histoire de la Marine Française* of René Jouan.

The literature of the Napoleonic period is so huge that even compiling a supplementary reading list from it is a formidable task. The present author has covered the military and naval background in two books; *Empire and the Sea* and *Empire and the Glory*.

The literature of the American Civil War is almost as extensive as that devoted to Napoleon. But Grant's *Personal Memoirs* may be mentioned, also a recent volume by E. S. Miers, *Web of Victory*. More nearly contemporary are F. V. Greene's *The Mississippi*, and *Battles and Leaders of the Civil War*.

Further reading on Midway can be done in S. E. Morison's *Coral Sea, Midway and Submarine Actions*, a part of his history of the naval war; also Fuchida and Okumiya, *Midway: the Battle that Doomed Japan*, and the interrogations of Japanese naval officers, an official publication.

INDEX

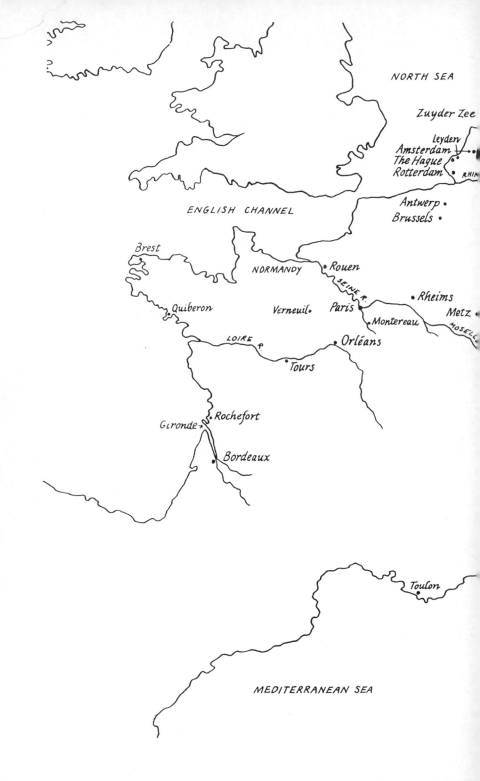

A CATALOG OF SELECTED
DOVER BOOKS
IN ALL FIELDS OF INTEREST

A CATALOG OF SELECTED DOVER
BOOKS IN ALL FIELDS OF INTEREST

CONCERNING THE SPIRITUAL IN ART, Wassily Kandinsky. Pioneering work by father of abstract art. Thoughts on color theory, nature of art. Analysis of earlier masters. 12 illustrations. 80pp. of text. 5⅜ x 8½.   0-486-23411-8

CELTIC ART: The Methods of Construction, George Bain. Simple geometric techniques for making Celtic interlacements, spirals, Kells-type initials, animals, humans, etc. Over 500 illustrations. 160pp. 9 x 12. (Available in U.S. only.)   0-486-22923-8

AN ATLAS OF ANATOMY FOR ARTISTS, Fritz Schider. Most thorough reference work on art anatomy in the world. Hundreds of illustrations, including selections from works by Vesalius, Leonardo, Goya, Ingres, Michelangelo, others. 593 illustrations. 192pp. 7⅛ x 10¼.   0-486-20241-0

CELTIC HAND STROKE-BY-STROKE (Irish Half-Uncial from "The Book of Kells"): An Arthur Baker Calligraphy Manual, Arthur Baker. Complete guide to creating each letter of the alphabet in distinctive Celtic manner. Covers hand position, strokes, pens, inks, paper, more. Illustrated. 48pp. 8¼ x 11.   0-486-24336-2

EASY ORIGAMI, John Montroll. Charming collection of 32 projects (hat, cup, pelican, piano, swan, many more) specially designed for the novice origami hobbyist. Clearly illustrated easy-to-follow instructions insure that even beginning papercrafters will achieve successful results. 48pp. 8¼ x 11.   0-486-27298-2

BLOOMINGDALE'S ILLUSTRATED 1886 CATALOG: Fashions, Dry Goods and Housewares, Bloomingdale Brothers. Famed merchants' extremely rare catalog depicting about 1,700 products: clothing, housewares, firearms, dry goods, jewelry, more. Invaluable for dating, identifying vintage items. Also, copyright-free graphics for artists, designers. Co-published with Henry Ford Museum & Greenfield Village. 160pp. 8¼ x 11.   0-486-25780-0

THE ART OF WORLDLY WISDOM, Baltasar Gracian. "Think with the few and speak with the many," "Friends are a second existence," and "Be able to forget" are among this 1637 volume's 300 pithy maxims. A perfect source of mental and spiritual refreshment, it can be opened at random and appreciated either in brief or at length. 128pp. 5⅜ x 8½.   0-486-44034-6

JOHNSON'S DICTIONARY: A Modern Selection, Samuel Johnson (E. L. McAdam and George Milne, eds.). This modern version reduces the original 1755 edition's 2,300 pages of definitions and literary examples to a more manageable length, retaining the verbal pleasure and historical curiosity of the original. 480pp. 5⁵⁄₁₆ x 8¼.   0-486-44089-3

ADVENTURES OF HUCKLEBERRY FINN, Mark Twain, Illustrated by E. W. Kemble. A work of eternal richness and complexity, a source of ongoing critical debate, and a literary landmark, Twain's 1885 masterpiece about a barefoot boy's journey of self-discovery has enthralled readers around the world. This handsome clothbound reproduction of the first edition features all 174 of the original black-and-white illustrations. 368pp. 5⅜ x 8½.   0-486-44322-1

STICKLEY CRAFTSMAN FURNITURE CATALOGS, Gustav Stickley and L. & J. G. Stickley. Beautiful, functional furniture in two authentic catalogs from 1910. 594 illustrations, including 277 photos, show settles, rockers, armchairs, reclining chairs, bookcases, desks, tables. 183pp. 6½ x 9¼. 0-486-23838-5

AMERICAN LOCOMOTIVES IN HISTORIC PHOTOGRAPHS: 1858 to 1949, Ron Ziel (ed.). A rare collection of 126 meticulously detailed official photographs, called "builder portraits," of American locomotives that majestically chronicle the rise of steam locomotive power in America. Introduction. Detailed captions. xi+ 129pp. 9 x 12. 0-486-27393-8

AMERICA'S LIGHTHOUSES: An Illustrated History, Francis Ross Holland, Jr. Delightfully written, profusely illustrated fact-filled survey of over 200 American lighthouses since 1716. History, anecdotes, technological advances, more. 240pp. 8 x 10¾. 0-486-25576-X

TOWARDS A NEW ARCHITECTURE, Le Corbusier. Pioneering manifesto by founder of "International School." Technical and aesthetic theories, views of industry, economics, relation of form to function, "mass-production split" and much more. Profusely illustrated. 320pp. 6⅛ x 9¼. (Available in U.S. only.) 0-486-25023-7

HOW THE OTHER HALF LIVES, Jacob Riis. Famous journalistic record, exposing poverty and degradation of New York slums around 1900, by major social reformer. 100 striking and influential photographs. 233pp. 10 x 7⅞. 0-486-22012-5

FRUIT KEY AND TWIG KEY TO TREES AND SHRUBS, William M. Harlow. One of the handiest and most widely used identification aids. Fruit key covers 120 deciduous and evergreen species; twig key 160 deciduous species. Easily used. Over 300 photographs. 126pp. 5⅜ x 8½. 0-486-20511-8

COMMON BIRD SONGS, Dr. Donald J. Borror. Songs of 60 most common U.S. birds: robins, sparrows, cardinals, bluejays, finches, more—arranged in order of increasing complexity. Up to 9 variations of songs of each species.
Cassette and manual 0-486-99911-4

ORCHIDS AS HOUSE PLANTS, Rebecca Tyson Northen. Grow cattleyas and many other kinds of orchids—in a window, in a case, or under artificial light. 63 illustrations. 148pp. 5⅜ x 8½. 0-486-23261-1

MONSTER MAZES, Dave Phillips. Masterful mazes at four levels of difficulty. Avoid deadly perils and evil creatures to find magical treasures. Solutions for all 32 exciting illustrated puzzles. 48pp. 8¼ x 11. 0-486-26005-4

MOZART'S DON GIOVANNI (DOVER OPERA LIBRETTO SERIES), Wolfgang Amadeus Mozart. Introduced and translated by Ellen H. Bleiler. Standard Italian libretto, with complete English translation. Convenient and thoroughly portable—an ideal companion for reading along with a recording or the performance itself. Introduction. List of characters. Plot summary. 121pp. 5¼ x 8½. 0-486-24944-1

FRANK LLOYD WRIGHT'S DANA HOUSE, Donald Hoffmann. Pictorial essay of residential masterpiece with over 160 interior and exterior photos, plans, elevations, sketches and studies. 128pp. 9¼ x 10¾. 0-486-29120-0

THE CLARINET AND CLARINET PLAYING, David Pino. Lively, comprehensive work features suggestions about technique, musicianship, and musical interpretation, as well as guidelines for teaching, making your own reeds, and preparing for public performance. Includes an intriguing look at clarinet history. "A godsend," *The Clarinet*, Journal of the International Clarinet Society. Appendixes. 7 illus. 320pp. 5⅜ x 8½. 0-486-40270-3

HOLLYWOOD GLAMOR PORTRAITS, John Kobal (ed.). 145 photos from 1926-49. Harlow, Gable, Bogart, Bacall; 94 stars in all. Full background on photographers, technical aspects. 160pp. 8⅜ x 11¼. 0-486-23352-9

THE RAVEN AND OTHER FAVORITE POEMS, Edgar Allan Poe. Over 40 of the author's most memorable poems: "The Bells," "Ulalume," "Israfel," "To Helen," "The Conqueror Worm," "Eldorado," "Annabel Lee," many more. Alphabetic lists of titles and first lines. 64pp. 5³⁄₁₆ x 8¼. 0-486-26685-0

PERSONAL MEMOIRS OF U. S. GRANT, Ulysses Simpson Grant. Intelligent, deeply moving firsthand account of Civil War campaigns, considered by many the finest military memoirs ever written. Includes letters, historic photographs, maps and more. 528pp. 6⅛ x 9¼. 0-486-28587-1

ANCIENT EGYPTIAN MATERIALS AND INDUSTRIES, A. Lucas and J. Harris. Fascinating, comprehensive, thoroughly documented text describes this ancient civilization's vast resources and the processes that incorporated them in daily life, including the use of animal products, building materials, cosmetics, perfumes and incense, fibers, glazed ware, glass and its manufacture, materials used in the mummification process, and much more. 544pp. 6¹⁄₈ x 9¹⁄₄. (Available in U.S. only.) 0-486-40446-3

RUSSIAN STORIES/RUSSKIE RASSKAZY: A Dual-Language Book, edited by Gleb Struve. Twelve tales by such masters as Chekhov, Tolstoy, Dostoevsky, Pushkin, others. Excellent word-for-word English translations on facing pages, plus teaching and study aids, Russian/English vocabulary, biographical/critical introductions, more. 416pp. 5⅜ x 8½. 0-486-26244-8

PHILADELPHIA THEN AND NOW: 60 Sites Photographed in the Past and Present, Kenneth Finkel and Susan Oyama. Rare photographs of City Hall, Logan Square, Independence Hall, Betsy Ross House, other landmarks juxtaposed with contemporary views. Captures changing face of historic city. Introduction. Captions. 128pp. 8¼ x 11. 0-486-25790-8

NORTH AMERICAN INDIAN LIFE: Customs and Traditions of 23 Tribes, Elsie Clews Parsons (ed.). 27 fictionalized essays by noted anthropologists examine religion, customs, government, additional facets of life among the Winnebago, Crow, Zuni, Eskimo, other tribes. 480pp. 6⅛ x 9¼. 0-486-27377-6

TECHNICAL MANUAL AND DICTIONARY OF CLASSICAL BALLET, Gail Grant. Defines, explains, comments on steps, movements, poses and concepts. 15-page pictorial section. Basic book for student, viewer. 127pp. 5⅜ x 8½.
0-486-21843-0

THE MALE AND FEMALE FIGURE IN MOTION: 60 Classic Photographic Sequences, Eadweard Muybridge. 60 true-action photographs of men and women walking, running, climbing, bending, turning, etc., reproduced from rare 19th-century masterpiece. vi + 121pp. 9 x 12. 0-486-24745-7

ANIMALS: 1,419 Copyright-Free Illustrations of Mammals, Birds, Fish, Insects, etc., Jim Harter (ed.). Clear wood engravings present, in extremely lifelike poses, over 1,000 species of animals. One of the most extensive pictorial sourcebooks of its kind. Captions. Index. 284pp. 9 x 12. 0-486-23766-4

1001 QUESTIONS ANSWERED ABOUT THE SEASHORE, N. J. Berrill and Jacquelyn Berrill. Queries answered about dolphins, sea snails, sponges, starfish, fishes, shore birds, many others. Covers appearance, breeding, growth, feeding, much more. 305pp. 5¼ x 8¼. 0-486-23366-9

ATTRACTING BIRDS TO YOUR YARD, William J. Weber. Easy-to-follow guide offers advice on how to attract the greatest diversity of birds: birdhouses, feeders, water and waterers, much more. 96pp. 5³⁄₁₆ x 8¼. 0-486-28927-3

MEDICINAL AND OTHER USES OF NORTH AMERICAN PLANTS: A Historical Survey with Special Reference to the Eastern Indian Tribes, Charlotte Erichsen-Brown. Chronological historical citations document 500 years of usage of plants, trees, shrubs native to eastern Canada, northeastern U.S. Also complete identifying information. 343 illustrations. 544pp. 6½ x 9¼. 0-486-25951-X

STORYBOOK MAZES, Dave Phillips. 23 stories and mazes on two-page spreads: Wizard of Oz, Treasure Island, Robin Hood, etc. Solutions. 64pp. 8¼ x 11. 0-486-23628-5

AMERICAN NEGRO SONGS: 230 Folk Songs and Spirituals, Religious and Secular, John W. Work. This authoritative study traces the African influences of songs sung and played by black Americans at work, in church, and as entertainment. The author discusses the lyric significance of such songs as "Swing Low, Sweet Chariot," "John Henry," and others and offers the words and music for 230 songs. Bibliography. Index of Song Titles. 272pp. 6½ x 9¼. 0-486-40271-1

MOVIE-STAR PORTRAITS OF THE FORTIES, John Kobal (ed.). 163 glamor, studio photos of 106 stars of the 1940s: Rita Hayworth, Ava Gardner, Marlon Brando, Clark Gable, many more. 176pp. 8⅜ x 11¼. 0-486-23546-7

YEKL and THE IMPORTED BRIDEGROOM AND OTHER STORIES OF YIDDISH NEW YORK, Abraham Cahan. Film Hester Street based on *Yekl* (1896). Novel, other stories among first about Jewish immigrants on N.Y.'s East Side. 240pp. 5⅜ x 8½. 0-486-22427-9

SELECTED POEMS, Walt Whitman. Generous sampling from *Leaves of Grass*. Twenty-four poems include "I Hear America Singing," "Song of the Open Road," "I Sing the Body Electric," "When Lilacs Last in the Dooryard Bloom'd," "O Captain! My Captain!"—all reprinted from an authoritative edition. Lists of titles and first lines. 128pp. 5³⁄₁₆ x 8¼. 0-486-26878-0

SONGS OF EXPERIENCE: Facsimile Reproduction with 26 Plates in Full Color, William Blake. 26 full-color plates from a rare 1826 edition. Includes "The Tyger," "London," "Holy Thursday," and other poems. Printed text of poems. 48pp. 5¼ x 7. 0-486-24636-1

THE BEST TALES OF HOFFMANN, E. T. A. Hoffmann. 10 of Hoffmann's most important stories: "Nutcracker and the King of Mice," "The Golden Flowerpot," etc. 458pp. 5⅜ x 8½. 0-486-21793-0

THE BOOK OF TEA, Kakuzo Okakura. Minor classic of the Orient: entertaining, charming explanation, interpretation of traditional Japanese culture in terms of tea ceremony. 94pp. 5⅜ x 8½. 0-486-20070-1

CATALOG OF DOVER BOOKS

FRENCH STORIES/CONTES FRANÇAIS: A Dual-Language Book, Wallace Fowlie. Ten stories by French masters, Voltaire to Camus: "Micromegas" by Voltaire; "The Atheist's Mass" by Balzac; "Minuet" by de Maupassant; "The Guest" by Camus, six more. Excellent English translations on facing pages. Also French-English vocabulary list, exercises, more. 352pp. 5⅜ x 8½. 0-486-26443-2

CHICAGO AT THE TURN OF THE CENTURY IN PHOTOGRAPHS: 122 Historic Views from the Collections of the Chicago Historical Society, Larry A. Viskochil. Rare large-format prints offer detailed views of City Hall, State Street, the Loop, Hull House, Union Station, many other landmarks, circa 1904-1913. Introduction. Captions. Maps. 144pp. 9⅜ x 12¼. 0-486-24656-6

OLD BROOKLYN IN EARLY PHOTOGRAPHS, 1865-1929, William Lee Younger. Luna Park, Gravesend race track, construction of Grand Army Plaza, moving of Hotel Brighton, etc. 157 previously unpublished photographs. 165pp. 8⅞ x 11¾. 0-486-23587-4

THE MYTHS OF THE NORTH AMERICAN INDIANS, Lewis Spence. Rich anthology of the myths and legends of the Algonquins, Iroquois, Pawnees and Sioux, prefaced by an extensive historical and ethnological commentary. 36 illustrations. 480pp. 5⅜ x 8½. 0-486-25967-6

AN ENCYCLOPEDIA OF BATTLES: Accounts of Over 1,560 Battles from 1479 B.C. to the Present, David Eggenberger. Essential details of every major battle in recorded history from the first battle of Megiddo in 1479 B.C. to Grenada in 1984. List of Battle Maps. New Appendix covering the years 1967-1984. Index. 99 illustrations. 544pp. 6½ x 9¼. 0-486-24913-1

SAILING ALONE AROUND THE WORLD, Captain Joshua Slocum. First man to sail around the world, alone, in small boat. One of great feats of seamanship told in delightful manner. 67 illustrations. 294pp. 5⅜ x 8½. 0-486-20326-3

ANARCHISM AND OTHER ESSAYS, Emma Goldman. Powerful, penetrating, prophetic essays on direct action, role of minorities, prison reform, puritan hypocrisy, violence, etc. 271pp. 5⅜ x 8½. 0-486-22484-8

MYTHS OF THE HINDUS AND BUDDHISTS, Ananda K. Coomaraswamy and Sister Nivedita. Great stories of the epics; deeds of Krishna, Shiva, taken from puranas, Vedas, folk tales; etc. 32 illustrations. 400pp. 5⅜ x 8½. 0-486-21759-0

MY BONDAGE AND MY FREEDOM, Frederick Douglass. Born a slave, Douglass became outspoken force in antislavery movement. The best of Douglass' autobiographies. Graphic description of slave life. 464pp. 5⅜ x 8½. 0-486-22457-0

FOLLOWING THE EQUATOR: A Journey Around the World, Mark Twain. Fascinating humorous account of 1897 voyage to Hawaii, Australia, India, New Zealand, etc. Ironic, bemused reports on peoples, customs, climate, flora and fauna, politics, much more. 197 illustrations. 720pp. 5⅜ x 8½. 0-486-26113-1

THE PEOPLE CALLED SHAKERS, Edward D. Andrews. Definitive study of Shakers: origins, beliefs, practices, dances, social organization, furniture and crafts, etc. 33 illustrations. 351pp. 5⅜ x 8½. 0-486-21081-2

THE MYTHS OF GREECE AND ROME, H. A. Guerber. A classic of mythology, generously illustrated, long prized for its simple, graphic, accurate retelling of the principal myths of Greece and Rome, and for its commentary on their origins and significance. With 64 illustrations by Michelangelo, Raphael, Titian, Rubens, Canova, Bernini and others. 480pp. 5⅜ x 8½. 0-486-27584-1

PSYCHOLOGY OF MUSIC, Carl E. Seashore. Classic work discusses music as a medium from psychological viewpoint. Clear treatment of physical acoustics, auditory apparatus, sound perception, development of musical skills, nature of musical feeling, host of other topics. 88 figures. 408pp. 5⅜ x 8½. 0-486-21851-1

LIFE IN ANCIENT EGYPT, Adolf Erman. Fullest, most thorough, detailed older account with much not in more recent books, domestic life, religion, magic, medicine, commerce, much more. Many illustrations reproduce tomb paintings, carvings, hieroglyphs, etc. 597pp. 5⅜ x 8½. 0-486-22632-8

SUNDIALS, Their Theory and Construction, Albert Waugh. Far and away the best, most thorough coverage of ideas, mathematics concerned, types, construction, adjusting anywhere. Simple, nontechnical treatment allows even children to build several of these dials. Over 100 illustrations. 230pp. 5⅜ x 8½. 0-486-22947-5

THEORETICAL HYDRODYNAMICS, L. M. Milne-Thomson. Classic exposition of the mathematical theory of fluid motion, applicable to both hydrodynamics and aerodynamics. Over 600 exercises. 768pp. 6⅛ x 9¼. 0-486-68970-0

OLD-TIME VIGNETTES IN FULL COLOR, Carol Belanger Grafton (ed.). Over 390 charming, often sentimental illustrations, selected from archives of Victorian graphics—pretty women posing, children playing, food, flowers, kittens and puppies, smiling cherubs, birds and butterflies, much more. All copyright-free. 48pp. 9¼ x 12¼. 0-486-27269-9

PERSPECTIVE FOR ARTISTS, Rex Vicat Cole. Depth, perspective of sky and sea, shadows, much more, not usually covered. 391 diagrams, 81 reproductions of drawings and paintings. 279pp. 5⅜ x 8½. 0-486-22487-2

DRAWING THE LIVING FIGURE, Joseph Sheppard. Innovative approach to artistic anatomy focuses on specifics of surface anatomy, rather than muscles and bones. Over 170 drawings of live models in front, back and side views, and in widely varying poses. Accompanying diagrams. 177 illustrations. Introduction. Index. 144pp. 8⅜ x11¼. 0-486-26723-7

GOTHIC AND OLD ENGLISH ALPHABETS: 100 Complete Fonts, Dan X. Solo. Add power, elegance to posters, signs, other graphics with 100 stunning copyright-free alphabets: Blackstone, Dolbey, Germania, 97 more—including many lower-case, numerals, punctuation marks. 104pp. 8⅛ x 11. 0-486-24695-7

THE BOOK OF WOOD CARVING, Charles Marshall Sayers. Finest book for beginners discusses fundamentals and offers 34 designs. "Absolutely first rate . . . well thought out and well executed."–E. J. Tangerman. 118pp. 7¾ x 10⅝. 0-486-23654-4

ILLUSTRATED CATALOG OF CIVIL WAR MILITARY GOODS: Union Army Weapons, Insignia, Uniform Accessories, and Other Equipment, Schuyler, Hartley, and Graham. Rare, profusely illustrated 1846 catalog includes Union Army uniform and dress regulations, arms and ammunition, coats, insignia, flags, swords, rifles, etc. 226 illustrations. 160pp. 9 x 12. 0-486-24939-5

WOMEN'S FASHIONS OF THE EARLY 1900s: An Unabridged Republication of "New York Fashions, 1909," National Cloak & Suit Co. Rare catalog of mail-order fashions documents women's and children's clothing styles shortly after the turn of the century. Captions offer full descriptions, prices. Invaluable resource for fashion, costume historians. Approximately 725 illustrations. 128pp. 8⅜ x 11¼. 0-486-27276-1

HOW TO DO BEADWORK, Mary White. Fundamental book on craft from simple projects to five-bead chains and woven works. 106 illustrations. 142pp. 5⅜ x 8. 0-486-20697-1

THE 1912 AND 1915 GUSTAV STICKLEY FURNITURE CATALOGS, Gustav Stickley. With over 200 detailed illustrations and descriptions, these two catalogs are essential reading and reference materials and identification guides for Stickley furniture. Captions cite materials, dimensions and prices. 112pp. 6½ x 9¼. 0-486-26676-1

EARLY AMERICAN LOCOMOTIVES, John H. White, Jr. Finest locomotive engravings from early 19th century: historical (1804–74), main-line (after 1870), special, foreign, etc. 147 plates. 142pp. 11⅜ x 8¼. 0-486-22772-3

LITTLE BOOK OF EARLY AMERICAN CRAFTS AND TRADES, Peter Stockham (ed.). 1807 children's book explains crafts and trades: baker, hatter, cooper, potter, and many others. 23 copperplate illustrations. 140pp. 4⅝ x 6. 0-486-23336-7

VICTORIAN FASHIONS AND COSTUMES FROM HARPER'S BAZAR, 1867–1898, Stella Blum (ed.). Day costumes, evening wear, sports clothes, shoes, hats, other accessories in over 1,000 detailed engravings. 320pp. 9⅜ x 12¼. 0-486-22990-4

THE LONG ISLAND RAIL ROAD IN EARLY PHOTOGRAPHS, Ron Ziel. Over 220 rare photos, informative text document origin (1844) and development of rail service on Long Island. Vintage views of early trains, locomotives, stations, passengers, crews, much more. Captions. 8⅞ x 11¾. 0-486-26301-0

VOYAGE OF THE LIBERDADE, Joshua Slocum. Great 19th-century mariner's thrilling, first-hand account of the wreck of his ship off South America, the 35-foot boat he built from the wreckage, and its remarkable voyage home. 128pp. 5⅜ x 8½. 0-486-40022-0

TEN BOOKS ON ARCHITECTURE, Vitruvius. The most important book ever written on architecture. Early Roman aesthetics, technology, classical orders, site selection, all other aspects. Morgan translation. 331pp. 5⅜ x 8½. 0-486-20645-9

THE HUMAN FIGURE IN MOTION, Eadweard Muybridge. More than 4,500 stopped-action photos, in action series, showing undraped men, women, children jumping, lying down, throwing, sitting, wrestling, carrying, etc. 390pp. 7⅞ x 10⅝. 0-486-20204-6 Clothbd.

TREES OF THE EASTERN AND CENTRAL UNITED STATES AND CANADA, William M. Harlow. Best one-volume guide to 140 trees. Full descriptions, woodlore, range, etc. Over 600 illustrations. Handy size. 288pp. 4½ x 6⅜. 0-486-20395-6

GROWING AND USING HERBS AND SPICES, Milo Miloradovich. Versatile handbook provides all the information needed for cultivation and use of all the herbs and spices available in North America. 4 illustrations. Index. Glossary. 236pp. 5⅜ x 8½. 0-486-25058-X

BIG BOOK OF MAZES AND LABYRINTHS, Walter Shepherd. 50 mazes and labyrinths in all–classical, solid, ripple, and more–in one great volume. Perfect inexpensive puzzler for clever youngsters. Full solutions. 112pp. 8⅛ x 11. 0-486-22951-3

PIANO TUNING, J. Cree Fischer. Clearest, best book for beginner, amateur. Simple repairs, raising dropped notes, tuning by easy method of flattened fifths. No previous skills needed. 4 illustrations. 201pp. 5⅜ x 8½. 0-486-23267-0

HINTS TO SINGERS, Lillian Nordica. Selecting the right teacher, developing confidence, overcoming stage fright, and many other important skills receive thoughtful discussion in this indispensible guide, written by a world-famous diva of four decades' experience. 96pp. 5⅜ x 8½. 0-486-40094-8

THE COMPLETE NONSENSE OF EDWARD LEAR, Edward Lear. All nonsense limericks, zany alphabets, Owl and Pussycat, songs, nonsense botany, etc., illustrated by Lear. Total of 320pp. 5⅜ x 8½. (Available in U.S. only.) 0-486-20167-8

VICTORIAN PARLOUR POETRY: An Annotated Anthology, Michael R. Turner. 117 gems by Longfellow, Tennyson, Browning, many lesser-known poets. "The Village Blacksmith," "Curfew Must Not Ring Tonight," "Only a Baby Small," dozens more, often difficult to find elsewhere. Index of poets, titles, first lines. xxiii + 325pp. 5⅜ x 8¼. 0-486-27044-0

DUBLINERS, James Joyce. Fifteen stories offer vivid, tightly focused observations of the lives of Dublin's poorer classes. At least one, "The Dead," is considered a masterpiece. Reprinted complete and unabridged from standard edition. 160pp. 5³⁄₁₆ x 8¼.
0-486-26870-5

GREAT WEIRD TALES: 14 Stories by Lovecraft, Blackwood, Machen and Others, S. T. Joshi (ed.). 14 spellbinding tales, including "The Sin Eater," by Fiona McLeod, "The Eye Above the Mantel," by Frank Belknap Long, as well as renowned works by R. H. Barlow, Lord Dunsany, Arthur Machen, W. C. Morrow and eight other masters of the genre. 256pp. 5⅜ x 8½. (Available in U.S. only.) 0-486-40436-6

THE BOOK OF THE SACRED MAGIC OF ABRAMELIN THE MAGE, translated by S. MacGregor Mathers. Medieval manuscript of ceremonial magic. Basic document in Aleister Crowley, Golden Dawn groups. 268pp. 5⅜ x 8½.
0 486 23211 5

THE BATTLES THAT CHANGED HISTORY, Fletcher Pratt. Eminent historian profiles 16 crucial conflicts, ancient to modern, that changed the course of civilization. 352pp. 5⅜ x 8½. 0-486-41129-X

NEW RUSSIAN-ENGLISH AND ENGLISH-RUSSIAN DICTIONARY, M. A. O'Brien. This is a remarkably handy Russian dictionary, containing a surprising amount of information, including over 70,000 entries. 366pp. 4½ x 6¼.
0-486-20208-9

NEW YORK IN THE FORTIES, Andreas Feininger. 162 brilliant photographs by the well-known photographer, formerly with *Life* magazine. Commuters, shoppers, Times Square at night, much else from city at its peak. Captions by John von Hartz. 181pp. 9¼ x 10¾. 0-486-23585-8

INDIAN SIGN LANGUAGE, William Tomkins. Over 525 signs developed by Sioux and other tribes. Written instructions and diagrams. Also 290 pictographs. 111pp. 6⅛ x 9¼. 0-486-22029-X

ANATOMY: A Complete Guide for Artists, Joseph Sheppard. A master of figure drawing shows artists how to render human anatomy convincingly. Over 460 illustrations. 224pp. 8⅜ x 11¼. 0-486-27279-6

MEDIEVAL CALLIGRAPHY: Its History and Technique, Marc Drogin. Spirited history, comprehensive instruction manual covers 13 styles (ca. 4th century through 15th). Excellent photographs; directions for duplicating medieval techniques with modern tools. 224pp. 8⅜ x 11¼. 0-486-26142-5

DRIED FLOWERS: How to Prepare Them, Sarah Whitlock and Martha Rankin. Complete instructions on how to use silica gel, meal and borax, perlite aggregate, sand and borax, glycerine and water to create attractive permanent flower arrangements. 12 illustrations. 32pp. 5⅜ x 8½. 0-486-21802-3

EASY-TO-MAKE BIRD FEEDERS FOR WOODWORKERS, Scott D. Campbell. Detailed, simple-to-use guide for designing, constructing, caring for and using feeders. Text, illustrations for 12 classic and contemporary designs. 96pp. 5⅜ x 8½. 0-486-25847-5

THE COMPLETE BOOK OF BIRDHOUSE CONSTRUCTION FOR WOODWORKERS, Scott D. Campbell. Detailed instructions, illustrations, tables. Also data on bird habitat and instinct patterns. Bibliography. 3 tables. 63 illustrations in 15 figures. 48pp. 5¼ x 8½. 0-486-24407-5

SCOTTISH WONDER TALES FROM MYTH AND LEGEND, Donald A. Mackenzie. 16 lively tales tell of giants rumbling down mountainsides, of a magic wand that turns stone pillars into warriors, of gods and goddesses, evil hags, powerful forces and more. 240pp. 5⅜ x 8½. 0-486-29677-6

THE HISTORY OF UNDERCLOTHES, C. Willett Cunnington and Phyllis Cunnington. Fascinating, well-documented survey covering six centuries of English undergarments, enhanced with over 100 illustrations: 12th-century laced-up bodice, footed long drawers (1795), 19th-century bustles, 19th-century corsets for men, Victorian "bust improvers," much more. 272pp. 5⅜ x 8¼. 0-486-27124-2

ARTS AND CRAFTS FURNITURE: The Complete Brooks Catalog of 1912, Brooks Manufacturing Co. Photos and detailed descriptions of more than 150 now very collectible furniture designs from the Arts and Crafts movement depict davenports, settees, buffets, desks, tables, chairs, bedsteads, dressers and more, all built of solid, quarter-sawed oak. Invaluable for students and enthusiasts of antiques, Americana and the decorative arts. 80pp. 6½ x 9¼. 0-486-27471-3

WILBUR AND ORVILLE: A Biography of the Wright Brothers, Fred Howard. Definitive, crisply written study tells the full story of the brothers' lives and work. A vividly written biography, unparalleled in scope and color, that also captures the spirit of an extraordinary era. 560pp. 6⅛ x 9¼. 0-486-40297-5

THE ARTS OF THE SAILOR: Knotting, Splicing and Ropework, Hervey Garrett Smith. Indispensable shipboard reference covers tools, basic knots and useful hitches; handsewing and canvas work, more. Over 100 illustrations. Delightful reading for sea lovers. 256pp. 5⅜ x 8½. 0-486-26440-8

FRANK LLOYD WRIGHT'S FALLINGWATER: The House and Its History, Second, Revised Edition, Donald Hoffmann. A total revision–both in text and illustrations–of the standard document on Fallingwater, the boldest, most personal architectural statement of Wright's mature years, updated with valuable new material from the recently opened Frank Lloyd Wright Archives. "Fascinating"–*The New York Times.* 116 illustrations. 128pp. 9¼ x 10¾. 0-486-27430-6

PHOTOGRAPHIC SKETCHBOOK OF THE CIVIL WAR, Alexander Gardner. 100 photos taken on field during the Civil War. Famous shots of Manassas Harper's Ferry, Lincoln, Richmond, slave pens, etc. 244pp. 10⅝ x 8¼. 0-486-22731-6

FIVE ACRES AND INDEPENDENCE, Maurice G. Kains. Great back-to-the-land classic explains basics of self-sufficient farming. The one book to get. 95 illustrations. 397pp. 5⅜ x 8½. 0-486-20974-1

CATALOG OF DOVER BOOKS

A MODERN HERBAL, Margaret Grieve. Much the fullest, most exact, most useful compilation of herbal material. Gigantic alphabetical encyclopedia, from aconite to zedoary, gives botanical information, medical properties, folklore, economic uses, much else. Indispensable to serious reader. 161 illustrations. 888pp. 6½ x 9¼. 2-vol. set. (Available in U.S. only.) Vol. I: 0-486-22798-7 Vol. II: 0-486-22799-5

HIDDEN TREASURE MAZE BOOK, Dave Phillips. Solve 34 challenging mazes accompanied by heroic tales of adventure. Evil dragons, people-eating plants, bloodthirsty giants, many more dangerous adversaries lurk at every twist and turn. 34 mazes, stories, solutions. 48pp. 8¼ x 11. 0-486-24566-7

LETTERS OF W. A. MOZART, Wolfgang A. Mozart. Remarkable letters show bawdy wit, humor, imagination, musical insights, contemporary musical world; includes some letters from Leopold Mozart. 276pp. 5⅜ x 8½. 0-486-22859-2

BASIC PRINCIPLES OF CLASSICAL BALLET, Agrippina Vaganova. Great Russian theoretician, teacher explains methods for teaching classical ballet. 118 illustrations. 175pp. 5⅜ x 8½. 0-486-22036-2

THE JUMPING FROG, Mark Twain. Revenge edition. The original story of The Celebrated Jumping Frog of Calaveras County, a hapless French translation, and Twain's hilarious "retranslation" from the French. 12 illustrations. 66pp. 5⅜ x 8½. 0-486-22686-7

BEST REMEMBERED POEMS, Martin Gardner (ed.). The 126 poems in this superb collection of 19th- and 20th-century British and American verse range from Shelley's "To a Skylark" to the impassioned "Renascence" of Edna St. Vincent Millay and to Edward Lear's whimsical "The Owl and the Pussycat." 224pp. 5⅜ x 8½. 0-486-27165-X

COMPLETE SONNETS, William Shakespeare. Over 150 exquisite poems deal with love, friendship, the tyranny of time, beauty's evanescence, death and other themes in language of remarkable power, precision and beauty. Glossary of archaic terms. 80pp. 5³⁄₁₆ x 8¼. 0-486-26686-9

HISTORIC HOMES OF THE AMERICAN PRESIDENTS, Second, Revised Edition, Irvin Haas. A traveler's guide to American Presidential homes, most open to the public, depicting and describing homes occupied by every American President from George Washington to George Bush. With visiting hours, admission charges, travel routes. 175 photographs. Index. 160pp. 8¼ x 11. 0-486-26751-2

THE WIT AND HUMOR OF OSCAR WILDE, Alvin Redman (ed.). More than 1,000 ripostes, paradoxes, wisecracks: Work is the curse of the drinking classes; I can resist everything except temptation; etc. 258pp. 5⅜ x 8½. 0-486-20602-5

SHAKESPEARE LEXICON AND QUOTATION DICTIONARY, Alexander Schmidt. Full definitions, locations, shades of meaning in every word in plays and poems. More than 50,000 exact quotations. 1,485pp. 6½ x 9¼. 2-vol. set.
Vol. 1: 0-486-22726-X Vol. 2: 0-486-22727-8

SELECTED POEMS, Emily Dickinson. Over 100 best-known, best-loved poems by one of America's foremost poets, reprinted from authoritative early editions. No comparable edition at this price. Index of first lines. 64pp. 5³⁄₁₆ x 8¼. 0-486-26466-1

THE INSIDIOUS DR. FU-MANCHU, Sax Rohmer. The first of the popular mystery series introduces a pair of English detectives to their archnemesis, the diabolical Dr. Fu-Manchu. Flavorful atmosphere, fast-paced action, and colorful characters enliven this classic of the genre. 208pp. 5³⁄₁₆ x 8¼. 0-486-29898-1

THE MALLEUS MALEFICARUM OF KRAMER AND SPRENGER, translated by Montague Summers. Full text of most important witchhunter's "bible," used by both Catholics and Protestants. 278pp. 6⅝ x 10.　　　　　　0-486-22802-9

SPANISH STORIES/CUENTOS ESPAÑOLES: A Dual-Language Book, Angel Flores (ed.). Unique format offers 13 great stories in Spanish by Cervantes, Borges, others. Faithful English translations on facing pages. 352pp. 5⅜ x 8½.

0-486-25399-6

GARDEN CITY, LONG ISLAND, IN EARLY PHOTOGRAPHS, 1869–1919, Mildred H. Smith. Handsome treasury of 118 vintage pictures, accompanied by carefully researched captions, document the Garden City Hotel fire (1899), the Vanderbilt Cup Race (1908), the first airmail flight departing from the Nassau Boulevard Aerodrome (1911), and much more. 96pp. 8⅞ x 11¾.　　　　　　0-486-40669-5

OLD QUEENS, N.Y., IN EARLY PHOTOGRAPHS, Vincent F. Seyfried and William Asadorian. Over 160 rare photographs of Maspeth, Jamaica, Jackson Heights, and other areas. Vintage views of DeWitt Clinton mansion, 1939 World's Fair and more. Captions. 192pp. 8⅞ x 11.　　　　　　0-486-26358-4

CAPTURED BY THE INDIANS: 15 Firsthand Accounts, 1750-1870, Frederick Drimmer. Astounding true historical accounts of grisly torture, bloody conflicts, relentless pursuits, miraculous escapes and more, by people who lived to tell the tale. 384pp. 5⅜ x 8½.　　　　　　0-486-24901-8

THE WORLD'S GREAT SPEECHES (Fourth Enlarged Edition), Lewis Copeland, Lawrence W. Lamm, and Stephen J. McKenna. Nearly 300 speeches provide public speakers with a wealth of updated quotes and inspiration—from Pericles' funeral oration and William Jennings Bryan's "Cross of Gold Speech" to Malcolm X's powerful words on the Black Revolution and Earl of Spenser's tribute to his sister, Diana, Princess of Wales. 944pp. 5⅜ x 8⅜.　　　　　　0-486-40903-1

THE BOOK OF THE SWORD, Sir Richard F. Burton. Great Victorian scholar/adventurer's eloquent, erudite history of the "queen of weapons"—from prehistory to early Roman Empire. Evolution and development of early swords, variations (sabre, broadsword, cutlass, scimitar, etc.), much more. 336pp. 6⅛ x 9¼.

0-486-25434-8

AUTOBIOGRAPHY: The Story of My Experiments with Truth, Mohandas K. Gandhi. Boyhood, legal studies, purification, the growth of the Satyagraha (nonviolent protest) movement. Critical, inspiring work of the man responsible for the freedom of India. 480pp. 5⅜ x 8½. (Available in U.S. only.)　　　　　　0-486-24593-4

CELTIC MYTHS AND LEGENDS, T. W. Rolleston. Masterful retelling of Irish and Welsh stories and tales. Cuchulain, King Arthur, Deirdre, the Grail, many more. First paperback edition. 58 full-page illustrations. 512pp. 5⅜ x 8½.　　　　　　0-486-26507-2

THE PRINCIPLES OF PSYCHOLOGY, William James. Famous long course complete, unabridged. Stream of thought, time perception, memory, experimental methods; great work decades ahead of its time. 94 figures. 1,391pp. 5⅜ x 8½. 2-vol. set.
Vol. I: 0-486-20381-6　　　Vol. II: 0-486-20382-4

THE WORLD AS WILL AND REPRESENTATION, Arthur Schopenhauer. Definitive English translation of Schopenhauer's life work, correcting more than 1,000 errors, omissions in earlier translations. Translated by E. F. J. Payne. Total of 1,269pp. 5⅜ x 8½. 2-vol. set.　　　Vol. 1: 0-486-21761-2　　　Vol. 2: 0-486-21762-0

MAGIC AND MYSTERY IN TIBET, Madame Alexandra David-Neel. Experiences among lamas, magicians, sages, sorcerers, Bonpa wizards. A true psychic discovery. 32 illustrations. 321pp. 5⅜ x 8½. (Available in U.S. only.) 0-486-22682-4

THE EGYPTIAN BOOK OF THE DEAD, E. A. Wallis Budge. Complete reproduction of Ani's papyrus, finest ever found. Full hieroglyphic text, interlinear transliteration, word-for-word translation, smooth translation. 533pp. 6½ x 9¼. 0-486-21866-X

HISTORIC COSTUME IN PICTURES, Braun & Schneider. Over 1,450 costumed figures in clearly detailed engravings–from dawn of civilization to end of 19th century. Captions. Many folk costumes. 256pp. 8⅜ x 11¾. 0-486-23150-X

MATHEMATICS FOR THE NONMATHEMATICIAN, Morris Kline. Detailed, college-level treatment of mathematics in cultural and historical context, with numerous exercises. Recommended Reading Lists. Tables. Numerous figures. 641pp. 5⅜ x 8½. 0-486-24823-2

PROBABILISTIC METHODS IN THE THEORY OF STRUCTURES, Isaac Elishakoff. Well-written introduction covers the elements of the theory of probability from two or more random variables, the reliability of such multivariable structures, the theory of random function, Monte Carlo methods of treating problems incapable of exact solution, and more. Examples. 502pp. 5⅜ x 8½. 0-486-40691-1

THE RIME OF THE ANCIENT MARINER, Gustave Doré, S. T. Coleridge. Doré's finest work; 34 plates capture moods, subtleties of poem. Flawless full-size reproductions printed on facing pages with authoritative text of poem. "Beautiful. Simply beautiful."–*Publisher's Weekly*. 77pp. 9¼ x 12. 0-486-22305-1

SCULPTURE: Principles and Practice, Louis Slobodkin. Step-by-step approach to clay, plaster, metals, stone; classical and modern. 253 drawings, photos. 255pp. 8⅛ x 11. 0-486-22960-2

THE INFLUENCE OF SEA POWER UPON HISTORY, 1660–1783, A. T. Mahan. Influential classic of naval history and tactics still used as text in war colleges. First paperback edition. 4 maps. 24 battle plans. 640pp. 5⅜ x 8½. 0-486-25509-3

THE STORY OF THE TITANIC AS TOLD BY ITS SURVIVORS, Jack Winocour (ed.). What it was really like. Panic, despair, shocking inefficiency, and a little heroism. More thrilling than any fictional account. 26 illustrations. 320pp. 5⅜ x 8½. 0-486-20610-6

ONE TWO THREE . . . INFINITY: Facts and Speculations of Science, George Gamow. Great physicist's fascinating, readable overview of contemporary science: number theory, relativity, fourth dimension, entropy, genes, atomic structure, much more. 128 illustrations. Index. 352pp. 5⅜ x 8½. 0-486-25664-2

DALÍ ON MODERN ART: The Cuckolds of Antiquated Modern Art, Salvador Dalí. Influential painter skewers modern art and its practitioners. Outrageous evaluations of Picasso, Cézanne, Turner, more. 15 renderings of paintings discussed. 44 calligraphic decorations by Dalí. 96pp. 5⅜ x 8½. (Available in U.S. only.) 0-486-29220-7

ANTIQUE PLAYING CARDS: A Pictorial History, Henry René D'Allemagne. Over 900 elaborate, decorative images from rare playing cards (14th–20th centuries): Bacchus, death, dancing dogs, hunting scenes, royal coats of arms, players cheating, much more. 96pp. 9¼ x 12¼. 0-486-29265-7

MAKING FURNITURE MASTERPIECES: 30 Projects with Measured Drawings, Franklin H. Gottshall. Step-by-step instructions, illustrations for constructing handsome, useful pieces, among them a Sheraton desk, Chippendale chair, Spanish desk, Queen Anne table and a William and Mary dressing mirror. 224pp. 8⅛ x 11¼.
0-486-29338-6

NORTH AMERICAN INDIAN DESIGNS FOR ARTISTS AND CRAFTSPEOPLE, Eva Wilson. Over 360 authentic copyright-free designs adapted from Navajo blankets, Hopi pottery, Sioux buffalo hides, more. Geometrics, symbolic figures, plant and animal motifs, etc. 128pp. 8⅜ x 11. (Not for sale in the United Kingdom.) 0-486-25341-4

THE FOSSIL BOOK: A Record of Prehistoric Life, Patricia V. Rich et al. Profusely illustrated definitive guide covers everything from single-celled organisms and dinosaurs to birds and mammals and the interplay between climate and man. Over 1,500 illustrations. 760pp. 7½ x 10⅛. 0-486-29371-8

VICTORIAN ARCHITECTURAL DETAILS: Designs for Over 700 Stairs, Mantels, Doors, Windows, Cornices, Porches, and Other Decorative Elements, A. J. Bicknell & Company. Everything from dormer windows and piazzas to balconies and gable ornaments. Also includes elevations and floor plans for handsome, private residences and commercial structures. 80pp. 9⅜ x 12¼. 0-486-44015-X

WESTERN ISLAMIC ARCHITECTURE: A Concise Introduction, John D. Hoag. Profusely illustrated critical appraisal compares and contrasts Islamic mosques and palaces—from Spain and Egypt to other areas in the Middle East. 139 illustrations. 128pp. 6 x 9. 0-486-43760-4

CHINESE ARCHITECTURE: A Pictorial History, Liang Ssu-ch'eng. More than 240 rare photographs and drawings depict temples, pagodas, tombs, bridges, and imperial palaces comprising much of China's architectural heritage. 152 halftones, 94 diagrams. 232pp. 10¾ x 9⅞. 0-486-43999-2

THE RENAISSANCE: Studies in Art and Poetry, Walter Pater. One of the most talked-about books of the 19th century, *The Renaissance* combines scholarship and philosophy in an innovative work of cultural criticism that examines the achievements of Botticelli, Leonardo, Michelangelo, and other artists. "The holy writ of beauty."—Oscar Wilde. 160pp. 5⅜ x 8½. 0-486-44025-7

A TREATISE ON PAINTING, Leonardo da Vinci. The great Renaissance artist's practical advice on drawing and painting techniques covers anatomy, perspective, composition, light and shadow, and color. A classic of art instruction, it features 48 drawings by Nicholas Poussin and Leon Battista Alberti. 192pp. 5⅜ x 8½.
0-486-44155-5

THE MIND OF LEONARDO DA VINCI, Edward McCurdy. More than just a biography, this classic study by a distinguished historian draws upon Leonardo's extensive writings to offer numerous demonstrations of the Renaissance master's achievements, not only in sculpture and painting, but also in music, engineering, and even experimental aviation. 384pp. 5⅜ x 8½. 0-486-44142-3

WASHINGTON IRVING'S RIP VAN WINKLE, Illustrated by Arthur Rackham. Lovely prints that established artist as a leading illustrator of the time and forever etched into the popular imagination a classic of Catskill lore. 51 full-color plates. 80pp. 8⅜ x 11. 0-486-44242-X

HENSCHE ON PAINTING, John W. Robichaux. Basic painting philosophy and methodology of a great teacher, as expounded in his famous classes and workshops on Cape Cod. 7 illustrations in color on covers. 80pp. 5⅜ x 8½. 0-486-43728-0

LIGHT AND SHADE: A Classic Approach to Three-Dimensional Drawing, Mrs. Mary P. Merrifield. Handy reference clearly demonstrates principles of light and shade by revealing effects of common daylight, sunshine, and candle or artificial light on geometrical solids. 13 plates. 64pp. 5⅜ x 8½. 0-486-44143-1

ASTROLOGY AND ASTRONOMY: A Pictorial Archive of Signs and Symbols, Ernst and Johanna Lehner. Treasure trove of stories, lore, and myth, accompanied by more than 300 rare illustrations of planets, the Milky Way, signs of the zodiac, comets, meteors, and other astronomical phenomena. 192pp. 8⅜ x 11. 0-486-43981-X

JEWELRY MAKING: Techniques for Metal, Tim McCreight. Easy-to-follow instructions and carefully executed illustrations describe tools and techniques, use of gems and enamels, wire inlay, casting, and other topics. 72 line illustrations and diagrams. 176pp. 8¼ x 10⅞. 0-486-44043-5

MAKING BIRDHOUSES: Easy and Advanced Projects, Gladstone Califf. Easy-to-follow instructions include diagrams for everything from a one-room house for bluebirds to a forty-two-room structure for purple martins. 56 plates; 4 figures. 80pp. 8¾ x 6⅜. 0-486-44183-0

LITTLE BOOK OF LOG CABINS: How to Build and Furnish Them, William S. Wicks. Handy how-to manual, with instructions and illustrations for building cabins in the Adirondack style, fireplaces, stairways, furniture, beamed ceilings, and more. 102 line drawings. 96pp. 8¾ x 6⅜. 0-486-44259-4

THE SEASONS OF AMERICA PAST, Eric Sloane. From "sugaring time" and strawberry picking to Indian summer and fall harvest, a whole year's activities described in charming prose and enhanced with 79 of the author's own illustrations. 160pp. 8¼ x 11. 0-486-44220-9

THE METROPOLIS OF TOMORROW, Hugh Ferriss. Generous, prophetic vision of the metropolis of the future, as perceived in 1929. Powerful illustrations of towering structures, wide avenues, and rooftop parks–all features in many of today's modern cities. 59 illustrations. 144pp. 8¼ x 11. 0-486-43727-2

THE PATH TO ROME, Hilaire Belloc. This 1902 memoir abounds in lively vignettes from a vanished time, recounting a pilgrimage on foot across the Alps and Apennines in order to "see all Europe which the Christian Faith has saved." 77 of the author's original line drawings complement his sparkling prose. 272pp. 5⅜ x 8½. 0-486-44001-X

THE HISTORY OF RASSELAS: Prince of Abissinia, Samuel Johnson. Distinguished English writer attacks eighteenth-century optimism and man's unrealistic estimates of what life has to offer. 112pp. 5⅜ x 8½. 0-486-44094-X

A VOYAGE TO ARCTURUS, David Lindsay. A brilliant flight of pure fancy, where wild creatures crowd the fantastic landscape and demented torturers dominate victims with their bizarre mental powers. 272pp. 5⅜ x 8½. 0-486-44198-9

Paperbound unless otherwise indicated. Available at your book dealer, online at **www.doverpublications.com**, or by writing to Dept. GI, Dover Publications, Inc., 31 East 2nd Street, Mineola, NY 11501. For current price information or for free catalogs (please indicate field of interest), write to Dover Publications or log on to **www.doverpublications.com** and see every Dover book in print. Dover publishes more than 500 books each year on science, elementary and advanced mathematics, biology, music, art, literary history, social sciences, and other areas.